A Critical Introduction to Skepticism

Bloomsbury Critical Introductions to Contemporary Epistemology
Series Editor:
Stephen Hetherington, The University of New South Wales, Australia

Editorial Board:
Anthony Brueckner, University of California, Santa Barbara, USA; Richard Fumerton, The University of Iowa, USA; John Greco, Saint Louis University, USA; Jonathan Kvanvig, Baylor University, USA; Ram Neta, University of North Carolina, Chapel Hill, USA; Duncan Pritchard, The University of Edinburgh, UK

Bloomsbury Critical Introductions to Contemporary Epistemology introduces and advances the central topics within one of the most dynamic areas of contemporary philosophy.

Each critical introduction provides a comprehensive survey to an important epistemic subject, covering the historical, methodological, and practical contexts and exploring the major approaches, theories, and debates. By clearly illustrating the changes to the ways human knowledge is being studied, each volume places an emphasis on the historical background and makes important connections between contemporary issues and the wider history of modern philosophy.

Designed for use in contemporary epistemology courses, the introductions are defined by a clarity of argument and equipped with easy-to-follow chapter summaries, annotated guides to reading, and glossaries to facilitate and encourage further study. This series is ideal for upper-level undergraduates and postgraduates wishing to stay informed of the thinkers, issues, and arguments shaping twenty-first-century epistemology.

New titles in the series include:
A Critical Introduction to the Epistemology of Perception, Ali Hasan
A Critical Introduction to Formal Epistemology, Darren Bradley
A Critical Introduction to Knowledge-How, J. Adam Carter and Ted Poston
A Critical Introduction to Testimony, Axel Gelfert

BLOOMSBURY CRITICAL INTRODUCTIONS TO CONTEMPORARY EPISTEMOLOGY

A Critical Introduction to Skepticism

ALLAN HAZLETT

B L O O M S B U R Y

LONDON • NEW DELHI • NEW YORK • SYDNEY

Bloomsbury Academic

An imprint of Bloomsbury Publishing Plc

50 Bedford Square
London
WC1B 3DP
UK

1385 Broadway
New York
NY 10018
USA

www.bloomsbury.com

Bloomsbury is a registered trade mark of Bloomsbury Publishing Plc

First published 2014

© Allan Hazlett, 2014

Allan Hazlett has asserted his right under the Copyright, Designs and Patents Act, 1988, to be identified as Author of this work.

British Library Cataloguing-in-Publication Data
A catalogue record for this book is available from the British Library.

ISBN: HB: 978-1-4411-3832-3
PB: 978-1-4411-4053-1
ePDF: 978-1-4411-4407-2
ePub: 978-1-4411-5489-7

Library of Congress Cataloging-in-Publication Data
Hazlett, Allan.
A critical introduction to skepticism / Allan Hazlett.
pages cm.– (Bloomsbury Critical Introductions to Contemporary Epistemology)
Summary: "A comprehensive introductory survey of the skeptical problems, arguments, and responses at the centre of contemporary epistemology"– Provided by publisher.
Includes bibliographical references and index.
ISBN 978-1-4411-3832-3 (hardback)– ISBN 978-1-4411-4053-1 (paperback)– ISBN 978-1-4411-5489-7 (epub) 1. Skepticism. 2. Knowledge, Theory of. I. Title.
BD201.H39 2014
149'.73–dc23
2013034323

Typeset by Fakenham Prepress Solutions, Fakenham, Norfolk NR21 8NN

*I should like to pause here and spend some time in the
contemplation of God; to reflect on his attributes, and to gaze
with wonder and adoration on the beauty of this immense light,
so far as the eye of my darkened intellect can bear it. For just as
we believe through faith that the supreme happiness of the next
life consists solely in the contemplation of the divine majesty,
so experience tells us that this same contemplation, albeit much
less perfect, enables us to know the greatest joy of which we are
capable in this life.*

— DESCARTES, THIRD MEDITATION

*In a word, human life is more governed by fortune than by
reason; is to be regarded more as a dull pastime than as
a serious occupation; and is more influenced by particular
humour, than by general principles. Shall we engage ourselves
in it with passion and anxiety? It is not worthy of so much
concern. Shall we be indifferent about what happens? We lose
all the pleasure of the game by our phlegm and carelessness.
While we are reasoning concerning life, life is gone; and death,
though perhaps they receive him differently, yet treats alike the
fool and the philosopher. To reduce life to exact rule and method,
is commonly a painful, oft a fruitless occupation: And is it not
also a proof, that we overvalue the prize for which we contend?
Even to reason so carefully concerning it, and to fix with accuracy
its just idea, would be overvaluing it, were it not that, to some
tempers, this occupation is one of the most amusing, in which
life could possibly be employed.*

— HUME, "THE SCEPTIC"

a companion to the philosophical texts that it discusses. If your only source of information about the problem of skepticism is this book, apologies, but again: you're doomed. You need to read the texts listed under "Readings" at the end of each chapter. I do not think you should even begin without laying your hands on copies of Hume's *Enquiry concerning Human Understanding* (see Chapter 3) and Descartes' *Meditations on First Philosophy* (see Chapter 4).

You should make use of the *Stanford Encyclopedia of Philosophy* (http:// plato.stanford.edu/) and *Philosophy Compass* (http://onlinelibrary.wiley.com/ journal/10.1111/(ISSN)1747-9991), but there is no substitute for careful, sometimes painful, engagement with the original work of other philosophers.

This book offers an introduction to skepticism in contemporary episte-mology, and presupposes no prior familiarity with the subject, but it is argumentative. I say many controversial things in this book; in some cases I give arguments for what I say, in other cases I simply note how things seem to me. I do not pretend to be neutral; those who engage in that sort of pretense rarely succeed in fooling anyone, and usually end up misleading at least some of their readers. But although this book is a kind of polemic, my aim isn't to convince you of anything: my aim is to give you some tools that will enable you to sensibly make up your own mind. And you will need to make up your own mind about the problem posed by skepticism; otherwise, you guessed it, you're doomed.

There are many important and interesting philosophical issues that are not discussed here. However, I have provided a bibliography that I think will be sufficient to get you started on your further research into skepticism and related epistemological issues. (Citations are given by author and year, and refer to entries in the bibliography.)

While writing this book I enjoyed the hospitality of the philosophy department at the University of New Mexico; to the philosophers there I owe thanks. I should also like to thank Brian Johnson and Duncan Pritchard, who provided feedback on earlier versions of this material.

Allan Hazlett

March 2013

Albuquerque, New Mexico

PART ONE

Skepticism

that followed him, skepticism was a way of life, the essence of which was suspension of judgment (ἐποχή). Moreover, such suspension of judgment was taken to lead to tranquility (ἀταραξία), or freedom from disturbance. Theirs was thus an ethical philosophy, in the sense that it offered an answer to the question of how to live, or to flourish, or to be happy.

In this book we'll not examine the idea that suspension of judgment leads to tranquility, but I'll very briefly sketch two Pyrrhonian ideas. The first is that we are often disturbed as a result of our evaluative beliefs, i.e. our beliefs about what is good or bad. Diogenes Laertius relates the following story about Pyrrho:

> When his fellow-passengers on board a ship were all unnerved by a storm, he kept calm and confident, pointing to a little pig in the ship that went on eating, and telling them that such was the unperturbed state in which the wise man should keep himself. (*Lives*, XI 68)[6]

What explained the difference between Pyrrho (and the pig) and the other passengers? So the story goes, this was down to their cognitive difference: Pyrrho (and the pig) lacked beliefs to the effect that going down with the ship would be bad, while the other passengers held this opinion, and so were terrified. Evaluative beliefs have emotional consequences—someone who thinks honor is good will be frustrated when she fails to acquire honor—but if you remove the evaluative beliefs, so the argument goes, you'll remove their emotional consequences (Sextus, *Outlines*, I 27, III 237–8). But suspension of judgment is not always calming, even when it comes to evaluative matters: if you very much want to eat at the best restaurant in town, suspension of judgment about the question of which restaurant is the best will hardly bring you tranquility. The second Pyrrhonian idea is that unsuccessful inquiry or unresolved disagreement about certain questions is disturbing, but that suspension of judgment can alleviate this (Sextus, *Outlines*, I 25). Suspension of judgment about a controversial issue can put an end to the frustration of trying to settle the matter. But this will not always work: if you are deeply curious about some question, suspension of judgment will not bring you tranquility, since it is your lack of belief about said question that is the source of your disturbance.

In any event, probably the most important thing about the Ancient skeptics was their rejection of the view that knowledge is necessary, if not sufficient, for living a good life. Stoics and Peripatetics defended this, Christians later took this view up, and many contemporary philosophers defend it. The Ancient skeptics rejected it.[7]

1.2 Ancient skeptical arguments

Our most important sources of information about Ancient skepticism are the writings of **Sextus Empiricus** (second century AD). Most of what we know about Pyrrhonian skepticism is based on Sextus' sympathetic presentation of it. In this section, we'll take a quick look at some of the skeptical arguments that Sextus presents in his most famous book, *Outlines of Scepticism*. These include the ten modes (§1.2.1) and the five modes, under which heading we'll discuss "Agrippa's trilemma" and the "problem of the criterion" (§1.2.2). These arguments have had a tremendous influence on subsequent philosophers, and the ten modes are the historical ancestors of the "Cartesian skeptical argument" (§4.2.1) that has been at the center of contemporary discussions of skepticism. I should note that, in distinguishing these arguments—the ten modes, the five modes, Agrippa's trilemma, the problem of the criterion—I do not mean to suggest that it would not be right to say that these are really just different ways of articulating the same basic skeptical idea. (The Pyrrhonians, for their part, would have seen the modes as a battery of tools for inducing suspension of judgment.) However, although there are many different arguments that are recognizable as "skeptical arguments", it would be foolish to try to find out which of these was "the" skeptical argument. It would be foolish to argue about which articulation was most "genuine" or "real". In any event, we'll adopt the practice here of engaging with arguments as they are articulated, and not worry too much about how individual articulations are related to one another, or to some unarticulated skeptical ideal.

1.2.1 *The ten modes*

The **ten modes** (*Outlines*, I 35–163) are not ten distinct skeptical arguments, but more like ten ways of applying a particular form of skeptical argument. The ten modes are sometimes attributed to Aenesidemus, and are thought to have their origin in Academic skepticism. These "modes" would have been methods of bringing about suspension of judgment (or for arguing for the conclusion that nothing can be known). The ten modes have the following three-step structure:

1 Each mode begins with the skeptic drawing our attention to some form of difference in opinion or difference in how things appear, in other words, some form of disagreement. Colors appear differently to human beings and other animals ("the mode depending on variations among animals"), food tastes different depending on what you've just eaten ("the mode depending on circumstances"), people from

different cultures consider different practices immoral ("the mode depending on persuasions and customs and laws and belief in myths and dogmatic suppositions").

2 The skeptic then argues that there is no legitimate way to decide which side of the disagreement is right; she thus reaches a state of equipollence in which the considerations on both sides of the disagreement appear equally compelling.

3 Finally, as a result, the skeptic suspends judgment about the relevant question (or concludes that knowledge about the answer to that question is impossible): about the color of the object, or the flavor of the food, or the morality of such-and-such practice.

That is the basic three-step structure of the ten modes: a disagreement, where there is no legitimate way to decide which side of the disagreement is right, resulting in suspension of judgment.

Let's look more closely at one of these modes. Sextus argues that "objects appear different" depending on their "positions and intervals and places" (I 118).[8] For example (when it comes to intervals):

[T]he same colonnade appears foreshortened when seen from one end, but completely symmetrical when seen from the middle. The same boat appears from a distance small and stationary, but from close at hand large and in motion. The same tower appears from a distance round, but from close at hand square. (*Ibid.*)

But it is "impossible ... to give preference to some of these appearances over others", and therefore:

Since ... all apparent things are observed in some place and for some interval and in some position, and each of these produces a great deal of variation in appearances ... we shall be forced to arrive at suspension of judgment. (I 121)

But why not give preference to some of these appearances over others? Don't we, for example, have a *better* view of the boat and the tower when they are close at hand? What Sextus says here (and in connection with others of the ten modes) is that legitimately giving preference to one appearance over another would require giving a proof that your choice was right, and that this would in turn require giving a proof that your proof was sound, and so on *ad infinitum* (I 122). This is a version of the "mode from infinite regress", one of the five modes, which suggests that the ten modes must be supplemented by the five modes, and in particular by Agrippa's trilemma (§1.2.2).

Although much of Sextus' discussion of the ten modes focuses on differences in sense perception, two other sorts of difference receive significant attention. First, there is considerable emphasis placed on cultural difference, especially in connection with "[t]he tenth mode, which especially bears on ethics" (but also on religious metaphysics), which "is the one depending on persuasions and customs and laws and beliefs in myth and dogmatic suppositions" (I 145; see e.g. I 145–62, III 199–228) Sextus offers a battery of examples of cultural difference: "Ethiopians tattoo their babies, while we do not" (I 148), "no male here would wear a brightly-colored full-length dress, although among the Persians this, which among us is shameful, is thought highly becoming" (III 204), and "[n]one of the devotees of Zeus Casius at Pelusim would consume an onion, just as no Priest of Libyan Aphrodite would taste garlic" (III 224). Sextus would have been familiar with the surprising stories of difference related in the *Histories* of Herodotus, and of "the wonderful forms of different nations" described in Pliny's *Natural History* (Book 7, Chapter 2). Second, similar emphasis is placed on philosophical differences about ethical (as well as metaphysical and theological) matters (cf. §1.1, and see e.g. III 179–232). The Pyrrhonian skeptic, as described by Sextus, is deeply suspicious of the efforts of theoretical philosophers, and in particular of ethicists who theorize about what is good and bad "by nature". Attending to the reality of difference, both cultural and philosophical, puts the lie to all such ethical theories, with their pretentions to universality. In this connection, we should consider also the mode "depending on the differences among humans", where emphasis is placed on individual differences in perception, emotion, and preference (I 79–90). In any event, this skeptical emphasis on various kinds of difference, as against would-be universal theories of the good life, would be revived in the Early Modern period (cf. §1.6). And the debate between ethicists who appeal to human nature and those who reject such appeals continues in contemporary philosophy; consider, for example, the dispute between neo-Aristotelian virtue ethicists and anti-essentialist inheritors of existentialism.

A final comment on the ten modes. The Ancient skeptics anticipated Early Modern and contemporary discussions of skepticism in many ways (cf. §1.2.2), but when it comes to the "Cartesian skeptical argument", which was to play such a decisive role in Early Modern and contemporary epistemology, there is no version obviously to be found in Ancient philosophy (cf. Burnyeat 1982, Bermudez 2008, Williams 2010). Two Ancient skeptical arguments are worth mentioning in this connection. First, Sextus argues that "[d]ifferent appearances come about depending on sleeping or waking", and thus "the existence or non-existence of the objects becomes not absolute but relative"

(I 104; see also Cicero, *On Academic Scepticism*, 2.88). Second, the Ancient skeptics seemed to have appealed to the possibility of misleading sense impressions, indistinguishable from veridical sense impressions, in advancing their skeptical agenda. Here is **Cicero** (106–43 BC):

> [S]ome impressions are true, others false; and a false impression isn't apprehensible; but every true impression is such that one could also have had a false impression just like it. And when two impressions are such that they don't differ at all, it isn't possible that one of them is apprehensible, while the other isn't. Therefore, no impression is apprehensible. (*Scepticism*, 2.40)[9]

The seeds of the "Cartesian skeptical argument" are here. We'll return to that argument, below (§4.2.1).

1.2.2 *The five modes*

The most influential set of Ancient skeptical arguments is the **five modes** (Sextus, *Outlines*, I 164–77; cf. Diogenes, *Lives*, IX 88–9), often called the five modes of **Agrippa** (first century AD). About Agrippa we know nothing apart from the fact that the five modes are attributed to him by Diogenes Laertius (*Lives*, IX 88). Here we shall briefly survey the five modes—they all have descendants in later philosophy, and we'll give them further scrutiny below. The five modes are:

1   The mode from dispute

2   The mode from infinite regress

3   The mode from relativity

4   The mode from hypothesis

5   The reciprocal mode

The mode from infinite regress, the mode from hypothesis, and the reciprocal mode together constitute a powerful and important skeptical argument known as **Agrippa's trilemma**.[10] The best way to see how the trilemma works is to imagine a conversation between a Pyrrhonian skeptic and someone who asserts that p; call the latter the "claimant". The skeptic asks the claimant to defend her assertion that p. Suppose she appeals at this point to the fact that q_1. The skeptic then asks the claimant to defend her assertion that q_1. And so on for additional assertions that q_2, that q_3, and so on. At any point at which the claimant appeals to the fact that q_i, and the skeptic asks her to defend her assertion that q_i, one of three things might happen:

1   The claimant cannot defend q_i. Perhaps she thinks q_i is obviously true; perhaps she thinks that there are good reasons for q_i but doesn't know what they are; perhaps she thinks that there are good reasons for q_i that she can't put into words. In any event, the claimant's defense of her original assertion that p comes to an end with her making an assertion that she cannot defend; she has begun "from something which [she does not] establish but claim[s] to assume simply and without proof in virtue of a concession" (Sextus, *Outlines*, I 168). This, so the argument goes, makes the claimant's defense illegitimate, and by applying the **mode from hypothesis**, the skeptic suspends judgment about whether p.

2   The claimant appeals to the fact that p, in defense of her claim that q_i. The claimant's defense of her original claim that p involves her appealing to the fact that p, and so "what ought to be confirmatory of the object under investigation needs to be made convincing by the object under investigation" (I 169). This, so the argument goes, makes the claimant's defense illegitimate, and by applying the **reciprocal mode**, the skeptic suspends judgment about whether p.

3   The claimant appeals to the fact that q_{i+1}, in defense of her claim that qi, and then to the fact that q_{i+2}, in defense of her claim that q_{i+1}, and so on. The claimant's defense of her original claim never comes to an end, and "what is brought forward as a source of conviction for the matter proposed itself needs another source, which itself needs another, and so *ad infinitum*, so that we have no point from which to begin to establish anything" (I 166). This, so the argument goes, makes the claimant's defense illegitimate, and by applying the **mode from infinite regress**, the skeptic suspends judgment about whether p.

Furthermore, it is suggested, these are the only three possibilities: either the claimant's defense terminates with her appeal to the fact that q_i (in which case the mode from hypothesis kicks in), her defense terminates with her appeal to the fact that p (in which case the reciprocal mode kicks in), or her defense does not terminate (in which case the mode deriving from infinite regress kicks in). Therefore, in any event, the skeptic will suspend judgment about whether p. As well, it is notable that we needed to assume nothing about the proposition that p to advance the argument. If the argument is sound, it would apply with complete generality for any proposition (cf. §1.3.2).

Agrippa's trilemma is a fascinating argument, and epistemologists have struggled with it for millennia. Each horn of the trilemma makes an assumption about the legitimacy of a certain form of argument: the first horn assumes that an argument is illegitimate if you can't argue for its premises, the second horn assumes that that circular arguments are illegitimate, and the third horn assumes that arguments with an infinite number of premises are illegitimate. These assumptions could be challenged—and the critical discussion of these assumptions composes the contemporary epistemological issue of the "structure of justification." (For more on this issue, see this chapter's "Readings".) But the trilemma, as formulated, also seems to make a more basic assumption: that you ought to suspend judgment about whether p if a legitimate defense of the assertion that p cannot be provided. When we turn to Hume's version of this argument (§3.1), I'll argue that an assumption like this is ultimately what weakens it (§3.2.2).

The trilemma is implicated in another Ancient skeptical argument: the **problem of the criterion**. Probably the most exciting topic for Ancient epistemologists was the question of whether there is a "criterion" or "standard of truth", and if so, what that standard is.[11] The problem of the criterion grows out of a closely-related problem, the so-called **paradox of inquiry**, articulated by Meno:

> How will you look for it, Socrates, when you do not know at all what it is? How will you aim to search for something you do not know at all? If you should meet with it, how will you know that this is the thing that you did not know? (Plato, *Meno*, 80d)

The problem of the criterion similarly arises from a concern that knowledge always requires prior knowledge—which suggests that knowledge is impossible. A "standard of truth", as Sextus puts it, is something "by which ... reality and unreality are judged" (*Outlines*, II 14). Consider some proposition that p—one, say, that you are inclined to believe. What defense can you offer of your would-be belief that p? Whatever defense you offer, it will presuppose some principle to the effect that such-and-such is sufficient for reasonable belief. In other words, it will presuppose some standard of truth. For example, suppose you are inclined to believe that you are presently seated. In defense of this belief, you might cite the fact that you see and feel that you are seated. This defense presupposes the principle that seeing and feeling that p is sufficient for reasonable belief that p. In other words, it presupposes that sense perception is a standard of truth. But what defense can you offer for this standard? At this point, Agrippa's trilemma kicks in, and the skeptic concludes that there is no defensible standard of truth—but an indefensible standard is no standard at all, and so there is no standard of truth (*Outlines*, I 178–9, II 14–79), and so knowledge is impossible.

As **Roderick Chisholm** (1916–99) (1982, pp. 61–5) argues, the problem of the criterion leads to the reciprocal mode: knowledge seems to require that we employ some procedure for distinguishing truth from falsity, but the legitimate employment of such a procedure seems to require that we know that said procedure is reliable, but knowing *that* seems to require that we already possess the very knowledge that we sought in the first place. A defense of sense perception as a standard of truth would surely cite, in the first instance, the reliability of sense perception. But how do we know that sense perception is reliable? It seems the only way we could know *that* would involve the employment of sense perception—but this seems to bring us straightaway to the reciprocal mode. Below, we'll further consider the problem of the criterion (§2.1) and Chisholm's articulation of it (§5.1).

The most eloquent skeptical defender of Agrippa's trilemma was David Hume, and we'll return to his argument for skepticism (§3.1), which centers on an application of the reciprocal mode.

On the **mode from relativity**, Sextus writes that "the existing object appears to be such-and-such relative to the subject judging" (*Outlines*, I 167), which is suggestive of the common structure of the ten modes (§1.2.1). The idea that perception can provide only subject-relative information, rather than knowledge of the external world, eventually found its most eloquent expression in the *Meditations* of René Descartes, to which we'll return (§4.1). The **mode from dispute**, where "undecidable dissension … both in ordinary life and among philosophers" (I 165) leads to suspension of judgment, has received considerable attention recently; we'll return to it below (Chapter 2).

1.3 Four distinctions

In this section we'll draw four distinctions that we'll need to make sense of the various species of skepticism. We'll discuss the order of skepticism (§1.3.1), the scope of skepticism (§1.3.2), the distinction between Academic and Pyrrhonian skepticism (§1.3.3), and the modality of skepticism (§1.3.4).

1.3.1 The order of skepticism

Imagine that you believe that whales evolved from land mammals. This is what philosophers call a "first-order" belief. To see why they call it that, imagine that you reflect on the question of what you believe about whale evolution, and now know that this is what you believe. You now have a "second-order" belief: you believe that you believe that whales evolved from land mammals. A **second-order belief** is a belief *about* beliefs; a **first-order belief** is a belief that isn't second-order. Let's assume that beliefs about *knowledge* are second-order beliefs: knowledge requires belief, and this provides the sense in which beliefs about knowledge are beliefs about beliefs. There is a plurality of species of skepticism, depending on (what I'll call) their order.

We might understand skepticism as essentially a matter of your second-order beliefs—or, in any event, as essentially a matter of your attitude toward your first-order beliefs. One way to do this would be to understand skepticism as a view, e.g. as a view about the extent of our knowledge, e.g. that knowledge is impossible (cf. §1.1). A skeptic, then, would be someone who believes or defends or otherwise accepts that view. Another way would be to understand the skeptic as one who suspends judgment about the extent of our knowledge, as one who lacks the dogmatic conviction that her first-order beliefs amount to knowledge. Along these lines, consider Michael Frede's (1979) explanation:

> What fundamentally distinguishes the sceptic from other people are not the beliefs he has but his attitude towards them. He no longer has the more or less naive and partially dogmatic attitude of the "ordinary" man; his relation to his beliefs is permeated by an awareness that things are quite possibly different in reality, but this possibility no longer worries him. (p. 23; see also p. 19)

These species of skepticism deserve to be called species of **second-order skepticism**. We must contrast them with species of skepticism such that skepticism is essentially a matter of your first-order beliefs, or species of **first-order skepticism**. Consider the proposition that whales evolved from land mammals. We might understand skepticism such that the skeptic must suspend judgment about whether whales evolved from land mammals. This would be a species of first-order skepticism. If skepticism merely requires that you hold this belief non-dogmatically, e.g. that you not take yourself to know that whales evolved from land mammals, we would be dealing with a species of second-order skepticism.

The distinction between first-order and second-order skepticism is closely related to another distinction, between "doxastic" and "linguistic" skepticism. **Doxastic** means involving or pertaining to belief; **linguistic** means involving or pertaining to language. So far we have been speaking of skepticism as a matter of your beliefs—i.e. as a doxastic matter—and thus have considered only species of **doxastic skepticism**. But we might understand skepticism as a linguistic matter, and thus consider species of **linguistic skepticism**. One way to do this would be to understand the skeptic as someone who refrains from assertion—perhaps from all assertion, or perhaps from assertion about certain topics, or perhaps from a certain kind of assertion. And a more specific way to do this would be to understand the skeptic as someone who refrains from claiming knowledge—again, perhaps from claiming any knowledge at all, or perhaps from claiming knowledge about certain topics, or perhaps from a certain kind of claim of knowledge.[12]

1.3.2 *The scope of skepticism*

There are different ways we can interpret the Ancient skeptics when it comes to the scope of their skepticism, and in general we can articulate a plurality of species of skepticism, depending on their scope. The scope of a species of skepticism is determined by a set of propositions—the set of propositions targeted by that species of skepticism, where the set of propositions **targeted** by a species of skepticism are those propositions said to be unknowable, or those propositions about which judgment is suspended, or whatever. Skepticism is thus always **skepticism about** some set of propositions.

Skepticism that targets the set of *all* propositions is **rustic**.[13] So the rustic skeptic says that no proposition whatsoever can be known, or she suspends judgment about every proposition, or whatever. Rustic skepticism is sometimes called "radical skepticism"—a name that is also sometimes applied to "Cartesian skepticism" (cf. §4.2.3).

When skepticism targets some proper subset of the set of all propositions, it is **non-rustic**. The non-rustic skeptic is always a skeptic about some proper subset of the set of all propositions. Jonathan Barnes (1982) writes that:

> The **urbane** Pyrrhonist is happy to believe most of the things that ordinary people assent to in the ordinary course of events: he directs his [suspension of judgment] towards a specific target—roughly speaking towards philosophical and scientific matters. (pp. 61–2)

And if philosophy and science concern themselves with the "real properties, or essences" of things, this implies what R. J. Hankinson (1995) calls **essential** skepticism. This idea will provide one kind of reply to two important objections to skepticism (§1.4).

Following Barnes, we might identify the skeptic's target in more-or-less **disciplinary** terms: the skeptic might target only the propositions of ethics, or of psychology, or of literary criticism. Recall our sketch of the Ancient philosophical scene (§1.1), and the skeptic's frustration with the dogmatic claims

of metaphysicians and ethicists. We can call skepticism about the propositions of discipline C "skepticism about C". Relatedly, we might identify the
skeptic's target in terms of putative **sources** of belief, like sense perception,
testimony, or clairvoyance. Many people are skeptics about the propositional
contents of the beliefs yielded by clairvoyance; some are skeptics about the
propositional contents of the beliefs yielded by sense perception. We can call
skepticism about the propositional contents of source S "skepticism about S".
Finally, we might identify the skeptic's target in terms of an intuitive **domain**
of propositions. "Skepticism about other minds" targets only propositions
concerning the contents of other people's minds; "religious skepticism"
targets only propositions concerning "religious" matters; a certain kind of
skeptic about morality targets only "absolute" or "universal" moral propositions. We can call skepticism about domain D "skepticism about D".

Once we allow that skepticism can be quite localized, it seems that
everyone is some species of skeptic (Annas and Barnes 1985, p. 1; Barnes
1990, p. 9): everyone thinks that there are some propositions about which
knowledge is impossible; everyone suspends judgment about some propositions. We can speak of species of skepticism as being more or less urbane:
species of skepticism SK_1 is less urbane than species SK_2 (and thus SK_2 more
urbane than SK_1) iff[14] the propositions targeted by SK_1 are a proper subset of
the propositions targeted by SK_2. (Note that not all species of skepticism will
be comparable in terms of urbanity.)

1.3.3 Academic vs. Pyrrhonian skepticism

I spoke above of Academic and Pyrrhonian skepticism (§1.1). What's the
difference? We can identify paradigm Academic skeptics—e.g. Arcesilaus—
and Pyrrhonian skeptics—e.g. Aenesidemus—but the distinction between
Academics and Pyrrhonians was controversial even for the Ancients. How
should we understand it?

A bad idea, it seems to me, would be to say that the Academics were
concerned with knowledge (e.g. in rejecting the possibility of knowledge)
and that the Pyrrhonians were concerned with belief (e.g. in suspending
judgment). Pyrrhonian skeptics, like the Academics, were opposed to the
Stoic view that knowledge is possible, and Academic skeptics, like the
Pyrrhonians, were in favor of suspension of judgment: Diogenes Laertius
says that Arcesilaus "was the first to suspend judgment owing to the
contradictions of opposing arguments" (*Lives*, IV 28), and that "[a]ccording
to some, one result of his suspending judgment on all matters was that
he never so much as wrote a book" (*ibid.* 32), and Cicero says that the
Academics suspension of assent was based on the argument that "if nothing

is apprehensible ... we must do away with assent" (*Scepticism*, 2.59). However, the following are better ideas about how to distinguish Academic from Pyrrhonian skepticism.

First, we might say that there is no significant difference between Academic and Pyrrhonian skepticism. For example, Sextus—who carefully distinguishes between a number of Academic philosophies (*Outlines*, I 220–35)—writes of Arcesilaus that "his persuasion and ours are virtually the same" (I 232; cf. Bayle, *Historical and Critical Dictionary*, p. 194). The view that the distinction between Academics and Pyrrhonians is spurious can be motivated by appealing to the idea that what appear to be Academic arguments for the conclusion that knowledge is impossible are actually *ad hominem* devices, designed to show that *if* one accepts Stoic epistemology, *then* knowledge is impossible (which contradicts the Stoics' own view that knowledge is possible).[15] Among other virtues, this interpretation jibes with the idea that the Academics claimed that "one ought to argue pro and contra everything, for the sake of discovering the truth" (Cicero, *Scepticism*, 2.60; see also Diogenes Laertius, *Lives*, IV 28; cf. Striker 2010, p. 201). Such arguments, on this interpretation, are not designed to establish their conclusion but rather to induce suspension of judgment.

Second, we might say that the only significant difference between Academic and Pyrrhonian skepticism is ethical: for the Pyrrhonians, but not for the Academics, suspension of judgment leads to tranquility (Annas and Barnes 1985, p. 14; Striker 1996, p. 148). More generally, we could say that Pyrrhonian skepticism is a way of life, whereas Academic skepticism, whether understood as a view or as a practice, is something more professional or scholastic.

Third, we might appeal to a distinction between "mitigated" and "unmitigated" skepticism. Consider the view that, while knowledge is impossible, some beliefs are reasonable and some unreasonable (or that some beliefs are more reasonable than others). This is a species of **mitigated** skepticism, by contrast with the corresponding species of **unmitigated** skepticism, which rejects not only the view that knowledge is possible, but also the view that reasonable belief is possible. The mitigated and unmitigated skeptic seem to disagree about the following principle:

Knowledge-belief principle: If you don't know whether p, it is not reasonable for you to believe that p.

And assuming that you ought to suspend judgment about whether p if neither believing nor disbelieving that p is reasonable for you, their disagreement is over the question of whether there is a gap between unknowability and suspension of judgment (cf. Barnes 1990, p. 10). For the unmitigated skeptic, there is no such gap: about what cannot be known, we ought to suspend judgment. For the mitigated skeptic, there is: I can reasonably believe that p, even if I do not know that p. In any event, given this distinction, we might understand Academic skepticism as essentially mitigated, and Pyrrhonian skepticism as essentially unmitigated.[16] There will thus be situations in which the Pyrrhonian skeptic suspends judgment about whether p, but in which the Academic skeptic believes that p, perhaps while suspending judgment about whether she knows that p. We'll return to the distinction between mitigated and unmitigated skepticism below (§9.1.2).

Fourth, and finally, we might follow Sextus and understand the Academic skeptic, but not the Pyrrhonian skeptic, as believing or asserting some proposition—e.g. that nothing can be known. Here is his famous set-up:

> When people are investigating any subject, the likely result is either a discovery, or a denial of a discovery and a confession of inapprehensibility, or else a continuation of the investigation. [...] Those who are called Dogmatists in the proper sense of the word think that they have discovered the truth—for example, the schools of Aristotle and Epicurus and the Stoics, and some others. The schools of Clitomachus and Carneades, and other Academics, have asserted that things cannot be apprehended. And the Sceptics are still investigating. (*Outlines*, I 1)

The Academic skeptics, on this interpretation, did not suspend judgment (at least not about the possibility of knowledge), but rather believed or asserted that knowledge is impossible, while the Pyrrhonian skeptics did no such thing.

For our purposes here, we can set aside the issue of whether Sextus' interpretation of his Academic interlocutors was historically accurate.[17] We'll use the language of "Academic" and "Pyrrhonian" to mark a closely related distinction: we'll treat **Academic** skepticism as a view—as a theory, a claim, an assertion, a belief, a proposition—and we'll treat **Pyrrhonian** skepticism as a practice, or a way of life, or, as Sextus puts it, as an ability:

> Scepticism is the ability to set out oppositions among things which appear and are thought of in any way at all, an ability by which, because of the equipollence of the opposed objects and accounts, we come first to suspension of judgment and afterwards to tranquility. (I 8)

Perhaps for reasons to which we'll turn in a moment (§1.5), contemporary epistemological discussions of skepticism have focused on species of Academic skepticism. In particular they have focused on versions of the thesis that knowledge is impossible. But there are other species of Academic skepticism, e.g. the claim that one ought to suspend judgment about some set of propositions.

1.3.4 The modality of skepticism

We can distinguish species of Academic skepticism in terms of their **modality**. Consider:

- Knowledge is impossible

- Knowledge is impossible for humans

- No humans actually have any knowledge

The first claim is modally stronger than the second, and the second is modally stronger than the third. We won't pay much attention to the modality of skepticism in this book, although we will return to it briefly (§4.2.3), but it's something to keep in mind in thinking about the varieties of skepticism, and the varieties of skeptical argument.

1.4 Two objections to skepticism

In this section I'll introduce two of the most important objections to skepticism. They're still around, but were first pressed by the Stoics. We'll first consider the charge that skepticism is self-refuting (§1.4.1), and then the charge that skepticism is incompatible with action (§1.4.2).

1.4.1 The self-refutation objection

Consider the following proposition:

S No proposition can be known by anyone.

Critics of skepticism are quick to point out that if (S) is true, then no one can know (S). (S) applies to (S) just as much as to any other proposition, and so (S) entails that (S) cannot be known by anyone. Thus a **self-refutation objection** to skepticism, which appeals to the premise that if (S) is true, (S) cannot be known. How serious is this objection?

It seems that this objection does not threaten rustic Pyrrhonian skepticism (§1.3.2, §1.3.3), or indeed any Pyrrhonian skeptic who suspends judgment about (S). The rustic Pyrrhonian suspends judgment about whether (S) is true, so the fact that, if (S) is true, (S) cannot be known, does no damage to the Pyrrhonian's position. It is the Academic skeptic who maintains (S), or something like it; what distinguishes the Pyrrhonian is precisely her suspension of judgment about propositions of this kind (Barnes 1990, p. 10).

However, things are a bit more complicated than that, given that the Pyrrhonian, as Sextus describes her, is disposed to "use" (more on this in a moment) various "**skeptical phrases**", including:

1   "No more this than that" (*Outlines*, I 188)

2   "I suspend judgment" (I 196)

3   "Everything is undetermined" (I 198)

4   "Everything is inapprehensible" (I 200)

The self-refutation objection can be rearticulated, for example, when it comes to (4): if (4) is true, then (4) is inapprehensible. Is this a problem for the Pyrrhonian?

There are several avenues of reply open here. One reply is articulated by Sextus:

> [J]ust as the phrase "Everything is false" says that it too, along with every-thing else, is false … so also "In no way more" says that it too, along with everything else, is no more so than not so, and hence it cancels itself out along with everything else. And we say the same of the other Sceptical phrases. (I 14)

In other words, the Pyrrhonian skeptic does not claim that (4) is apprehen-sible, and so there is no threat to her position from the fact that, if (4) is true, then (4) is inapprehensible. Another reply is suggested elsewhere (I 188–200): the skeptic's "use" of a given skeptical phrase is merely a "report" of the skeptic's "feeling", and not an "assertion" or "affirmation". So the skeptic is not even committed to the truth of (4)—and thus her position is unthreatened by the fact that, if (4) is true, then (4) is inapprehensible.

This second reply, however, raises the question of just what the skeptic is doing when she "uses" the skeptical phrases. In uttering (4), how is she not committed to believing that (4) is true? It seems to me that there are two quite different possibilities here. I assume that when someone asserts that p she represents herself as believing that p.

The first possibility is that the skeptic's utterances of the skeptical phrases are assertions, and thus commit her to believing that they are true. In devel-oping this reply to the self-refutation objection, the Pyrrhonian could adopt a form of non-rustic skepticism (§1.3.2), on which propositions about appearances are not targeted, and amend or clarify (4) to:

4* "It appears to me that everything is inapprehensible"

This jibes with what Sextus says in several passages (e.g. I 193, I 197, I 199, I 200).[18] Alternatively, the Pyrrhonian could adopt a form of non-rustic skepticism, on which the proposition expressed by (4) is simply not targeted (cf. Burnyeat 1980, p. 56). We'll return to this idea below, in connection with Academic skepticism.

The second possibility is that the skeptic's utterance of (4) is not an assertion, and involves no commitment to believing that (4) is true. To assert that p, the skeptic concedes, is to represent oneself as believing that p, and thus the rustic Pyrrhonian's suspension of judgment commits her to not asserting anything (cf. Sextus, *Outlines* I 192). But what then is the skeptic up to, when she utters (4), and the other skeptical phrases? The Pyrrhonian could say that she is *reporting the appearance* that (4) is true, where reporting the appearance that p is distinct both from asserting that p and from asserting that it appears that p. But what does "reporting the appearance that p" mean? Perhaps it involves "confessions" or "avowals" (Barnes 1982, p. 65) or perhaps assumption, pretense, hypothesis, or "approval." (Perin 2010, pp. 149–50) Alternatively (but consistent with the previous strategy), the Pyrrhonian could say that her utterance of the skeptical phrases is part of a purely rhetorical or dialectical strategy against her Stoic and Academic interlocutors, designed to bring about suspension of judgment (cf. §1.3.3). Finally (but consistent with both the previous strategies), the Pyrrhonian could say that her utterance of the skeptical phrases involves a temporary commitment to their truth, which commitment is part of a course of skeptical treatment. Here is Sextus:

> In the case of the skeptical phrases, you should understand that we do not affirm definitely that they are true—after all, we say that they can be destroyed by themselves, being cancelled out along with what they are applied to, just as purgative drugs do not merely drain the humors from the body but drive themselves out too along with the humors. (I 206; see also Diogenes Laertius, *Lives*, IX 76)

And elsewhere Sextus compares the skeptical phrases to a ladder that one climbs and then discards (*Against the Logicians* 2.481).

It seems then that the Pyrrhonian has a wealth of options available to her, when it comes to replying to the self-refutation objection. What about the Academic skeptic? Let's grant that she believes that (S) is true. If (S) is true, then (S) cannot be known. Does this threaten the Academic skeptic?[19]

In virtue of her belief that (S) is true, the Academic skeptic seems committed to the claim that (S) cannot be known (Cicero, *Scepticism*, 2.28). If so, she believes that p while being committed to the claim that she does not know that p. If the knowledge-belief principle (§1.3.3) is true, she seems thus committed to the claim that her belief that p is not reasonable. But mitigated skepticism, which rejects the knowledge-belief principle, does not seem to be affected by this worry. We'll return to the plausibility of mitigated skepticism below (Chapter 9).

Note well, for the time being, that (S) is importantly different from:

N No proposition is true

Someone who believes that (N) is true is committed to the claim that (N) is not true. She seems thereby to have contradicted herself. But believing that (S) is true involves no such contradiction. The person who believes that (S) is true is committed to the claim that (S) is not known. That (S) is not known does not imply that (S) is not true.

Alternatively, the Academic might opt for a species of non-rustic skepticism (§1.3.2), and amend (S) accordingly.[20] For example, she might opt for the view that perceptual knowledge is impossible, or the view that ethical knowledge is impossible. Since the proposition that perceptual knowledge is impossible is not itself an item of would-be perceptual knowledge, and the proposition that ethical knowledge is impossible is not itself an item of would-be ethical knowledge, the self-refutation objection would not apply. Similarly, if skepticism is confined to propositions concerning "how things really are" or "how things are in nature" (Frede 1979; Barnes 1982; cf. Burnyeat 1980), the Academic can amend her view to:

S* No proposition concerning "how things really are" can be known by anyone

and argue that (S*) is not itself a proposition concerning "how things really are". Again, the self-refutation objection would not apply.

In any event, it seems then that the Academic has a wealth of options available to her, when it comes to replying to the self-refutation objection.

Before turning to the second of our two objections to skepticism, it is worth mentioning a cousin of the self-refutation objection. Suppose the skeptic offers an argument for some conclusion, e.g. that knowledge is impossible. Her conclusion commits her to the claim that she does not know that the premises of her argument are true. But if the skeptic does not know the premises of her argument, why should anyone be convinced by said argument? Call this the **self-undermining objection** to skepticism (cf. Cicero, *Scepticism*, 2.43; Bayle, *Dictionary*, pp. 205–6).

We'll return to this argument below (§4.4.1), but four observations should be made here. First, the self-undermining objection does not suggest that skepticism is false; at most it suggests that skepticism cannot be defended. Second, in connection with this, the premises of an argument might be true, even if they are not known, so the self-undermining objection does not suggest that the premises of the skeptic's argument are false. Third, the self-undermining objection does not seem to threaten Pyrrhonian skepticism. As Jonathan Barnes (1982) argues:

When a philosopher offers us an argument, he normally implies that, if we accept the premises, we ought to accept the conclusion. It is thus natural to suppose that a Pyrrhonist's arguments similarly imply an intellectual *ought*: 'Consider these premises', the Sceptic urges, 'and you will see that you should suspend judgment'. [But] Sextus usually says, not 'you *should* suspend judgment', but 'you *will* (or: *must*) suspend judgment'. […] The onset of ἐποχή is something which simply *happens* to us. (pp. 58–9)

The modes employed by the Pyrrhonian skeptic, on this interpretation, are not arguments for some conclusion, but techniques or methods or strategies designed to cause suspension of judgment. The self-undermining objection, therefore, is a *non sequitur* when it comes to Pyrrhonian skepticism. Fourth, all the replies to the self-refutation objection that we considered above could be used, *mutatis mutandis*, against the self-undermining objection.

1.4.2 The apraxia objection

Probably the most instinctive and common and historically important objection to skepticism is the charge that skepticism is, in some sense, impractical. The skeptic, so the objection goes, will be unable to act, or she will be unable to live a normal life, or she will become immoral and irreligious. Here is Socrates:

[W]e will be better men, braver and less idle, if we believe that one must search for the things that one does not know, rather than if we believe that it is not possible to find out what we do not know and that we must not look for it. (*Meno*, 86b–c)

Worries about the corrupting influence of skepticism, present in Ancient times (Cicero, *Scepticism*, 2.27), became hyperbolic in the Early Modern period, with anti-skeptical philosophers denouncing the bad effects of skepticism (cf. §9.2.1). A more basic version of this thought is the idea that skepticism is incompatible with action. Aristotle pressed this kind of objection, against someone who would both believe that p and believe that ~p:

> [I]f he makes no judgment but thinks and does not think, indifferently, what difference will there be between him and plants? [...] For why does a man walk to Megara and not stay at home thinking he ought to walk? Why does he not walk early some morning into a well or over a precipice, if one happens to be in his way? Why do we observe him guarding against this, evidently not thinking that falling in is alike good and not good? Evidently he judges one thing to be better and another worse. (*Metaphysics* IV.4, 1008b 10–19)[21]

But this seems to apply, *mutatis mutandis*, to the rustic skeptic who suspends judgment, and the Ancient Stoics pressed this objection against their Academic interlocutors. Pyrrho's critics lampooned him as "taking no precaution, but facing all risks as they came", and as being "kept out of harm's way by his friends" (Diogenes Laertius, *Lives*, IX 62). We can articulate this objection in the form of a dilemma. Faced with some situation in which a non-skeptic would, say, turn left to avoid walking over a cliff, on the basis of her belief that there is a cliff in her way, either:

i   The skeptic turns left, thus suggesting that she too believes that there is a cliff in her way, and therefore is no skeptic, or

ii The skeptic walks over the cliff, thus suggesting that suspension of judgment does not lead to (the relevant sort of) tranquility.

This is the **apraxia objection** to skepticism; "praxis" means "action" and "apraxia" means "without action", i.e. paralysis or inactivity.

Note well that this objection does not threaten mitigated Academic skepticism (§1.3.3). Nor does it even threaten the unmitigated species of Academic skepticism that says that everyone ought to suspend judgment about everything, unless the skeptic also asserts the Pyrrhonian ethical idea that suspension of judgment leads to tranquility (cf. §4.5.2).

The apraxia objection can be bolstered if we assume the popular belief-desire model of action. According to this model, every intentional action is caused by at least one belief and at least one desire; in a paradigm case, a person will Φ as a result of desiring that p and believing that Φing will bring it about, or make it more likely, that p. In Aristotle's case, your desire to not fall off the cliff, combined with your belief that turning left will bring it about that you do not fall off the cliff, causes you to turn left. Mere belief can't bring about action (if you didn't want to avoid falling, you wouldn't avoid the cliff), but mere desire can't bring about action either (if you didn't know that turning left was a way to avoid falling, for example if you could not see the cliff, you'd not turn left either, despite wanting to not fall). If this model is assumed, then it seems to follow that the skeptic, who suspends judgment, will be incapable of intentional action.

For the Ancient Stoics this objection was especially compelling, because they gave belief an even more important role *vis-à-vis* intentional action. The belief-desire model is popular in contemporary philosophy, but the Stoics would have assumed what we might call a belief-belief model: in Aristotle's case, your action is the result of your belief that turning left is a way to avoid falling in conjunction with, not a desire, but (as Aristotle suggests) another belief: your belief that it would be bad to fall. But whichever of these two models we adopt, intentional action requires belief.

There are a number of replies available to the Pyrrhonian, which we'll briefly survey here; and we'll return to the charge of impracticality below (Chapter 9). Many of these replies are compatible and mutually supporting, but we'll distinguish between them for the sake of clarity.

First, the apraxia objection does not threaten any species of non-rustic skepticism that does not target the relevant propositions (§1.3.2). One way of developing this idea would be to adopt some version of urbane or essential skepticism, e.g. on which the skeptic only targets propositions concerning "how things really are" or how things are "in nature" (cf. Burnyeat 1980; Barnes 1982).[22] Sextus suggests such an interpretation in several places (e.g. *Outlines*, I 13, I 30, I 59, I 140, I 208). Suspension of judgment about the "real nature" of the cliff does not require not believing that turning left is a way to avoid falling over the cliff, nor does it require not believing that falling over the cliff would be bad. Another way of developing this idea would be to understand the skeptic as not targeting beliefs about appearances (Perin 2010).

Second, we might argue that suspension of judgment is consistent with belief (Frede 1979). We assumed, above (§1.1), that suspension of judgment about whether p required neither believing that p nor disbelieving that p. On the present interpretation, the skeptic suspends judgment, but not belief.[23] This interpretation gains plausibility on the assumption that judgment, unlike belief, is voluntary, given Sextus' insistence that the skeptic does not (*per impossibile*) suspend attitudes over which she has no control (I 13, I 19, I 22, I 193).

Third, the skeptic might argue that the belief-desire model of action, or the belief-belief model of action, should be rejected. Sextus suggests this (I 21–4), writing that the skeptic's standard of action is "what is apparent" or "the appearances" (I 22; see also Vogt 2010b). However, there are a few different ways of fleshing out this idea. One possibility is that "appearance that p" is an attitude, distinct from believing that p, but which can play belief's role in combining with desire to yield action. We might understand "appearances" such that they include sense impressions, thus when it comes to the skeptic walking towards the cliff, although she does not believe that turning left is a way to avoid falling, it appears to her that turning left is a way to avoid falling—and this is sufficient, along with her desire to avoid falling, to cause her to turn left. As Sextus puts it, "[b]y nature's guidance we are naturally capable of perceiving and thinking" (I 24). Without giving up the spirit of the belief-desire model, the skeptic can amend it: what is required for action is desire along with some representation of the world, but that representation need not be a belief: a sense impression, for example, will do the job.

But what about the belief-belief model, where evaluative beliefs are required for intentional action? Here Sextus has another idea available, when he speaks of "necessitation by feelings" (*Ibid*.). He writes that "hunger conducts us to food and thirst to drink," (*ibid*.) and elsewhere notes that a dog "can both grasp and relieve his own feelings", as when she removes a thorn from her paw, cleans a wound, favors a lame leg, or eats grass to relieve "inappropriate humors." (I 70) Intentionally drinking a glass of water does not require, *pace* the belief-belief model, that you believe that drinking water is good; it merely requires that you are thirsty (Barnes 1982, pp. 82–3n).[24]

Sextus makes two other suggestions (I 23–4) about how "appearances" can cause action in the absence of belief. The first is that a nonbeliever can still have professional expertise or know-how (cf. Barnes 1982, pp. 83–4); the second is that a nonbeliever can habitually follow the laws and customs of her society (*ibid*. pp. 86–7). Both of these ideas, it seems to me, require the Pyrrhonian to adopt some species of non-rustic skepticism (§1.3.2), since both know-how and habitual conformity will require the knower and the conformist, respectively, to have some beliefs.

In any event, it seems then that the Pyrrhonian skeptic has a wealth of options available to her, when it comes to replying to the apraxia objection.

The apraxia objection raises an important question when it comes to our understanding of Pyrrhonian skepticism. What is the practical difference (the difference in action), if any, between the Pyrrhonian skeptic and her non-skeptical counterpart? On the one hand, we know that in philosophical conversation the skeptic behaves in a distinctive way: she puts forward arguments on both sides of any issue, for example, and she utters the skeptical phrases (§1.4.1). And we're told that there will be situations in which the skeptic, but not her non-skeptical counterpart, will be tranquil, and such tranquility is at least partly a practical matter; consider the case of Pyrrho's tranquility during a storm at sea (§1.1). However, on the other hand, in response to the apraxia objection the skeptic is keen to show that she will be able to live an ordinary life: she'll avoid danger, she'll eat when hungry, she'll go to work and practice her trade, and she'll stick to social conventions.[25] We'll return to some of these issues below (Chapter 9).

1.5 A problem for rustic Pyrrhonian skepticism

We are now in a position to articulate a problem for rustic Pyrrhonian skepticism (cf. Woodruff 2010, pp. 210–11). The problem is that rustic Pyrrhonian skepticism can be neither criticized nor defended. Because she asserts no proposition, the rustic Pyrrhonian is immune to criticism: we cannot allege that her view is false, for she asserts no view. But because she asserts no proposition, the rustic Pyrrhonian cannot defend her position: she cannot offer an argument for her view, for she asserts no view. (Note that this would not necessarily be a problem for the non-rustic Pyrrhonian skeptic; cf. §1.3.2.)

This problem does not arise for Academic skepticism, for Academic skepticism is a view (§1.3.3). Pyrrhonian skepticism, by contrast, is a practice or way of life. And this problem does not (necessarily) arise for non-rustic Pyrrhonian skepticism, for the non-rustic Pyrrhonian is free to assert a philosophical view (Woodruff 2010, p. 211). The problem is that the rustic Pyrrhonian asserts no view, and is therefore both immune to criticism and incapable of self-defense.

You might object that practices and ways of life can be criticized and defended. But this will not help the *rustic* Pyrrhonian. For what can she say in defense of her skeptical practice? Perhaps that suspension of judgment leads to tranquility. But the rustic Pyrrhonian faces a dilemma. If, on the one hand, she is asserting that suspension of judgment leads to tranquility, then she represents herself as believing that suspension of judgment leads to tranquility. We can now have a philosophical debate about the proposition that suspension of judgment leads to tranquility, but our interlocutor has shifted to a species of non-rustic skepticism. If, on the other hand, she is not asserting that suspension of judgment leads to tranquility, then she has offered no defense of her skeptical practice. The same, *mutatis mutandis*, when it comes to the possibility of criticism of the skeptic's practice.

Critique and defense take place in a space of reasons given for and against the truth and falsity of propositions. To the extent that the skeptic refuses to assert the truth or falsity of any proposition, she is outside this space of reasons. As Myles Burnyeat (1980) puts it, "the sceptic who adheres strictly to appearance is withdrawing to the safety of a position not open to challenge or enquiry" (p. 41). And as Gisela Striker (1996) argues, the skeptic's position (of "conviction") is a "state of mind, comparable to a physical sensation"

(p. 146)—her suspension of judgment is not a proposition actively asserted, but a state that she finds herself in. Thus:

> [J]ust as it is absurd to try to talk a person out of his hunger, so [the skeptics] considered it absurd to try to persuade the skeptic that he's not convinced. And a counterargument would accomplish nothing at all, since after all the skeptic only takes her thesis to be convincing, not true. (*Ibid.*; cf. Burnyeat 1980, pp. 30–1)

This sounds at first like it's good news for the rustic Pyrrhonian—what philosopher wouldn't want to withdraw to a position safe from all objections—but it's really not. It takes more to win the argument than to not lose the argument, which is why you can't win the argument by not making one.

The rustic Pyrrhonian skeptic, perhaps, has given up trying to win the philosophical argument; she has given up playing that particular game. In this respect, she closely resembles the naïve non-philosopher, who never took up the game in the first place. Perhaps, for this, our intellectual attitude toward the Pyrrhonian should be the same as our attitude toward the naïve non-philosopher. It seems to me that this attitude should be one of indifference: the Pyrrhonian, like the non-philosopher, has lots of things to say, but since both are outside the space of reasons, we can ignore them when we're inside that space.

You might argue that winning the philosophical argument is impossible. But it seems to me that this is a weak reason not to try. Sisyphus had it right: trying the impossible is better than the alternative. We should try to argue, to engage in critique and defense, and for this reason we should not be rustic Pyrrhonian skeptics. In any event, our focus in what follows will be on species of Academic skepticism (which have been the focus of contemporary epistemological discussions of skepticism).

1.6 The Early Modern skeptical renaissance

Skepticism did not disappear from the philosophical landscape in Medieval Europe, but it definitely dropped off the radar. Although critics of Aristotle deployed skeptical arguments (cf. Popkin 1979, p. 18; Bermudez 2008, pp. 67–9), Aristotelian ideas dominated the epistemological scene. Academic skeptics appeared in the early sixteenth century, inspired by a renewed interest in Cicero's *On Academic Scepticism*, and the publication of a Latin translation of Sextus' *Outlines* in 1562 coincided with a renaissance of skeptical thinking.[26] Skepticism came back to life in the Early Modern period.

Two factors played a decisive role here. The first was the Protestant Reformation. Essential to the dispute between Reformers like **Martin Luther** (1483–1586) and **John Calvin** (1509–64), on the one hand, and Counter-Reformers, on the other, was a question about the standard of truth (§1.2.2): for the Protestants, the standard was individual conscience; for the Catholics (at least at first), the standard was tradition. Eventually, Christianity was radically fragmented, with Protestant denominations (Lutherans, Baptists, Presbyterians, Anabaptists, Quakers, etc.) proliferating. In the same way that Ancient skepticism was motivated by the persistence of philosophical disagreement (§1.1), Early Modern skepticism was motivated, at least at first, by the persistence—and eventual violence—of religious disagreement.

The first Early Modern skeptics were Catholics who saw skepticism as an argument against Reformation, with Luther cast in the role of the dogmatist. Some of these Catholic skeptics, like **Sebastian Castellio** (1515–63), **Francisco Sanchez** (1552–1623), **Marsene Mersenne** (1588–1648), and **Pierre Gassendi** (1592–1655), were **mitigated Academic skeptics**, inspired by Cicero. After 1562, however, a new species of Catholic skepticism developed, inspired by Sextus: a **Pyrrhonian fideism** most eloquently defended by **Michel de Montaigne** (1533–92) in his "Apology for Raymond Sebond" (1580).[27]

Montaigne's position can perhaps be best understood by contrasting it with the Augustinian maxim "crede, ut intelligas": believe so that you may understand. Montaigne's version of this would have been: suspend judgment so that you may believe. For Montaigne, Pyrrhonian suspension of judgment was the first step of a two-step process; the second step was faithful acceptance of religious truth (viz., Catholicism). Montaigne advances the skeptical modes (§1.2), with the aim of inducing suspension of judgment, and sarcastically rails against the weakness of reason and the intellectual vanity of human beings; "[t]o what degree of arrogance and insolence", he writes, "do we not carry our blindness and our brutish stupidity" (p. 623).[28] (As is typical of a certain kind of humanist, Montaigne is able to muster up a seething hatred of humans.) But Montaigne's skepticism is a prelude to faith, gracefully delivered:

No system discovered by Man has greater usefulness nor a greater appearance of truth [than Pyrrhonism,] which shows us Man naked, empty, aware of his natural weakness, fit to accept outside help from on high: Man, stripped of all human learning and so all the more able to lodge the divine within him, annihilating his intellect to make room for faith[. H]e is humble, obedient, teachable, keen to learn[.] He is a blank writing-tablet, made ready for the finger of God to carve such letters on him as he pleases. (p. 564)

An important feature of the Reformation crisis was the assumption, on both sides, that religious beliefs must be certain. This limited the options to two: Luther's infallibilism—on which knowledge requires certainty (cf. §4.3)—or Montaigne's Pyrrhonian fideism. The mitigated Catholic skeptics, mentioned above, saw the way out of this dilemma: reject the requirement of certainty; Montaigne, for his part, rejects that move (pp. 623–3).

Pyrrhonian fideism eventually found Protestant defenders as well. In his *Historical and Critical Dictionary* (1697), **Pierre Bayle** (1647–1706) wrote of Pyrrhonism that:

> [I]t may have its value in making men conscious of the darkness they are in, so that they will implore help from on high and submit to the authority of the faith. (p. 194; see also p. 206)[29, 30]

However, Bayle also suggests a species of non-rustic skepticism, targeting the propositions of "natural science … concerning the causes producing heat, cold, the tides, and the like",[31] and exempting propositions of "the divine science" (*Ibid.* p. 194; see also p. 422).

The second decisive factor in the skeptical renaissance was the discovery of the New World. As with their Ancient predecessors, Early Modern skeptics were impressed by the evidence of cultural difference. Montaigne dwells on the theme of individual and cultural difference (e.g. p. 547, pp. 582–3, pp. 656–8), and mentions the New World in this connection (pp. 587–8, p. 646). He also invokes exploration as evidence of our limited knowledge: Ptolemy thought he had "established the boundaries of the known world", but "in our century new discoveries have revealed, not an odd island or odd individual country, but an infinite land-mass, almost equal in size to the part we already know", and "[s]ince Ptolemy was once mistaken over his basic tenets, would it not be foolish to trust what moderns are saying now?" (p. 644).[32] As for Sextus, Montaigne's interest in difference stems from the premise that the existence of knowledge would bring about "universal assent" to the proposition known (p. 634). But the reality of individual and cultural difference ensures that there is disagreement about everything.[33]

The revival of Pyrrhonism had a tremendous impact on European philosophy, and in particular on René Descartes (cf. Chapter 4), whose anti-skeptical meditations constitute the most famous discussion of skepticism ever published, and David Hume (cf. Chapter 3), whose skepticism epitomized the Age of Enlightenment and announced the dawn of secularism.

To conclude this section, however, I'll make four comments on the social and political implications of Early Modern Pyrrhonian fideism.

First issue: toleration. The Early Modern skeptics were deeply concerned with "all the sects and schisms that our century has produced" (Montaigne, op. cit., p. 642; see also p. 656), which prompted their emphasis on ignorance about religious matters like the nature of God (*ibid.* p. 556, p. 573), the afterlife (pp. 580–3), and the soul (pp. 608–26). In some cases, skepticism about religion motivated religious tolerance. Castellio, as Popkin (1979) argues, "indicated that no one was really so sure of the truth in religious affairs that he was justified in killing another as a heretic" (p. 10). Bayle's early defenses of religious toleration, written in Holland as a religious refugee, were read sympathetically by **John Locke** (1632–1704), whose "Letter concerning Toleration" (1689) was, in turn, read sympathetically by **Thomas Jefferson** (1743–1826) and other early liberals.

Second issue: conservativism. Recall the idea that the Pyrrhonian will use "laws and customs" as a standard of action (§1.4.2). But given the diversity of laws and customs in the world, which laws and customs should you use as your standard? The Pyrrhonian's answer is that you should use the laws and customs of *your* society as your standard. But what this shows us is that the "laws and customs" standard implies a form of social and political conservativism.[34] For Montaigne, this is essential: suspension of judgment leads eventually to "the ancient beliefs of our religion" (p. 642; cf. Popkin 1979, p. 47), i.e. Catholicism, not to some new beliefs of someone else's religion. We can see why Montaigne is called a skeptic: he rejects the possibility of human knowledge. But we should also note that there is a sense in which he is no skeptic at all: he is certain that ignorance and Catholic piety are what is absolutely and universally good. With respect of his having metaphysical and ethical commitments, Montaigne seems to have failed utterly in his emulation of the Ancient skeptics.[35] For the same reason, he lacks a trait found in many skeptics (e.g., and especially, Hume): an aversion to testimony and, especially, the appeal to authority. Montaigne's emphasis on "submissiveness and obedience" (p. 557), and his manifest respect for ecclesiastical tradition and authority, make him look like a most credulous and trusting "skeptic". (As well, this makes the dispute between the Protestant infallibilists and the Catholic fideists look not like a dispute between dogmatists and skeptics but more like a dispute between two species of dogmatist, each wielding a different standard of truth: the Protestants choosing individual conscience, and the Catholics choosing tradition and authority.)

Third issue: anti-intellectualism. There is no doubt that that language of Montaigne is suggestive of the religious anti-intellectualism that still plagues many societies. "We would be better if we dropped our inquiries and let ourselves be moulded by the natural order of the world" (p. 564)—it sounds like a line from a speech in defense of education funding cuts. Intellectuals are mocked as self-promoters and deliberate obfuscators: "Not only Aristotle but most philosophers aim at being hard to understand; why?—if not to emphasize the vanity of their subject-matter and to give our minds something to do!" (p. 566). Montaigne is against inquiry, criticism, learning, and study; and he inherits the anti-intellectualism of Paul, who railed against wisdom-seeking Greeks (1 Cor. 1.22). In this respect, again, Montaigne's Pyrrhonian fideist does not resemble the Ancient skeptics.

Fourth issue: secularism. For some Early Modern writers, "skepticism" and "atheism" were synonymous, and the association of skepticism and secularism[36] is still strong (think of *The Skeptic* magazine). From what has been said so far, it is clear that no association can be made between Pyrrhonian fideism and secularism. Secular skepticism developed later (cf. Popkin 1979, p. xviii), although many Christian philosophers had opposed skepticism from the beginning (Annas and Barnes 1985, p. 18). In any event, by the close of the Early Modern period, skepticism was in the hands of the atheistic Hume (cf. Chapter 3), and skepticism and atheism were denounced in the same breath. Some religious people attempted to combat skeptical thinking, sometimes using censorship and other forms of political harassment. The intervention of the Presbyterian Church of Scotland, in 1742, against the appointment of Hume to the Chair of Ethical and Pneumatical Philosophy at the University of Edinburgh, is a famous example of this phenomenon.

1.7 Skepticism in Ancient, Modern, and contemporary epistemology

It is often said that Ancient skepticism is different, in important and fundamental ways, both from Modern and from contemporary skepticism. Although there is some truth in this idea, there is also some falsehood. In this section we'll briefly look at some would-be differences between Ancient, Modern, and contemporary skepticism.

It is sometimes said that Ancient skepticism concerns belief, while Modern skepticism concerns knowledge (e.g. Vogt 2010a). But as I suggested above, the Ancient skeptical slogan that "nothing is apprehensible" is just as well translated with "nothing can be known". I agree with Frede (1983) when he writes that "[t]he debate between the Stoics and skeptics primarily concerned the nature and possibility of knowledge" (p. 65). Moreover, "knowledge" is rarely used in certain crucial Modern texts, like Descartes' *Meditations*. Alternatively, it is sometimes said that Modern epistemologists were obsessed with certainty, in a way that Ancient epistemologists weren't. It certainly seems true that some Modern epistemologists—Descartes in particular—thought that certain knowledge was possible, and were concerned to make a case that this is so. But the Ancient skeptics also seemed to be interested in certainty, which is why they are concerned with "conviction", "determination", and "proof".

It seems to me that a certain kind of annoyance with Modern and contemporary epistemology derives from two facts: (i) that many Modern epistemologists seem to maintain that knowledge requires certainty; and (ii) that many contemporary discussions of skepticism have centered on an argument for a form of Academic skepticism formulated in terms of knowledge (cf. Chapter 4). If you assume that the contemporary epistemologists are assuming the Moderns' infallibilism, then you might think that contemporary epistemologists are focusing on certainty, at the expense of questions about reasonable belief that were of interest to the Ancients. However, most contemporary epistemologists reject infallibilism, and (more importantly) the aforementioned skeptical argument does not rely on infallibilism—a point that I'll argue for below (§4.3).

Julia Annas and Jonathan Barnes (1985, p. 7) identify the view that knowledge is impossible, but that reasonable belief is possible, as the essence of "modern" skepticism, with Ancient skeptics ruling out reasonable belief as well as knowledge. This is our distinction between mitigated and unmitigated skepticism (§1.3.3). Two things are in tension with Annas and Barnes' idea. First, although there were mitigated skeptics in the Early Modern period, both Descartes and Hume seem to think of skepticism as involving suspension of judgment. Second, there were mitigated Academic skeptics in Ancient times—including Philo of Larissa, and perhaps Carneades as well.[37]

It is sometimes said that Ancient skepticism was a way of life, whereas Modern skepticism is purely hypothetical. This sounds plausible if we focus only on Pyrrhonian skepticism and Descartes' *Meditations*, but not if we consider Ancient Academic skepticism (which was not a way of life) and the skepticism of Hume (who non-hypothetically described himself as an Academic skeptic).[38] Indeed, skeptics seem to have been commonplace in the Early Modern period: their anti-skeptical critics certainly thought they were real enough (Popkin 1979, pp. 110–28). In 1642 Descartes warned that "we should not assume that the sceptical philosophy is extinct", and that "it is vigorously alive today" (*Meditations on First Philosophy*, Seventh Replies, 548), and in 1770 James Beattie (a critic of Hume's) lamented that "SCEPTICISM is now the profession of every fashionable inquirer" (*Essay on the Immutability of Truth*).

I think there are two important kinds of difference between Ancient, Modern, and contemporary skepticism. First, there are ethical differences. Pyrrhonian skepticism was a way of life, designed to lead to tranquility; "Cartesian skepticism" (§4.2.1) makes no ethical suggestions and is not, in any obvious sense, a way of life (although cf. §9.2). Although there is something of the ethical aspect in Montaigne, nothing like this is implied by skepticism as under-stood in contemporary epistemology. Some Early Modern skeptics suggested ethical implications of their skepticism, but mainly it was their critics who said that skepticism would lead to immorality (cf. 9.2.1). In contemporary discus-sions, skepticism is understood as an epistemological, and not an ethical, view. Moreover, there are also few self-described skeptics, and even those sympa-thetic to skepticism—e.g. Barry Stroud (1984)—treat it as a puzzle or paradox more than a position (cf. §9.1.2). In contemporary debates, ethical questions are usually understood as orthogonal to the issue of skepticism.

Second, there are differences as to whom the skeptic's opponent is understood to be.[39] Ancient skeptics seem first and foremost to be opposed to theoretical philosophers (cf. §1.1, §1.2.1), and to other powerful elites who claimed knowledge (e.g. politicians). Hume inherited this tendency. By contrast, Early Modern skepticism about religious propositions (§1.6), whether fideist or secular, opposed ordinary people: heretical Protestants, enthusiasts, fanatics, superstitious Papists, etc. Contemporary epistemolo-gists similarly treat skepticism as a view about ordinary people's beliefs.[40]

However, in spite of these differences, there are common ideas that constantly reappear throughout the long history of skepticism. For the remainder of our discussion of skepticism (Part I), we'll be concerned with three of these ideas: disagreement (Chapter 2), circularity (Chapter 3), and the possibility of error (Chapter 4).

1.8 Conclusion

We'll now look at three skeptical arguments in more detail: the mode from dispute (Chapter 2), an argument inspired by Hume, which is a version of Agrippa's trilemma (Chapter 3), and an argument inspired by Descartes (Chapter 4). This last argument will serve as the basis for our discussion of contemporary anti-skepticism (Part II).

Readings

The student of skepticism will begin with the Ancient texts that inspired the rest. Annas and Barnes (1985) may be particularly useful; it collects transla-tions of several sources and includes introductory material and commentary.

- Diogenes Laertius, *Lives of Eminent Philosophers* (e.g. Diogenes Laertius 1925).

- Sextus Empiricus, *Outlines of Scepticism* (e.g. Sextus Empiricus 2000).

- Cicero, *On Academic Scepticism* (e.g. Cicero 2006).

- B. Inwood and L. P. Gerson, *Hellenistic Philosophy: Introductory Readings* (Inwood and Gerson 1997), §III.

- J. Annas and J. Barnes, *The Modes of Scepticism* (Annas and Barnes 1985).

- A. A. Long and D. N. Seddy, *The Hellenistic Philosophers* (Long and Seddy 1987), §§1–3 and §§39–42.

Consult the following for discussions of the views and arguments of the Ancient skeptics.

- M. Frede, "Stoics and Skeptics on Clear and Distinct Impressions" (Frede 1983).

- G. Striker, "The Problem of the Criterion" (Striker 1996, Essay 7).

- J. Barnes, *The Toils of Scepticism* (Barnes 1990).

- R. J. Hankinson, *The Sceptics* (Hankinson 1995).

- R. Bett (ed.), *The Cambridge Companion to Ancient Scepticism* (Bett 2010).

A study of the self-refutation objection (§1.4.1) and the apraxia objection (§1.4.2), as they arise in connection with Ancient skepticism, should begin with the following essays (which are reprinted in Burnyeat and Frede 1997).

- M. Frede, "The Sceptic's Beliefs" (Frede 1979).

- M. Burnyeat, "Can the Sceptic Live his Scepticism?" (Burnyeat 1980).

- J. Barnes, "The Beliefs of a Pyrrhonist" (Barnes 1982).

Above, I set aside the issue of the "structure of justification" (§1.2.2). The following will provide a start for your study of that issue.

- L. BonJour, "Can Empirical Knowledge Have a Foundation?" (BonJour 1978).

- E. Sosa, "The Raft and the Pyramid" (Sosa 1991, Chapter 10).

- P. Klein, "Human Knowledge and the Infinite Regress of Reasons" (Klein 1999).

- R. Fogelin, "Agrippa and the Problem of Justification" (Fogelin 1994, Part II).

On skepticism in the Early Modern period before Descartes and Hume (§1.6), consult the following.

- M. de Montaigne, "An Apology for Raymond Sebond" (see e.g. Montaigne 2003, pp. 489–683).

- R. Popkin, *Scepticism from Erasmus to Spinoza* (Popkin 1979).

- T. Penelhum, "Skepticism and Fideism" (Penelhum 1983).

2

The Mode from Dispute

Philosophers have always been interested in disagreement. A common theme is the canvassing of disagreement in preparation for an attempt at resolution; think here of how Aristotle standardly proceeds. Another is the analysis of the psychological origins of disagreement; think here of Locke and Hume's analyses of enthusiasm and superstition. Our interest in this chapter is epistemological: what can disagreement tell us about the possibility of knowledge or reasonable belief?

2.1 The significance of disagreement

We'll look at what Sextus Empiricus says about disagreement (§2.1.1), before articulating a skeptical argument, based on disagreement, that has attracted attention in contemporary epistemology (§2.1.2).

2.1.1 Sextus on disagreement and the problem of the criterion

Among the five modes (§1.2.2) is the "mode deriving from dispute":

> According to the mode deriving from dispute, we find that undecidable dissension about the matter proposed has come about both in ordinary life and among philosophers. Because of this we are not able either to choose or to rule out anything, and we end up with suspension of judgment. (Sextus Empiricus, *Outlines of Scepticism*, I 165)

The idea that suspension of judgment follows, or ought to follow, awareness of disagreement can be found throughout the *Outlines*. Recall, for example, the dispute about the fundamental constitution of material things (§1.1).

That the answer to this question is "inapprehensible is easy to see from the dispute that has gone on ... among the Dogmatists" (*Ibid.* III 30). Alternatively, consider religious disagreement. In his famous discussion of religious testimony (*Enquiry concerning Human Understanding*, §X), David Hume appeals to the idea that,

> [I]n matters of religion, whatever is different is contrary; and ... it is impossible that the religions of ancient Rome, or Turkey, or Siam, and of China should, all of them, be established on any solid foundation. (p. 121)

Hume, and other Early Modern skeptics about religious propositions (§1.6), follow Sextus on this point, who notes that "[m]atters of piety and service to the gods are also full of much dispute" (III 218), goes on to canvass various of these disagreements (III 218–22), and concludes that, when it comes to parties to these disputes, "[a]s long as they remain in undecidable dispute, we have no agreement from them as to what we should think" (III 3).

However, what exactly is the argument that takes us from disagreement to suspension of judgment? The fact that people disagree about whether p does not seem, on its own, to provide any reason to suspend judgment about whether p. People are often foolish, bigoted, or uninformed, and usually some combination of all three; when the wise disagree with the foolish, we should not suspend judgment, but side with the wise. (This point applies even if the disagreement in question is persistent, for people are often persistently foolish, bigoted, and uninformed.) If what the skeptic offers are merely lists of historical and contemporary disagreements, which reveal that people are capable of defending myriad absurd views, the epistemological implications are unclear; all we have is what Richard Popkin (1979) aptly describes as "an appeal to the history of human stupidity" (p. 37).

Jonathan Barnes (1990) identifies two Sextan arguments, and we'll consider them here. The first is based on the following:

> **Principle of disagreement:** If you are aware that there is an undecided dispute about whether p, then you ought to suspend judgment about whether p. (p. 21)

What is an "undecided" dispute? We can distinguish between an undecided dispute, a dispute that is undecidable given our present circumstances, and a dispute that is undecidable no matter what (Barnes 1990, pp. 17–20). Who will win next week's Super Bowl? On the radio there are people arguing about this right now, but it's an undecided dispute, and plausibly one that is undecidable given our present circumstances—the outcome of the game isn't the kind of thing that can be known in advance. (Perhaps if there were cheating or some kind of corruption, we would be able to know.) An example of a dispute that is undecidable no matter what would be controversial; many people feel that some debates in metaphysics (do material objects have temporal parts?) and theology (how many angels can fit on the head of a pin?) are undecidable no matter what. Still, what's meant by an "undecided" dispute? Barnes' example of an undecided dispute is the debate about whether Aristotle was the author of the *Magna Moralia*:

> [T]he dispute is still undecided: the parties have not come to any agreement, and no decisive argument or consideration for or against authenticity has yet been advanced. (p. 22)

So let's say that a dispute is undecided iff (i.e. if and only if) none of the disagreeing parties has advanced a decisive argument in favor of her position. However, on this understanding of "undecided", the principle of disagreement is false (*pace* Barnes). On this understanding of "undecided", there is an undecided dispute about whether climate change is (partially) caused by human activity. The scientists who work on this question say that climate change is (partially) caused by human activity, but there are "climate change skeptics" who deny this. The scientists do not have a decisive argument in favor of their position. However, it is not the case that you ought to suspend judgment about whether climate change is (partially) caused by human activity. You ought to believe that climate change is (partially) caused by human activity, because the empirical evidence, gathered by the scientists, overwhelmingly supports that proposition.

A Pyrrhonian objection: you must think that the scientists have advanced decisive arguments in favor of their position, otherwise it would not be reasonable to agree with them. A Popperian reply (cf. Popper 1963, Chapter 1): this misunderstands the epistemology of science. Science does not trade in *decisive* arguments, but rather in *probable* conclusions on the basis of existing evidence. A scientist who claimed to have a decisive argument would not be a legitimate scientist. Our best scientific theories are well supported by empirical evidence, but there is no decisive argument in their favor. But it is not the case that we ought to suspend judgment about our best scientific theories (cf. §4.3).

Barnes' second Sextan argument appeals to a version of the **problem of the criterion** (§1.2.2). Suppose that you disagree with someone about some question, i.e. that you are party to some dispute. Here is Barnes (1990):

> [W]here there is disagreement, there we require some criterion or sign or proof; we require a mode or means of deciding the issue: we require, as I

shall put it, a yardstick. [...] For what is the alternative? Only, it seems, an arbitrary decision to opt for one side of the dispute or another—and that can hardly count as a resolution of the dispute. (p. 27)

However, "every attempt to produce a yardstick has been subject to deep disagreement", and "if the disagreement over yardsticks is undecided, then we surely cannot properly use a yardstick. Hence every dispute is undecided" (*ibid.*).

We need not understand "undecided" as we did above (which proved problematic) to articulate this argument. The leading idea doesn't have to do with decisiveness, but with standards: the methods or principles we use to settle disagreements. Here's the upshot. To reasonably believe that p, in the face of disagreement about whether p, you must legitimately employ some standard that supports believing that p. But legitimately employing a standard C requires that you reasonably believe that it is legitimate to employ C. And, for any C, there is disagreement about whether it is legitimate to employ C.

Now at this point the skeptic can finish the argument in either of two ways. First (Barnes 1990, p. 28), she could argue that the disagreement about standards is undecided, and appeal to the principle of disagreement, yielding the conclusion that you cannot reasonably believe that p, in the face of disagreement about whether p. Second, she could appeal to **Agrippa's trilemma** (§1.2.2): reasonable belief about the legitimacy of your standard will require the legitimate employment of another standard (in which case infinite regress), or the same standard (in which case the reciprocal mode), or no standard (in which case the mode from hypothesis), again yielding the conclusion that you cannot reasonably believe that p, in the face of disagreement about whether p.

However, we should never have allowed the argument to get this far. We should reject the following premise:

Legitimately employing a standard C requires that you reasonably believe that it is legitimate to employ C.

Whether or not this premise, or something like it (see "internalism", below), is true is one of the deepest questions in epistemology. The premise says that if your use of some method or principle can yield reasonable belief, then you must reasonably believe that said method or principle can do so. Is that true? Many people find this premise totally obvious and utterly compelling, while many others (myself included) feel the exact opposite: the premise is obviously wrong and based on a confusion—in this case, between a standard's *being* legitimate and its being *reasonably believed to be* legitimate (or *known* to be legitimate).

In any event, we can articulate a principle that, it seems to me, is the idea that makes premises like this look plausible. It's this (put in terms of knowledge):

Internalism: If S knows (that p) only if q, then S knows (that p) only if S knows that q.

Internalism says that knowledge requires knowledge of all the necessary conditions of knowledge. This is what's motivating the problem of the criterion. Knowledge requires the use of a legitimate standard; therefore (given internalism), knowledge requires knowledge that the standard you've used is legitimate. Knowing that the cat is on the mat, for example, requires the use of a legitimate standard, e.g. sense perception; therefore (given internalism), knowing that the cat is on the mat requires knowing that sense perception is a legitimate standard. But internalism could be applied, no matter what you think is necessary for knowledge. If belief is necessary for knowledge, then internalism implies that knowing that p requires knowing that you believe that p. If justification is necessary for knowledge, then internalism implies that knowing that p requires knowing that you are justified in believing p. If reliability is necessary for knowledge (cf. §5.2.3), then internalism implies that knowing that p requires knowing that your belief was reliably formed.

There is a short argument from internalism to a species of rustic Academic skepticism. Internalism implies that S knows that p only if S knows that S knows that p (because S knows that p only if S knows that p). This is sometimes called the **KK principle**. Given the premise that no one can know an infinite number of distinct propositions, this implies that knowledge is impossible, since knowing that p would require knowing that you know that p, and this in turn would require knowing that you know that you know that p, and so on, *ad infinitum*.

The negation of internalism is **externalism**. I think Barnes (1990) hits the nail on the head when he writes that "the status of epistemological externalism can be seen to be the deep and fundamental issue raised by Agrippan scepticism" (p. 141). The question of internalism will persistently arise in our study of skepticism (§2.2, §5.2.3). It would be a mistake to try to convince you that internalism is false (although I think it is, indeed, false): it's too controversial, and intuitions about it run too deep. It is more important that we highlight the role that this idea, and others like it, have to play in skeptical arguments. After we've covered more ground, you can make up your own mind about internalism.

We have seen, however, that the mode from dispute ends up relying on the problem of the criterion and Agrippa's trilemma. We have identified internalism as the principle that motivates the problem of the criterion; a diagnosis of Agrippa's trilemma will come later (Chapter 3).

2.1.2 Peer disagreement

In his *Essays on the Intellectual Powers of Man* (1785), **Thomas Reid** (1710–96) offers the following, on the significance of disagreement:

> Suppose a mathematician has made a discovery in that science which he thinks important; that he has put his demonstration in just order; and, after examining it with an attentive eye, has found no flaw in it. [...] He commits his demonstration to the examination of a mathematical friend, whom he esteems a competent judge, and waits with impatience the issue of his judgment. Here I would ask ... Whether the verdict of his friend, according as it is favorable or unfavorable, will not greatly increase or diminish his confidence in his own judgment? Most certainly it will, and it ought. (6.4)

We are here most interested in Reid's claim that disagreement with his friend should diminish the mathematician's confidence. This claim seems true, but what explains the fact that it is true (if indeed it is)?

It is important that the mathematician and his friend really do disagree. For example, the mathematician's confidence should not be diminished if there was a typo in the version of the proof that he sent to his friend, suggesting a different conclusion to the proof. It is also important that their disagreement is a disagreement in belief. Suppose I prepare a curry that my friend finds too spicy. There seems to be a sense in which we disagree about the curry, but this shouldn't affect either of our attitudes towards the curry. "There's no accounting for taste," we'll both say, and leave it at that. The same point applies to what we might call "practical disagreement": I want to watch *Die Hard* and you want to watch *Love Actually*. Neither of us should stop wanting to watch what we originally wanted to watch (although one of us must agree to watch something she would rather not watch). In any event, in what follows, when we say that two people disagree about whether p, we'll mean that one of them believes that p and the other believes that ~p.

There are two additional features of Reid's case that at least partially explain why his claim is plausible. First, the mathematical friend has examined the mathematician's work. It would not diminish the mathematician's confidence at all if his friend were to disagree with him, without having seen the would-be proof. What makes Reid's claim compelling is the fact that both the mathematician and his friend have the same evidence: both have carefully examined the would-be proof. Second, the mathematical friend is a "competent judge" when it comes to mathematics. It would not diminish the mathematician's confidence at all if his friend were not good at mathematics—if he were not at least as good at mathematics as the mathematician himself.

In virtue of these two features, the mathematician and his friend are what contemporary epistemologists call "epistemic peers". Different epistemologists define this jargon in different ways,[1] and for our purposes here we'll understand "epistemic peers" by appealing to the two features just described. First, epistemic peers must have the same evidence: a novice mathematician and an expert mathematician are not epistemic peers, for example. Second, epistemic peers must be equally intellectually virtuous: a prejudiced mathematician and an open-minded mathematician are not epistemic peers, for example. Epistemic peers must be equally intelligent and equally well-informed; they must (following Reid) be equally competent judges.

Both of these conditions must be relativized: what matters is not that the mathematician and his friend have equally good evidence *in general*, but that they have equally good evidence relative to the question of whether the proof is correct (e.g. it would not matter that the friend has not yet read today's sports page); and what matters is not that the mathematician and his friend are equally intellectually virtuous *in general*, but that they are equally intellectually virtuous when it comes to mathematics, and in particular when it comes to the question of whether the proof is correct (e.g. it would not matter if the friend is an incompetent art critic, or if he were biased in his political thinking).

Putting all this together, we can define epistemic peerhood as follows:

S_1 and S_2 are **epistemic peers** (relative to the question of whether p) (sometimes, below, just "peers") iff S_1 and S_2 have the same evidence (relevant to the question of whether p) and S_1 and S_2 are equally intellectually virtuous (when it comes to the question of whether p).

We're now in a position to speculate, based on our intuition about Reid's case: is it perhaps the case that disagreement (about whether p) with an epistemic peer (relative to the question of whether p) should always diminish your confidence (in your answer to the question of whether p)? If this were true, it would explain why Reid's mathematician's confidence about the correctness of his proof should be diminished: because he disagrees with an epistemic peer about whether the proof is correct.

Richard Feldman (2006, 2007) has articulated an argument for a general principle of this kind. Suppose that you disagree with an epistemic peer about whether p: you believe that p, and she believes that ~p. You both are aware of the disagreement, and of the fact that you are epistemic peers. Feldman then argues that at most one of your beliefs is reasonable, by appeal to the following principle:

Uniqueness principle: Given a body of evidence (relevant to the question of whether p), there is only one reasonable attitude to take toward the proposition that p.[2]

In particular, it cannot be both reasonable to believe that p and reasonable to believe that ~p. Either your belief (that p) is not reasonable, or your peer's belief (that ~p) is not reasonable (or both are not reasonable). So at most one of your beliefs is reasonable: which belief is it? Given that you and your peer are equally intellectually virtuous (when it comes to the question of whether p), it seems like it would be arbitrary to believe that your belief, and not your peer's, is reasonable. At most one of your beliefs is reasonable, but you're equally intellectually virtuous (when it comes to the relevant question), so it seems equally likely that your peer's belief is reasonable as that your belief is reasonable. So it would be arbitrary to believe that your belief, and not your peer's, is reasonable. And it would be equally arbitrary to think that your peer's belief, and not yours, is the reasonable one. The reasonable thing to do, then, is to suspend judgment about whether your belief is reasonable. However, Feldman argues, once you suspend judgment about whether your belief (that p) is reasonable, you cannot reasonably continue to believe that p: you should suspend judgment about whether p, as well.

Feldman's argument has an elegant and simple structure:

1   If you disagree with an epistemic peer about whether p, then you ought to suspend judgment about whether it is reasonable for you to believe that p.

2   If you suspend judgment about whether it is reasonable for you to believe that p, then you ought to suspend judgment about whether p.

3   Therefore, if you disagree with an epistemic peer about whether p, then you ought to suspend judgment about whether p.

The argument is valid, so if its premises are true, then its conclusion is true as well. But if its conclusion is true, then a form of non-rustic Academic skepticism seems true as well. The reason is that many of our beliefs are controversial: we have many beliefs (that p) where we disagree with epistemic peers about whether p. Consider your beliefs about religion, politics, and morality, for example. For the vast majority of these beliefs, you have epistemic peers who believe the negation of what you believe: equally intelligent and equally well-informed people have different beliefs. Consider three propositions: (i) that God exists, (ii) that assault weapons ought to be illegal, and (iii) that abortion is sometimes morally permissible. If you believe or disbelieve any of these propositions, then it is likely that you have epistemic peers with whom you disagree. If so, then Feldman's conclusion implies that you ought to suspend judgment about these propositions. Thus it seems that Feldman's conclusion implies a form of skepticism about religion, politics, and morality, on which you ought to suspend judgment about the propositions of religion, politics, and morality.

This skeptical conclusion is at odds with the common sense of contemporary liberal democracies, where we are committed to the idea that reasonable people can "agree to disagree." As **John Rawls** (1921–2002) puts it in *Political Liberalism* (1996):

> Political liberalism assumes that, for political purposes, a plurality of reasonable yet incompatible comprehensive doctrines is the normal result of the exercise of human reason within the framework of the free institutions of a constitutional democratic regime. (p. xviii)

Reasonable disagreement about matters religious, political, and moral is a basic assumption of liberalism. You might say that reasonable disagreement is impossible (as suggested by Feldman's conclusion), but that the possibility of reasonable disagreement should be assumed "for political purposes." That is an uncomfortable position, so the tension between Feldman's conclusion and political liberalism is good reason to sympathetically consider what might be said against his argument.

2.2 Anti-skeptical strategies

We'll briefly consider three anti-skeptical strategies that might be employed in response to Feldman's argument (§2.1.2). First, we'll consider rejecting its first premise (§2.2.1), and then its second premise (§2.2.2). Finally, we'll consider the possibility of avoiding the skeptical conclusion by saying that we have few epistemic peers (§2.2.3). This will allow us to better articulate the epistemological problem posed by disagreement (§2.2.4).

2.2.1 Objective reasonableness

Imagine that you believe that climate change is (partially) caused by human activity. Your belief is based on the same evidence on which most people who believe this proposition base their belief: you've read some magazine and newspaper articles about climate change, which gave an overview of the evidence that climate change is (partially) caused by human activity; you know that this is the consensus of scientists who work on climate change; you saw the Al Gore movie; etc. You've never discussed this with your best friend Simone, but you consider her your epistemic peer, relative to a variety of questions, but in particular relative to the question of whether climate change is (partially) caused by human activity. You and Simone share roughly the same moral and political and religious worldview, and you rarely disagree about anything of substance. Imagine now that you ask Simone about climate change and she tells you that she's a skeptic: she believes that climate change is not caused by human activity, but instead by increased solar activity. You discuss the matter, and it is clear that you and Simone have access to the same evidence: you also read that article on solar activity (but dismissed it as quackery); Simone also saw the Al Gore movie (but was unconvinced).

Given the principle of uniqueness, at most one of your beliefs is reasonable. Is your belief, but not Simone's, reasonable? What should you believe about this question? Here's a possibility: you should believe that your belief, and non Simone's, is reasonable. Simone is intelligent and well-informed and very much your epistemic peer, but she has been duped by the climate change skeptics, and her belief is not reasonable. You are thus under no pressure to give up your belief that climate change is (partially) caused by human activity.

Note well the idea: you can consistently think someone your epistemic peer, relative to the question of whether p, while thinking that she is unreasonable and wrong in her belief about whether p. Peers have the same evidence and are equally virtuous (§2.1.2): but this is compatible with one party getting things right and the other getting them wrong.

But isn't it arbitrary for you to believe that your belief is reasonable, and Simone's not reasonable? "Arbitrary" suggests a choice made at random or without reason; but if our evidence actually makes it reasonable to believe that climate change is (partially) caused by human activity, why say that it's arbitrary for me to believe that my belief is reasonable? This belief isn't the result of a choice made at random or without reason, but rather the result of correctly evaluating the evidence.

That's the idea behind what we can call an **objective reasonableness** approach to peer disagreement (Kelly 2005a, 2010): whether your belief (that p) is actually reasonable can make a difference when it comes to the reasonableness of your beliefs about whether your belief (that p) is reasonable, such that sometimes it's reasonable to believe that your belief (that p) is reasonable and an epistemic peer's belief (that ~p) is not reasonable. The kind of case we must imagine here is one in which you have evidence that very strongly supports believing that p, where such support is so strong that you can reasonably conclude, on the basis of said evidence, that your peer's belief that ~p is unreasonable. You are thus under no pressure to give up your belief that p. If this is possible, then the first premise of Feldman's argument (§2.1.2) is false.

2.2.2 *Humility*

Alternatively, you might challenge the second premise of Feldman's argument (§2.1.2). The premise depends on this idea:

> Reasonable belief (that p) is incompatible with suspending judgment about whether it is reasonable for you to believe (that p).

Is this true? You might think the following is obviously true:

> Reasonable belief (that p) is incompatible with believing that it is not reasonable for you to believe (that p).

But this doesn't entail the second premise of Feldman's argument. Suspending judgment about whether it is reasonable for you to believe (that p) is not the same as believing that it is not reasonable for you to believe (that p). As Roderick Chisholm (1986) writes:

> One may object, "But it is unreasonable to proceed if you do not think you are justified in proceeding!" The answer is ... that that is not unreasonable. What is unreasonable is to proceed when you think you are not justified in proceeding. And from the fact that you do not think you are justified, it does not follow that you do think you are not justified. (p. 6)

Chisholm is making two claims in this passage. The first is that not believing that p does not entail believing that ~p, thus not believing that you're justified does not entail believing that you're not justified, and not believing that it is reasonable for you to believe (that p) does not entail believing that it is not reasonable for you to believe (that p). This is an important point (and not just in connection with the mode from dispute).[3] Suspending judgment about whether it is reasonable for you to believe (that p) indeed entails that you do not believe that it is reasonable for you to believe (that p), but this does not entail that you believe that it is not reasonable for you to believe (that p).

   The second claim Chisholm is making amounts to the rejection of a cousin of internalism (§2.1.1), on which it is reasonable to proceed only if you believe you are justified in proceeding. The second premise of Feldman's argument would be well-supported by the claim (another cousin of internalism) that you reasonably believe that p only if you reasonably believe that it is reasonable for you to believe that p. Chisholm would have us reject this requirement. For my part, I agree with him: reasonable belief does not require a higher-order belief to the effect that one's lower-order belief is reasonable. Elsewhere (Hazlett 2012), I appeal to this idea in a critique of the second premise of Feldman's argument. I argue that reasonable belief (that p) is compatible with suspending judgment about whether it is reasonable for you to believe (that p). On my view, suspending judgment about the reasonableness of your beliefs can be a manifestation of the virtue of **intellectual humility** (cf. §9.2.3). Imagine that you have been having an intense debate about some religious proposition, e.g. that a higher power created the universe. You believe this proposition, and your interlocutor believes its negation, but you now appreciate that the evidence relevant to whether a higher power created the universe is very complex and difficult to evaluate, and so you conclude your debate by saying: "I still think that a higher power created the universe, but I'm not so sure about whether this belief is reasonable, perhaps your atheism is actually the reasonable conclusion; so I suspend judgment about whether my belief is reasonable". I think the attitude you express in this case is coherent. If so, the second premise of Feldman's argument is false.

2.2.3 Peerlessness

A third strategy involves accepting the conclusion of Feldman's argument (§2.1.2) while rejecting that it has skeptical consequences. To get from Feldman's conclusion to skepticism about religion, politics, and morality, we assumed that you are party to many peer disagreements about religion, politics, and morality. You could resist this by arguing that those with whom you disagree (about religion, politics, and morality) are not your epistemic peers.

One way of defending this idea is to argue that people, especially people with divergent religious, political, and moral worldviews, rarely have the same evidence. Some people have had an experience of God's presence, for example, while other people have never had any experience like that. Alternatively, people are members of different communities, and are thus exposed to very different sources of information. But if we accept Feldman's conclusion, and want to retain our religious, political, and moral beliefs, on the grounds that we have different evidence from those with whom we disagree, it seems that we end up having to say something rather dogmatic: that the evidence possessed by those with whom we disagree is misleading evidence. (This strategy would be even more obviously dogmatic if we were to say that we are more intellectually virtuous than those with whom we disagree.)

The prospects for this strategy depend on how we understand the notion of an "epistemic peer", and the related notion of "intellectual virtue". We might drop the idea that peers must have the same evidence, in favor of the requirement that they have equally good evidence. The charge of dogmatism again threatens: on what grounds can we say that the evidence possessed by those with whom we disagree is not as good as the evidence that we possess? Alternatively, we might require that epistemic peers be equally reliable on the topic of disagreement. Religious, political, and moral disagreements could then be dismissed as not cases of peer disagreement, because such disagreements are often "deep": they involve systematic differences in worldview, such that the parties to a "deep" disagreement cannot be peers, since they cannot be equally reliable on the topic of disagreement. The charge of dogmatism, perhaps, is thus mitigated: is it dogmatic for me to say that those with whom I disagree are not my "epistemic peers", when all I mean is that our worldviews are systematically different?

2.2.4 Looking at (and not thinking about) disagreement

The conclusion of Feldman's argument (§2.1.2) is that, if you disagree with an epistemic peer about whether p, then you ought to suspend judgment about whether p. If you deny this, you face the following question: when ought you to suspend judgment about whether p, on the basis of peer disagreement about whether p? Not always—that's what it means to deny Feldman's conclusion. But also not never—and this is an important point. Reid's case (§2.1.2) makes it clear that sometimes we ought to change our views in response to peer disagreement. So not always, but not never. So when? This, I think, is the big epistemological question when it comes to disagreement.[4]

There's a famous line of Wittgenstein's: "don't think, look". He means that it can be important to set aside theory and think about the phenomena we're theorizing about. I want to suggest that, when it comes to disagreement, when we look without thinking, what we find is that disagreement sometimes, but not always, requires us to change our views, and that the philosophical challenge is to give an account of the difference between the two kinds of case. Compare Reid's case of two mathematical friends with a case of religious disagreement between two friends, a Hindu and a Muslim, over whether monotheism is true. Fill in the details so that the two religious friends are reflective and intelligent, but also deeply committed to their religion, through ties of community and history. It seems obvious that the mathematical friends should suspend judgment about whether the proof is correct, but it seems equally obvious that neither of the two religious friends should give up her faith. The question is: what's the relevant difference between the cases?

I'll close this section with two thoughts. First, the two mathematical friends have means at their disposal to settle their dispute: they can re-check the would-be proof. The religious friends have no such means; there is no way for them to "check" which of them is right. I don't know how this could make a difference, when it comes to whether suspension of judgment is required, but it strikes me as an important difference between the cases. Second, as David Christensen (2007) argues, in the case of the mathematician, it seems that the reason the discovery of disagreement requires him to change his view is that the discovery of disagreement amounts to the discovery of evidence that he made a mistake. He puts this point like this:

> Actual disagreement with peers is informative because it provides evidence that a certain possibility—the possibility of our having made an epistemic error—has been actualized. It makes what we already know possible more probable. (p. 208)

This seems like an excellent diagnosis of what goes on in the case of the mathematical friends. But as an account of the case of the religious friends, it strikes me as awkward, at best. That an equally intelligent and equally well-informed friend disagrees with me about religion does not seem like evidence that my religious views are mistaken. I think we are inclined to say that *of course* my friend disagrees with me about this: after all, she's a Muslim and I'm a Hindu. Mathematical disagreement is surprising in a way that religious disagreement isn't. Again, it's unclear why this would be, but if it's right, it's relevant to explaining the difference between the cases.

2.3 Expert disagreement

The mode from dispute is an exercise in **social epistemology**: the study of how knowledge and reasonable belief are related to our social environment. I said that our social environments are full of people who disagree with us about religion, politics, and morality, and who are our epistemic peers (§2.2.3). But our social environments also seem to be full of people who disagree with us, and who are our epistemic *superiors*, namely, people are *experts* on the topic of disagreement. What are the implications, when you disagree with an expert?

We can adapt our definition of epistemic peers (§2.1.2), and understand epistemic superiority as follows:

S_1 is S_2's **epistemic superior** (relative to the question of whether p) iff either S_1 has more evidence than S_2 (relevant to the question of whether p) or S_1 is more intellectually virtuous than S_2 (when it comes to the question of whether p). (cf. Frances 2005, p. 22)

You might think that when you find out that you disagree with an epistemic superior, you should defer to her, i.e. believe whatever your epistemic superior believes. This seems obviously right in some cases. If you believe that Hume was born in Glasgow, but find out that a world-renowned Hume scholar (i.e. someone who is obviously your epistemic superior when it comes to Hume's biography) believes that Hume was born in Edinburgh (e.g. she tells you that he was born in Edinburgh), you should believe that Hume was born in Edinburgh. But it seems obviously wrong in other cases. I disbelieve in the doctrine of transubstantiation (that bread and wine are transformed into the body and blood of Christ during the Eucharist), but Pope Francis believes in the doctrine, and he is certainly my epistemic superior when it comes to transubstantiation: he's studied the matter, he's thought long and hard about it, read lots of stuff that's been written about it, and so on. It would be crazy, however, for me (not even being Catholic) to defer to the Pope on this matter.

Liberals are instinctively skeptical of the idea of deference to religious, political, or moral experts. You might motivate this by rejecting the idea of religious, political, or moral expertise—perhaps we were wrong to say that the Pope is, in the relevant sense, my epistemic superior when it comes to transubstantiation. Or you might think that while there are religious, political and moral experts, there is no requirement to defer to them, although there is such a requirement in other domains. The task would then be to explain the difference.

However, perhaps what's going on in the transubstantiation case is that the Pope is not the only expert on transubstantiation, and some of the experts reject the doctrine. There are Lutherans who have studied and thought about and read up on transubstantiation just as much as the Pope, and who have come to disbelieve in transubstantiation. What should you do, then, when there is disagreement *among* your epistemic superiors?

Bryan Frances (2005) argues that you cannot know that p, nor can you know that q (where you know that q entails ~p), when there is disagreement about whether p among your epistemic superiors (pp. 24–5). If "well-informed, well-respected, non-crackpot, and highly intelligent genuine experts in the field(s) to which [the hypothesis that p] belongs" are still arguing about whether p (pp. 18–19), and you are not among those experts, then you cannot know that p, nor can you know anything which you know entails ~p. If this is right, then it seems that I cannot know that the doctrine of transubstantiation is false.

Above, I said that Feldman's conclusion (about peer disagreement) implies a counterintuitive species of non-rustic Academic skepticism about religion, politics, and morality. What sort of skepticism is implied by Frances' view (about expert disagreement)? One notable difference is that while Feldman's skepticism concerns suspension of judgment, Frances' skepticism concerns knowledge. Another is that the scope of skepticism based on expert disagreement is extremely broad—or so Frances argues. For one, there is disagreement among your epistemic superiors about eliminativism about belief (pp. 30–41), and so you cannot know that S believes that p, for any person S and proposition that p. For another, there is disagreement among your epistemic superiors over the reality of colors (pp. 69–72), and so you cannot know that x is c, for any object x and color c.

For my part, I think it is unclear whether the propositions debated by these experts are incompatible with the propositions we ordinarily believe. I think it's unclear whether the propositional content of my ordinary belief that Kobe believes that the Lakers will win entails the falsity of the propositional content at issue in the debate over eliminativism about belief, and I think it's unclear whether the propositional content of my ordinary belief that Kobe's jersey is yellow entails the falsity of the propositional content at issue in the debate over the realty of colors. Let me explain this with a slightly less controversial example. Imagine that Ishmael spots a massive sperm whale heading towards the Pequod, and exclaims: "My God, that's a mighty fish!" Ishmael, at least in some sense, believes that there is a mighty fish heading towards the Pequod. But as any zoologist will tell you, whales are not fish. Is what Ishmael believes incompatible with what the zoologist says (along with the fact that the animal heading toward the Pequod is a whale)? Perhaps there is a sense in which Ishmael's belief is false, but there also seems to be a sense in which his belief is true, and thus a sense in which what he believes is not incompatible with what the zoologist says (and with the fact that the animal is a whale). If so, something similar can be said about our ordinary beliefs about beliefs and about colors, and in general about apparent conflicts between ordinary beliefs and scientific or philosophical theories. None of this speaks against the idea that, if experts disagree about whether p, and you believe that q, and you know that q entails ~p, then you don't know that q. What I am suggesting is that we must be careful when it comes to figuring out what is entailed by the contents of our beliefs.[5]

This is just to say, again (§2.1.2), that before considering the significance of disagreement we must make sure we have real disagreement on our hands. I think that when we keep this in mind, the scope of disagreement-based skepticism will be relatively limited (cf. Chapters 3 and 4). In what domains is there ubiquitous peer disagreement? Perhaps in religion, morality, and politics. In what domains is there widespread expert disagreement? It is likely that wherever there are experts there is widespread expert disagreement (a point that the Ancient skeptics were fond of emphasizing). But if one accepts my suggestion that our ordinary beliefs are not threatened by this, then we can conclude (at most) that we non-experts know nothing in these domains— that I do not know whether p, for any proposition that p such that whether p is a controversial question among experts, in (say) physics, or economics, or theology. Perhaps that is right; it jibes with what seems right, which is that I am ignorant of those fields.

2.4 Conclusion

We have here considered the mode from dispute and the problem of the criterion (§2.1.1), and some contemporary species of skepticism based on disagreement (§2.1.2, §2.3). We'll now turn to the skepticism of David Hume.

Readings

The following are essential readings in the contemporary epistemology of disagreement. As suggested above (§2.1.1), the Ancient mode from dispute is well covered in Chapter 1 of Barnes 1990.

- T. Kelly, "The Epistemological Significance of Disagreement" (Kelly 2005a).

- B. Frances, *Scepticism Comes Alive* (Frances 2005).

- R. Feldman, "Epistemological Puzzles about Disagreement" (Feldman 2006).

- R. Feldman, "Reasonable Religious Disagreements" (Feldman 2007).

- A. Elga, "Reflection and Disagreement" (Elga 2007).

- D. Christensen, "Epistemology of Disagreement: The Good News" (Christensen 2007).

For more, consult the following. Christensen 2009 is an overview of the recent literature; the other two pieces are collections of new papers on disagreement.

- D. Christensen, "Disagreement as Evidence: The Epistemology of Controversy" (Christensen 2009).

- R. Feldman and T. A. Warfield (eds), *Disagreement* (Feldman and Warfield 2010).

- D. Christensen (ed.), *The Epistemology of Disagreement*, special issue of *Episteme*, 6(3) (2009).

3

Our Infirm Understanding

We turn now to one of the most important and celebrated skeptical arguments in the history of philosophy: **David Hume**'s (1711–76) argument concerning induction. Like most interesting people, Hume delights his fans and infuriates his detractors. His contributions to the history of philosophy were many, and they include the first development, or at least the first Modern development, of a thoroughly secular (or naturalistic) philosophical worldview: Hume has (positive, non-skeptical) things to say in epistemology, ethics, aesthetics, political philosophy, metaphysics, and the philosophy of mind, and none of these things depend on, or imply, any religious claim (or any claim about the supernatural). In this respect, he stands apart not only from non-skeptical religious philosophers like Aquinas, Berkeley, and Descartes (cf. §4.1), but also from skeptical fideists like Montaigne and Bayle (§1.6).[1, 2]

Hume was a proponent and defender of the relatively new practice of empirical science, and his discussion of induction reflects his desire both to explain the legitimacy of the experimental method and to "introduce the experimental Method of Reasoning into Moral Subjects" (see below), which subjects include what we now call epistemology (along with most of the rest of what we now call philosophy). Hume's philosophical views, regardless of how we interpret them (cf. §3.1.2), were intended to be, and were, revolutionary ideas.

We are here interested in one of the skeptical arguments that Hume offers; although the description of Hume's argument as "skeptical" is controversial (§3.1.2). The argument concerns induction—drawing conclusions about things unobserved on the basis of observation—and our beliefs based on induction (or "inductive beliefs", as I'll call them below). This much is uncontroversial: Hume argues that we can produce no good argument in defense of our inductive beliefs. In focusing on induction, we shall set aside three other aspects of Hume's (apparently) skeptical philosophy: his "scepticism with regard to reason" (*Treatise of Human Nature*, I.iv.1), his "scepticism with regard to the senses" (*ibid.* I.iv.2; see also *Enquiry concerning Human*

Understanding, §XII.1, pp. 152–3),[3] and his skepticism about religious propositions (*Enquiry*, §§X–XI, *Dialogues concerning Natural Religion*).

3.1 Hume on induction

Hume's argument concerning induction is presented in three places:

- in the *Treatise of Human Nature: Being an Attempt to Introduce the Experimental Method of Reasoning into Moral Subjects* (1739/40) (I.iii.6),

- in the *Abstract of a Book Lately Published; Entituled, A Treatise of Human Nature, &c. wherein the Chief Argument of that Book is Farther Illustrated and Explained* (1740) (pp. 651–2), and

- in the *Enquiry concerning Human Understanding* (originally *Philosophical Essays concerning Human Understanding*) (1748) (§IV).

Mainly to simplify things, I'm going to focus here on the presentation of the argument in the *Enquiry*.[4]

3.1.1 Skeptical doubts

Hume begins by outlining his question:

It may ... be a subject worthy of curiosity, to enquire what is the nature of that evidence which assures us of any real existence and matter of fact, beyond the present testimony of our senses, or the records of our memory. (*Enquiry*, §IV.1, p. 26)

He will end up giving a "negative answer" (*ibid.* §IV.2, p. 32) to this question. His argument relies on an assumption:

All the objects of human reason or enquiry may naturally be divided into two kinds, to wit, *Relations of Ideas*, and *Matters of Fact*. Of the first kind are the sciences of Geometry, Algebra, and Arithmetic; and in short, every affirmation which is either intuitively or demonstratively certain. [...] Propositions of this kind are discoverable by a mere operation of thought, without dependence on what is anywhere existent in the universe. [...] Matters of fact ... are not ascertained in the same manner; nor is our evidence of their truth, however great, of a like nature with the foregoing.

The contrary of every matter of fact is still possible; because it can never imply a contradiction[.] (*Ibid.* §IV.1, pp. 25–6)

All truths are either relations of ideas or matters of fact, and Hume here gives us two criteria by which to distinguish relations of ideas from matters of fact. First, relations of ideas can be certain, while matters of fact cannot be certain; at best they can be probable. Second, the contrary, i.e. negation, of any relation of ideas is a contradiction, while this is not the case when it comes to matters of fact. We can try out these two criteria on the examples Hume gives. For an example of a relation of ideas, he offers:

Three times five is equal to the half of thirty.

In other words, $3\times5=30/2$. After brief reflection, it does seem like this is something we can know with certainty—at least if we can know anything with certainty. It's a bit less obvious that the negation of this proposition is a contradiction, but I suppose we might make the point like this: 3×5 is 15, and $30/2$ is 15, so the negation of our proposition amounts to the proposition that 15 is not equal to 15, and that's a contradiction. In any event, when it comes to both of these criteria, there is a difference between the proposition that $3\times5=30/2$ and the following:

The sun will rise tomorrow.

The negation of this—that the sun will not rise tomorrow—is, as Hume puts it, "no less intelligible a proposition, and implies no more contradiction", than the proposition that the sun will rise tomorrow (*ibid.* p. 26). And brief reflection shows that we cannot know with certainty that the sun will rise tomorrow— there's always the chance, however improbable, that some celestial accident will happen later today (giant asteroid, solar burn-out). Although it is highly probable that the sun will rise tomorrow, it is not certain that it will rise.

This example—of the proposition that the sun will rise tomorrow—is what prompts Hume's question about our evidence concerning matters of fact, apart from what we perceive or remember. The proposition that the sun will rise tomorrow is just such a matter of fact, for we neither perceive nor remember that the sun will rise tomorrow (how could we, since it hasn't happened yet!). So we can restate Hume's question as one concerning this particular example: what evidence assures us that the sun will rise tomorrow?

Well, the proposition isn't a relation of ideas, as we just saw, so it must be a matter of fact—something probable, but not certain. Hume then makes an assumption, that "[a]ll reasonings concerning matters of fact seem to be founded on the relation of *Cause and Effect*" (*ibid.*), and that "*causes and effects are discoverable, not by reason but by experience*" (*Ibid.* p. 28), The details of Hume's argument here need not detain us (and in particular the argument that we neither perceive nor intuit the connection between cause and effect), because his conclusion seems right when applied to our example of the proposition that the sun will rise tomorrow. What's our evidence for this? Well, whatever exactly our evidence is, it's some kind of experiential evidence, e.g. the fact that we've seen the sun rise every day up till now.

But now a wrinkle appears, that Hume will ultimately exploit. Given what we've said about our evidence that the sun will rise tomorrow, it looks like we have the following to say, in defense of believing that proposition:

1 Up till now, the sun has risen every day.

2 Therefore, the sun will rise tomorrow.

However, Hume argues, this argument is no good without an assumption that implies that our observations of how the sun has behaved in the past are reliable indications of how the sun will behave in the future. As Hume puts it, this argument is weak without the assumption that "the future will be conformable to the past" (*ibid.* §IV.2, p. 35). Indeed, he argues, all arguments in defense of matters of fact (apart from those matters of fact that we perceive or remember) require (something like) this assumption (*ibid.*).

Now to exploit the wrinkle. What evidence assures us that the future will be conformable to the past? Presumably there must be some evidence that assures us of this, otherwise our argument that the sun will rise tomorrow is not a good argument. The proposition that the future will be conformable to the past isn't a relation of ideas, because its negation, that the future won't be conformable to the past, isn't a contradiction. So it must be a matter of fact. Moreover, it's not something we perceive or remember (again, because it hasn't happened yet). Given Hume's assumption about cause and effect, it follows that our evidence that the future will be conformable to the past is experiential evidence. And again, this sounds right: to the extent that we have evidence for this proposition, surely it's our past experience of the way that the future has been conformable to the past. But now we are caught in a version of the reciprocal mode (§1.2.2):

To endeavor, therefore, the proof of this last supposition [that the future will be conformable to the past] by probable arguments, or arguments regarding existence, must be evidently going in a circle, and taking that for granted, which is the very point in question. (*Ibid.* pp. 35–6)

Let's try it. Our defense would have to be something like:

1　Up till now, the future has been conformable to the past.

2　Therefore, the future will be conformable to the past.

But, as above, this argument is no good without the assumption that the future will be conformable to the past. But that assumption is the same as the conclusion of the argument! No good argument relies on an assumption that's the same as its conclusion; as Hume says, that's "going in a circle, and taking that for granted, which is the very point in question."

We cannot defend the assumption that the future will be conformable to the past, which we needed for our defense of believing that the sun will rise tomorrow. Hume concludes:

> [E]ven after we have had experience of the operations of cause and effect, our conclusions from that experience are *not* founded on reasoning, or any process of the understanding. (*Ibid.* p. 32)

We've only touched on half of Hume's view, for in addition to these "sceptical doubts," (*Enquiry*, §IV) Hume has a "sceptical solution of these doubts." (*ibid.* §V) Once we've looked at his "sceptical solution" (§3.1.2), I'll say a little bit about some interpretative issues, but our interest here isn't primarily historical, and we'll soon turn to the "Humean skeptical argument" (§3.2), even if it isn't an argument that Hume would have endorsed. But to conclude this section I'll make two defensive comments, when it comes to the argument of Hume's that we've been considering.

First, it's easy to mistakenly think that Hume has confused induction with deduction, or otherwise assumed the illegitimacy of induction. A good deductive argument is logically valid, i.e. it is one whose premises necessitate (entail) its conclusion, such that it is impossible for the premises of the argument to be true and the conclusion false. Inductive arguments do not have this feature; there are good inductive arguments whose premises do not necessitate their conclusions. Consider, again:

1　Up till now, the sun has risen every day.

2　Therefore, the sun will rise tomorrow.

When Hume argues that this argument is no good without the assumption that the future will be conformable to the past, isn't he implicitly assuming that this argument is meant to be deductive, or that it would have to be deductive to be any good? He complains, of arguments of this kind, that "[t]he consequence seems nowise necessary" and that "[t]he connection between these propositions is not intuitive" (§IV.2, p. 34). But there is no necessary connection between the premises and the conclusion of the very best inductive argument. However, we can amend Hume's argument to at least partially avoid this objection. It's true that the following looks like a deductive argument:

1   Up till now, the sun has risen every day.

A   The future is always conformable to the past in every respect.

2   Therefore, the sun will rise tomorrow.

But this is obviously a bad argument, since premise (A) is obviously false. Surely we can do better; consider:

1   Up till now, the sun has risen every day.

A*   The future tends to be comfortable to the past in most respects.

2   Therefore, probably, the sun will rise tomorrow.

Now we have a genuine inductive argument that the sun will rise tomorrow, and the important thing is that we can see the intuitive pull of Hume's idea that premise (A*) is required to make this a good argument. Adding the second premise looks like a reasonable case of making one's assumptions explicit—rather than an unreasonable case of trying to make an inductive argument into a deductive one.

Second, it's easy to think that Hume's (apparently) skeptical conclusion is not all that surprising, perhaps even commonsensical, if you think that it only applies to beliefs about the future. You might think: "Will the sun rise tomorrow? Who knows! It's impossible to know the future". But Hume's argument has a broader scope than that. It concerns our beliefs about "any real existence and matter of fact, beyond the present testimony of our senses, or the records of our memory", i.e. it concerns all our conclusions about what we have not directly observed, made on the basis of observation. It concerns, in other words, all the conclusions made by scientists, whether physical ("The Higgs boson exists"), astronomical ("Jupiter is made of gas"), natural-historical ("Whales evolved from land mammals"), zoological ("Tigers nurse their young"), historical ("Hume lived in Edinburgh"), or whatever. We focused above on the assumption that the future will be conformable to the past. But Hume's argument applies to a more general and more fundamental principle, which **Isaac Newton** (1642–1746) articulated as "Rule III", among his "Rules for Reasoning in Philosophy" (*Principia Mathematica*, Book III):

The qualities of bodies ... which are found to belong to all bodies within the reach of our experiments, are to be esteemed the universal qualities of all bodies whatsoever.

Compare Hume's formulation of the relevant principle in the *Treatise*:

[I]nstances, of which we have had no experience, must resemble those, of which we have had experience, and ... the course of nature continues always uniformly the same. (I.iii.6, p. 89; see also I.iii.8, p. 104)

Hume would have been aware of Newton's "Rules" (cf. *Enquiry concerning the Principles of Morals*, §III.2, p. 204), and of the essential role that induction—i.e. drawing conclusions about the unobserved world on the basis of observation—played in the new empirical scientific practice that Hume sought to vindicate and exemplify. At stake in Hume's argument is not merely our knowledge of the future, but a much broader and potentially more devastating swathe of our empirical knowledge.

3.1.2 *The skeptical solution*

Is Hume a skeptic? And, if he is, what sort of skeptic is he? These questions don't have obvious answers. Part of the reason is what Hume calls his "skeptical solution" to the "skeptical doubts" articulated above (§3.1.1). Concerning "the Academic or Sceptical philosophy", with which Hume seems sympathetic, he writes:

Nor need we fear that this philosophy ... should ever undermine the reasonings of common life, and carry its doubts so far as to destroy all action, as well as speculation. Nature will always maintain her rights, and prevail in the end over any abstract reasoning whatsoever. Though we should conclude ... that, in all reasonings from experience, there is a step taken by the mind which is not supported by any argument or process of the understanding; there is no danger that these reasonings, on which almost all knowledge depends, will ever be affected by such a discovery. (*Enquiry concerning Human Understanding*, §V.1, p. 41)

The explanation of this, Hume argues, is that our "reasonings" from experience are not actually the result of reason—they are "not supported by any argument or process of the understanding"—but rather an innate psychological tendency, which he calls "Custom or Habit. For whenever the repetition of any particular act or operation produces a propensity to renew the same act or operation … we always say, that this propensity is the effect of *Custom*" (*ibid.* p. 43; see also *Treatise* I.iii.8, *Abstract*, p. 652). We are so constituted that, if you show us the sun rising over and over again, we will inevitably expect it to rise the next day. It's not that we have an argument that the sun will rise again; it's that we've been habituated to believe that it will rise every day. So although Hume's conclusion seems skeptical, in some sense, it does not lead to suspension of judgment. However, "[w]ithout the influence of custom, we should be entirely ignorant of every matter of fact beyond what is immediately present to our memory and senses" (*Enquiry*, §V.1, p. 45), and thus "['t]is happy … that nature breaks the force of all skeptical arguments" (*Treatise*, I.iv.1, p. 187).

Essential to Hume's "skeptical solution" is his endorsement of **doxastic involuntarism**: the view that we have no direct voluntary control over what we believe. When we form an inductive belief on the basis of experience,

> [t]he belief is the necessary result of placing the mind in such circumstances. It is an operation of the soul, when we are so situated, as unavoidable as to feel the passion of love, when we receive benefits; or hatred, when we meet with injuries. (*Enquiry*, §V.1, p. 46)

In this way, "[n]ature, by an absolute and uncontroulable necessity has determin'd us to judge as well as to breathe and feel" (*Treatise*, I.iv.1, p. 183). Hume's "skeptical solution" is a descendant of the Pyrrhonian appeal to "appearances" as a standard for action in response to the apraxia objection (§1.4.2); essential to that appeal is the idea that appearances "depend on passive and unwilled feelings" (Sextus Empiricus, *Outlines of Scepticism*, I 22).[5] Hume expands this strategy to include not only appearance, but belief as well—which he describes as a "peculiar sentiment" (*Abstract*, p. 657; see also *Treatise* I.iii.7, Appendix, pp. 623–7, *Enquiry*, §V.2). Thus:

> [W]e assent to our faculties, and employ our reason only because we cannot help it. Philosophy wou'd render us entirely *Pyrrhonian*, were not nature too strong for it. (*Abstract*, p. 657)

And so:

> [T]he skeptic still continues to reason and believe, even tho' he asserts, that he cannot defend his reason by reason[.] Nature has not left this to his choice, and has doubtless esteem'd it an affair of too great importance to be trusted to our uncertain reasonings and speculations. (*Treatise*, I.iv.2, p. 187)

In these passages, Hume's innovative approach to the philosophy of human nature is on display: human beings, including their cognitive capacities, are entirely a part of the natural world, to be investigated by empirical science.

So is Hume a skeptic, and if so, what sort of skeptic is he? Interpretations of Hume, in connection with this question, fall into roughly three categories.

First, there are **skeptical** interpretations. Historically, a number of Hume's critics mistakenly understood Hume as a skeptic, and nothing more than a skeptic, effectively ignoring the "skeptical solution" we've just explored. Call this a **mere skeptical** interpretation. However, there is still a debate about whether Hume was *even* a skeptic, and some argue that he was (e.g. Fogelin 1985, 2009; cf. Norton 2002). Hume certainly seems to have taken himself to be some kind of skeptic: he describes the philosophy contained in the *Treatise* as "very sceptical" (*Abstract*, p. 657) and sympathetically describes "*mitigated* scepticism or *academical* philosophy" as "both durable and useful" (*Enquiry*, §XII.3, p. 161). If Hume is a skeptic, he is an Academic skeptic (§1.3.3).[6] What is his skeptical view? Perhaps merely that our inductive beliefs cannot be defended by argument, or more generally that "reason cannot be defended by reason". But this would make it obscure why "[p]hilosophy wou'd render us entirely *Pyrrhonian*, were not nature too strong for it", unless we assume, in addition, something like the principle that we ought to suspend judgment about what cannot be defended by argument.[7] This would explain why our inability to defend our inductive beliefs would even appear to threaten to "undermine the reasonings of common life". On this interpretation, Hume's skeptical view is that we ought to suspend judgment, to which he adds the psychological claim that such suspension is impossible.

Second, there are **naturalistic** interpretations, which understand Hume, in the texts we've been considering, not as engaged in epistemology so much as in psychology (e.g. Smith 1905a, 1905b, Stroud 1977, Garrett 1997). On this interpretation, Hume's central theses are not skeptical claims (about what we ought to believe, or about the possibility of knowledge), but psychological claims about the nature and causes of belief, e.g. that our inductive beliefs are the result of custom rather than reason. And on a **mere naturalistic** interpretation, Hume endorses no skeptical claim, only psychological claims. Naturalistic interpretations are motivated by Hume's stated aims in both the *Treatise* and the *Enquiry* (an empirical investigation of human understanding, as part of a "science of man") and by the fact that he frequently, if not exclusively, states his conclusion in psychological terms, for example:

When the mind ... passes from the idea or impression of one object to the idea or belief of another, it is not determin'd by reason, but by certain principles, which associate together the ideas of these objects, and unite them in the imagination. (*Treatise*, I.iii.vi, p. 92)

Third, there are **anti-skeptical** interpretations, which understand Hume as defending a non-skeptical epistemological claim (e.g. Beauchamp and Mappes 1975). For example, we could interpret Hume as arguing against a picture of knowledge, on which all knowledge must be based on reasoning. If this interpretation is right, Hume would reject what we'll call the "Humean skeptical argument" (§3.2.1), and probably for something like the reason that I suggest that it should be rejected (§3.2.2). In support of this idea, consider Hume's frequent claims about what one ought to believe—"A wise man … proportions his belief to the evidence" (*Enquiry*, §X.1, p. 110); "Rules by which to judge of causes and effects" (*Treatise*, I.iii.15)—and his concession (above) that "all our knowledge" depends on custom.

We need not enter into this interpretative controversy. But it is worth noting that the (non-mere) skeptical and (non-mere) naturalistic interpretations are not incompatible. We could understand Hume as making both an epistemological claim (e.g. that our inductive beliefs are not reasonable) and a psychological claim (e.g. that our inductive beliefs are the result of custom). As well, we could understand Hume as making both a skeptical epistemological claim and a non-skeptical epistemological claim, as Peter Millikan (2002) suggests: on his interpretation, Hume maintains both that "we can see no reason whatever … why induction should be a reliable method of inference" and that, given its irresistibility, "we should treat induction as our norm of factual reasoning" (p. 166). In any event, we'll now turn to an argument for skepticism that, whether or not it is Hume's, is inspired by his discussion of induction.

3.2 The Humean skeptical argument

In this section I'll articulate a skeptical argument, based on Hume's argument concerning induction, for a form of non-rustic Academic skepticism (§1.3.3), on which inductive knowledge is impossible (§3.2.1). This argument requires an assumption, which I'll call the "argumentative constraint on knowledge" (§3.2.2).

3.2.1 *The argument*

The argument assumes that inductive knowledge is a species of *a posteriori* knowledge. Following Hume, the argument will assume that all knowledge is either **a priori** (not based on experience) or **a posteriori** (based on experience), and that all *a posteriori* knowledge is either inductive or observational. **Observational knowledge** is perceptual knowledge (or memorial knowledge deriving from perceptual knowledge), and **inductive knowledge** is any *a posteriori* knowledge apart from this. Thus inductive knowledge is non-observational *a posteriori* knowledge. The argument appeals to the notion of an **inductive argument**: an argument for a conclusion about the unobserved world from premises based on observation.

The argument we'll look at contains no reference to causation. Hume's views about causation play a central role in his thinking about induction, but our interest lies elsewhere.

The argument's conclusion is that inductive knowledge is impossible. However, the argument does not assume infallibilism (cf. §4.3). Hume equates knowledge and certainty (*Treatise* I.iii.1, p. 70) and contrasts knowledge with opinion based on observation and experience (I.iii.3, p. 82). As is standard in contemporary epistemology, our use of "knowledge" is broader, and infallibilism is not assumed. Nor does the argument assume "deductivism", on which inductive knowledge is impossible (cf. §3.1.1), otherwise it would be circular.

Finally, the argument will target our knowledge of the following:

Principle of uniformity: The unobserved world tends to resemble the observed world.

Call this, then, the **Humean skeptical argument**:

1 All knowledge is either *a priori* or *a posteriori*. (Premise)

2 I do not know *a priori* that the sun will rise tomorrow. (Premise)

   a All *a posteriori* knowledge is either observational or inductive. (Premise)

   b I do not know observationally that the sun will rise tomorrow. (Premise)

   c If S has inductive knowledge that p, then S can give a good inductive argument that p. (Premise)

   d Any good inductive argument has the principle of uniformity as a premise. (Premise)

   e Any good argument has only known premises. (Premise)

   f Therefore, if I have inductive knowledge that the sun will rise tomorrow, I know that the principle of uniformity is true. (From c, d, e)

      i I do not know *a priori* that the principle of uniformity is true. (Premise)

ii I do not know observationally that the principle of uniformity is true. (Premise)

iii If I have inductive knowledge that the principle of uniformity is true, then I can give a good inductive argument that the principle of uniformity is true. (From c)

iv No good argument has its conclusion among its premises. (Premise)

v I cannot give a good inductive argument that the principle of uniformity is true. (From d, iv)

vi I do not have inductive knowledge that the principle of uniformity is true (From iii, v)

vii I do not know *a posteriori* that the principle of uniformity is true. (From a, ii, vi)

viii I do not know that the principle of uniformity is true. (From 1, i, vii)

g I do not have inductive knowledge that the sun will rise tomorrow. (From f, viii)

3 I do not know *a posteriori* that the sun will rise tomorrow. (From a, b, g)

4 I do not know that the sun will rise tomorrow. (From 1, 2, 3)

Above, I said that the argument's conclusion was that inductive knowledge is impossible. We need three steps to generalize to this conclusion. First, if what we've said here about the proposition that the sun will rise tomorrow is right, then we could say the same about any would-be object of inductive knowledge. So I do not have any inductive knowledge. Second, if that's true of me, it's surely true of any other human being. So no human being has any inductive knowledge. Third, the argument makes no contingent assumptions about human cognition. So inductive knowledge is impossible.

This formulation reveals the assumptions that motivate Hume's worries about induction. Given the way we defined our terms, premise (1) and premise (a) look solid. Premise (2) and premise (i) strike me as very plausible as well—whatever contingent *a priori* knowledge there might be, these are not the sorts of contingent propositions that can be known *a priori*. Premise (b) and premise (ii) are likewise in good shape: that the sun will rise tomorrow and that the principle of uniformity are true are not the sorts of propositions that can be perceived.

Premise (d) is controversial. Above, I briefly suggested its appeal: adding the principle of uniformity to an inductive argument looks like a standard case of making the assumptions of an argument explicit. Although I find this premise compelling, this is a promising place to challenge the Humean skeptical argument (cf. Van Cleve 1984, §II).

Premise (e) and premise (iv) affirm necessary conditions for a "good argument". (Students of skepticism will recognize them as two of G. E. Moore's (1939) conditions for a "rigorous proof".) Premise (e) prohibits arguments with unknown premises; premise (iv) prohibits circular arguments. These premises could be challenged as well, but we'll grant them for the sake of argument.

Finally, we must consider premise (c)—it seems to me that this is where the Humean skeptical argument goes wrong.

3.2.2 *The argumentative constraint on knowledge*

Premise (c) says that the ability to give a good inductive argument is a necessary condition on inductive knowledge. It is entailed by the following more general principle:

The argumentative constraint on knowledge: S knows that p only if S can give a good argument that p.

Something like this idea has had a tremendous influence on the history of philosophy. It is suggested by Plato's account of knowledge as true belief with an account (see e.g. *Meno* 98a, *Theatetus* 202a) and by Wittgenstein's remark that "[o]ne says 'I know' when one is ready to give compelling grounds" (*On Certainty*, §243). Consider the long-popular idea that knowledge requires justification. On one natural way of understanding "justification", this implies the argumentative constraint on knowledge. I have in mind what Ernest Sosa (1991) calls an "argumentative conception of justification":

One might so define justification that for a belief (assertion, assumption, claim, thought, or what have you) to have the status of being justified: (a) it must have *been justified*, a process of (its) justification must have taken place; and (b) this process must have involved the giving of reasons or arguments, must have involved conversation, at least *in foro interno*. (p. 90; see also p. 109, p. 253)

As Sosa points out (p. 253), this sense of "justification" is in line with what you will find in the dictionary (*OED*: "The action of justifying or showing something to be just, right, or proper"): knowing requires justification, justification requires being justified, and being justified requires having been justified, or at least being able to justify, and thus knowing that p requires the ability to give a good argument that p. Premise (c) places such a constraint on inductive knowledge.

You might object that I have been unfair here, in burdening the Humean skeptical argument with the assumption of the argumentative constraint on (inductive) knowledge. But I do not think there is any charitable way to understand this kind of argument without appealing to something like this assumption. The essence of Hume's argument (§3.1.1) is a prohibition on circularity, on "taking that for granted, which is the very point in question". For this to bear on the possibility of inductive knowledge, we must take inductive knowledge that p to require at least the ability to justify, defend, or give reasons or considerations in favor of the proposition that p, if not having actually justified, defended, or given reasons or considerations in favor of the proposition that p. For only in the course of justifying, defending, or giving reasons or considerations in favor of some proposition might one "take ... for granted" the "very point in question". The relevant notion of circularity is essentially a notion that applies to argumentation.

Given this point, we can now see the argumentative constraint on knowledge, or something like it, motivating **Agrippa's trilemma** (§1.2.2), where we imagined the skeptic and the claimant in conversation.

Whether the argumentative constraint on knowledge is true is a fundamental epistemological question. As with internalism (§2.1.1), I won't try to convince you that the argumentative constraint on knowledge is false (although it seems to me that it is false). What is important is that we note its role in the Humean skeptical argument. However, it is worth briefly mentioning one way of motivating the rejection of the argumentative constraint on knowledge—apart from the fact that it seems to lead straightaway to skepticism (cf. Sosa 1991, pp. 253–4).

There's always a point in cop shows where somebody is frustrated by the fact that some suspect, who obviously committed the crime, hasn't been arrested yet. "You know he's the killer!", the frustrated character urges. The streetwise old detective always answers with something like: "Knowing it and proving it in court are two different things". The detective has a point. Knowing that p and being able to prove that p are *completely* different things. Knowing that p is just a matter of you and your relationship with the proposition that p. But being able to prove that p is a matter not only of that, but of your relationship with other people: the people to whom you're trying to prove that p. The reason for this, or at least one reason for this, is that whether you can give a proof—or a good argument, or a good defense, or good reasons—depends on your audience. In the cop show, for example, the cops have conclusive evidence that so-and-so is the killer, but some crafty lawyer got the evidence excluded from court. They know so-and-so is the killer, but they can't prove that he is. Many philosophers have concluded that the essential link between argumentation and audiences means that knowledge cannot require the ability to give a good argument (cf. §5.2.2).[8]

3.3 Conclusion

In this chapter we have articulated the Humean skeptical argument (§3.2.1), and I have suggested that this argument relies on a controversial presupposition: the argumentative constraint on knowledge (§3.2.2). We turn now to a skeptical argument inspired by the work of René Descartes—one that does not presuppose the argumentative constraint on knowledge.

Readings

On the Humean skeptical argument (§3.2.1), you should start by reading Hume.

- *A Treatise of Human Nature* (e.g. Hume 1978).

- Hume's *Abstract* of the *Treatise* (in e.g., Hume 1978).

- *An Enquiry concerning Human Understanding* (in e.g. Hume 1975).

The following offer an entry into the secondary literature on Hume.

- N. Smith, "The Naturalism of Hume" (Smith 1905a; 1905b).

- B. Stroud, *Hume* (Stroud 1977).

- R. Fogelin, *Hume's Skepticism in the Treatise of Human Nature* (Fogelin 1985).

- M. Williams, "Hume's Skepticism" (Williams 2008).

- P. Millikan (ed.), *Reading Hume on Human Understanding* (Millikan 2002b).

Finally, the following two papers have inspired my treatment of the Humean skeptical argument (§3.2.2).

- J. Van Cleve, "Reliability, Justification, and the Problem of Induction" (Van Cleve 1984).

- E. Sosa, "Methodology and Apt Belief" (Sosa 1991, Essay 14).

4

Our Darkened Intellect

We turn now to an argument for a species of Academic skepticism (§1.3.3), one that has had tremendous influence in contemporary epistemology, and which will serve as a jumping-off point for our discussion of anti-skepticism (Part II). We'll call it the "Cartesian skeptical argument", after **René Descartes** (1596–1650), whose *Meditations* provide its inspiration.

The impact of Descartes' *Meditations* on our intellectual history was at once immediate, long-lasting, and far-reaching. In his own time, Descartes was perceived by some as a dangerous skeptic and by others as an uncritical dogmatist; the truth is that he was a conservative and openminded anti-skeptic whose intellectual goal was the reconciliation of the new science of Copernicus and Galileo with the old religion of the Catholic Church. Since then, the arguments of the *Meditations* have served as central foils in both epistemology and the philosophy of mind, and academics from every discipline have devoted their lives to (and made their reputations on) the celebration and the rejection of Cartesian philosophy. It remains fashionable to point out Descartes' supposed errors (and to make fun of him for his silly views about neurobiology and animal intelligence). Our aim here will be to extract the best skeptical argument we can from his skeptical meditations.

4.1 Descartes' skeptical meditations

Descartes was no skeptic, and in his *Meditations* he does not defend skepticism.[1] However, the first two Meditations (the work is divided into six of these) can be accurately described as "skeptical". In this section we'll look at these skeptical meditations: we'll look at Descartes' anti-skeptical use of skeptical arguments (§4.1.1), the First Meditation (§4.1.2), and the Second Meditation (§4.1.3).

4.1.1 Skepticism for the anti-skeptic

The student of skepticism sometimes stumbles over the fact that the canonical articulation of the skeptical argument that has most influenced contemporary epistemology appears in a decidedly *anti*-skeptical work: Descartes' *Meditations on First Philosophy, in Which Are Demonstrated the Existence of God and the Distinction Between the Human Soul and the Body* (1641). The fact that Descartes is not a skeptic—neither Academic nor Pyrrhonian, neither mitigated nor unmitigated—is right there in the title, for no skeptic would purport to demonstrate anything, much less the existence of God and the distinction between the soul and the body. Understanding Descartes' project in the *Meditations* is essential for understanding contemporary discussions of skepticism, because many contemporary epistemologists are engaged in a project that is importantly similar to that of Descartes.

What was distinctive about Descartes' project in the *Meditations* was not that he, an anti-skeptic, took skepticism seriously. That had been done before, for example, by **Augustine** (354–430) in *Against the Academics*.[2] Nor was it that Descartes, an anti-skeptic, used skeptical arguments to advance non-skeptical conclusions. Philosophers had done this before, when, for example, they argued that alternatives to their preferred epistemological theory would lead to skepticism (cf. Bermudez 2005, p. 68). The Reformers and Counter-Reformers were constantly accusing one another of holding views that would lead to skepticism (Popkin 1979, pp. 11–14). What seems to have been distinctive about Descartes' project was a kind of combination of these two things: he was an anti-skeptic who (i) treated its anti-skeptical credentials as the criterion of success for an epistemological theory and (ii) set the anti-skeptical bar extraordinarily high. He took the strongest and most extreme form of skepticism he could think up, and then set out to refute it.

In a dedicatory letter to the Sorbonne (which Descartes wrote with the aim of getting the *Meditations* adopted as a kind of textbook at the prestigious university), Descartes cites Scripture in support of the view that "everything that may be known of God can be demonstrated by reasoning which has no other source but our own mind" (*Meditations*, 2).[3] He then mentions the most important epistemological theme of the *Meditations*:

> Hence I thought it was most proper for me to inquire how this may be, and how God may be more easily and certainly known than the things of this world. (*Ibid.*)

As for the distinction between the soul and the body, Descartes says that some people "have even had the audacity to assert that ... there are persuasive grounds for holding that the soul dies along with the body and that the opposite view is based on faith alone" (*ibid.* 3). But since the Pope had "expressly enjoined Christian philosophers to refute their arguments", Descartes announces that he will attempt to do just that. He then goes on to say that "irreligious people" might be convinced by his arguments for God's existence and the distinctness of the soul and the body. Moreover, these arguments "have the force of demonstrations", and thus will yield certain knowledge of their conclusions. This anti-skeptical view about religious propositions, by Descartes' time, was highly controversial (cf. §1.6). Once this religious knowledge is established, Descartes goes on to argue, scientific knowledge—physics, astronomy, chemistry—can be established on this firm and stable foundation. Descartes thus has three targets in mind: unbelievers who reject the existence of God and the immortality of the soul, fideists (like Montaigne) who reject the possibility of religious knowledge in favor of faith, and mitigated skeptics (like Gassendi, and Descartes' friend Mersenne) who reject the possibility of scientific knowledge in favor of reasonable belief.

I mention this passage not to prove Descartes' piety,[4] but to indicate that the *Meditations* are wholly anti-skeptical. Elsewhere, in a synopsis of the *Meditations*, Descartes writes that:

> The great benefit of these arguments is not, in my view, that they prove what they establish—namely that there really is a world, and that human beings have bodies and so on—since no sane person has ever seriously doubted these things. The point is that in considering these arguments we come to realize that they are not as solid or as transparent as the arguments which lead us to knowledge of our own minds and of God, so that the latter are the most certain and evident of all possible objects of knowledge for the human intellect. (15–16)

There are four lessons here. The first, again, is that Descartes is no skeptic. The second is, again, that Descartes' aim is to defend a particular epistemological principle: the epistemic priority of theological and introspective knowledge over perceptual knowledge. (This is a quite striking thesis when you think about it.)

The third is that Descartes' method of doubt does not involve actually suspending judgment about anything. Although Descartes says, in the preface to the *Meditations*, that "I would not urge anyone to read this book except those who are able and willing to meditate seriously with me" (9), he is clear in the synopsis that he does not expect genuine doubt. His method of doubt, therefore, is importantly different from the practice of the Pyrrhonian skeptic. We'll call it **hypothetical doubt**. That said, "doubt" here means suspension of judgment; it's just that the suspension of judgment is hypothetical—more on which below (§4.1.2).

The fourth concerns what is distinctive of Descartes' project. What Descartes will attempt is to refute (better: to argue his way out of) rustic suspension of judgment. And yet "no sane person" has ever suspended judgment about everything. These two things, together, express what is distinctive about Descartes' project (cf. Williams 1978, Chapter 2): his epistemological view that a refutation of skepticism is needed, combined with the scope of his ambition: to refute the most insane species of skepticism ever imagined.

Contemporary discussions of skepticism inherit many aspects of Descartes' project. Most contemporary epistemologists reject skepticism, but think that skepticism has important epistemological lessons to teach us (cf. Greco 2007). Many epistemological views—theories of knowledge, for example—are evaluated based on their anti-skeptical credentials. And many contemporary epistemologists would argue that understanding how skepticism can be false is among the central projects in epistemology.

4.1.2 The evil demon

The opening paragraph of the First Meditation[5] is worth quoting in full:

> Some years ago I was struck by the large number of falsehoods that I had accepted as true in my childhood, and by the highly doubtful nature of the whole edifice that I had subsequently based on them. I realized that it was necessary, once in the course of my life, to demolish everything completely and start again right from the foundations if I wanted to establish anything at all in the sciences that was stable and likely to last. But the task looked an enormous one, and I began to wait until I should reach a mature enough age to ensure that no subsequent time of life would be more suitable for tackling such inquiries. This led me to put the project off for so long that I would now be to blame if by pondering over it any further I wasted the time still left for carrying it out. So today I have expressly rid my mind of all worries and arranged for myself a clear stretch of free time. I am here quite alone, and at last I will devote myself sincerely and without reservation to the general demolition of my opinions. (*Meditations*, 17–18)

This is an incredible little passage, and there's a lot to be said about it. Four comments. First, the genre of the *Meditations* is unfamiliar to most philosophical readers. Descartes addresses us as the first-person narrator of a story about a series of philosophical reflections, taking place over the course of six days. The story is interesting because of the philosophical ideas that the main character thinks about, and the first-person narration is an invitation for us to put ourselves in Descartes' position and, as he puts it, meditate along with him.[6]

Second, like the Ancient skeptics, Descartes was concerned with disagreement. In the *Rules for the Direction of the Mind* (1628) he writes that:

> [T]here is hardly any question in the sciences about which clever men have not frequently disagreed. But whenever two persons make opposite judgments about the same thing, it is certain that at least one of them is mistaken, and neither, it seems, has knowledge. For if the reasoning of one of them was certain and evident, he would be able to lay it before the other in such a way as eventually to convince his intellect as well. (363)

The reason for this was Descartes' conviction that all human beings shared a common intelligence. In his *Discourse on the Method of Rightly Conducting One's Reason and Seeking the Truth in the Sciences* (1637), he writes that "the power of judging well and of distinguishing the true from the false— which is what we properly call 'good sense' or 'reason'—is naturally equal in all men" (2). However, Descartes' *Meditations* describe a solitary project, undertaken "quite alone", and in articulating his skeptical doubts Descartes does not appeal to the familiar fact of persistent disagreement, although it was on his mind (cf. *Discourse*, 12–13, 16). The skepticism Descartes confronts is of a fundamentally different kind than skepticism based on the mode from dispute (Chapter 2).

Third, we must keep in mind that Descartes' doubt is hypothetical (§4.1.1): "the general demolition of my opinions" is not an actual demolition, but an imagined demolition.

However, fourth, this raises a crucial question: how do we get from the unobjectionable and obvious idea with which Descartes begins—that I have sometimes believed falsehoods in the past—to the surprising and radical conclusion—that I should in general demolish (or imagine demolishing) my opinions?

The *Meditations* were published with a set of objections (written by Mersenne, Gassendi, Thomas Hobbes, Antoine Arnauld, and others) along with Descartes' replies; in one of these replies (from the second edition, of 1642) he explains his method:

> I shall employ an everyday example to explain to my critic the rationale for my procedure[.] Suppose he had a basket of apples and, being worried that some of the apples were rotten, wanted to take out the rotten ones to

prevent the rot spreading. How would he proceed? Would he not begin by tipping the whole lot out of the basket? And would not the next step be to cast his eye over each apple in turn, and pick up and put back in the basket only those he saw to be sound, leaving the others? In just the same way, those who have never philosophized correctly have various opinions in their minds which they have begun to store up since childhood, and which they therefore have reason to believe may in many cases be false. They then attempt to separate the false beliefs from the others, so as to prevent their contaminating the rest and making the whole lot uncertain. Now the best way they can accomplish this is to reject all their beliefs together in one go, as if they were all uncertain and false. They can then go over each belief in turn and re-adopt only those which they recognize to be true and indubitable. (Seventh Replies, 481)

We can now see what Descartes is up to. I know my beliefs have been mistaken before. How can I determine whether my current beliefs are likewise mistaken? Descartes' method is simple: suspend judgment about everything, and then believe only what is certain and indubitable. This explains the surprising idea that "I should hold back assent from opinions which are not completely certain and indubitable just as carefully as I do from those which are patently false" (18). For only then can I be sure that my "basket of beliefs" is completely free of rot.

Descartes then adopts a strategy for sustaining the doubt that his method requires: he proceeds to articulate arguments designed to show that he cannot be certain of various things, with an emphasis on "the basic principles on which all my former beliefs rested" (*ibid.*). So, for example, he notes that "from time to time I have found that the senses deceive" (*ibid.*), which seems to suggest that he cannot be certain about any deliverance of his senses. But that Ancient skeptical thought (cf. §1.2.1) isn't right, in virtue of the fact that there are ideal conditions for the use of sense perception:

[A]lthough the senses deceive us with respect to objects which are very small or in the distance, there are many other beliefs about which doubt is quite impossible, even though they are derived from the senses—for example, that I am here, sitting by the fire, wearing a winter dressing-gown, holding this piece of paper in my hands, and so on. (*Ibid.*)

However, Descartes realizes that this anti-skeptical thought isn't right either, in virtue of the fact that we sometimes dream that we are in those ideal conditions:

How often, asleep at night, am I convinced of just such familiar events—that

I am here in my dressing-gown, sitting by the fire, when in fact I am lying undressed in bed! (19)

But is it really possible that I'm dreaming right now? Descartes shakes his head and stretches out his hand: isn't there a kind of clarity to our waking lives, that is absent in dreams? It's not (sadly) that I've never dreamed that I was in the office writing a book about skepticism. It's hard to say why exactly, but right now I feel absolutely certain that I'm not dreaming. Ask yourself: is there really any doubt that you're awake right now, reading this book? There are, of course, situations where we may be unsure whether we're awake or not, e.g. something totally incredible happens, or there's tremendous excitement or confusion, or you're stoned, or delirious with a fever, and you wonder whether you might be dreaming. But there are also situations, and right now seems like one of them, where you're 100 percent positive that you're awake. Descartes, for his part, doesn't buy this; he writes that "I see plainly that there are never any sure signs by means of which being awake can be distinguished from being asleep" (*ibid.*). Whether or not you agree with this principle, keep it in mind. We'll see that something like it is plausible.

Descartes next adopts another strategy for sustaining his doubt: he imagines not only suspending judgment about, for example, whether he's sitting by a fire, but that he actually *isn't* sitting by a fire.[7] He not only imagines suspending judgment about whether he's awake, but he actually imagines that he's dreaming. But even while imagining this, he argues that he can still be certain of some things. "[T]he visions which come in sleep are like paintings," he says, "[f]or when painters try to create sirens and satyrs … they simply jumble up the limbs of different animals", and if not, "at least the colors used in the composition are real", as well as the shapes, locations, times, and other "simpler and more universal things" (20). Therefore, Descartes concludes, "arithmetic, geometry and other subjects of this kind, which deal only with the simplest and most general things … contain something certain and indubitable" (*ibid.*).

But this, too, turns out to be too hasty:

[S]ince I sometimes believe that others go astray in cases where they think they have the most perfect knowledge, may I not similarly go wrong every time I add two and three or count the sides of a square, or in some even simpler matter, if that is imaginable? (21)

Descartes considers the possibility that God would not permit him to make such errors, but realizes that he cannot be certain that God even exists. Then, as part of his strategy of imagining that his former beliefs are false, he proceeds to imagine a scenario of total and seemingly unavoidable deception:

I will suppose therefore that ... some malicious demon of utmost power and cunning has employed all his energies in order to deceive me. I shall think that the sky, the air, the earth, colors, shapes, sounds and all external things are merely the delusions of dreams which he has devised to ensnare my judgment. I shall consider myself as not having hands or eyes, or flesh, or blood or senses, but as falsely believing that I have all these things. I shall stubbornly and firmly persist in this meditation; and even if it is not in my power to know any truth, I shall at least do what is in my power, that is, resolutely guard against assenting to any falsehoods, so that the deceiver, however powerful and cunning he may be, will be unable to impose on me in the slightest degree. (22–3)

We have arrived at the heart of Descartes' epistemological insight. Even if, as I argued, you can sometimes be certain that you're awake, there is no way you can be certain that you're not deceived by a demon, of the sort Descartes describes. The reason is simple: there are never any sure signs by means of which not being so deceived can be distinguished from being so deceived. The demon provides an absolutely convincing simulacrum of reality: sensations, emotions, thoughts, memories, everything. There is no way you can possibly know whether or not you are deceived by such a demon. Moreover, even your beliefs about the simplest and most general things are threatened by this possibility. For you cannot be certain that the demon does not cause you to go wrong every time you add two and three, or count the sides of a square. We've all made outrageous and silly mistakes about even very simple matters. We can imagine that the demon has the ability—he is of "utmost power", after all—to cause you to make these kinds of mistakes all the time. You can't be certain that you're not deceived by a demon, of the sort Descartes describes. But if you can't be certain of that, then you can't be certain of anything. That's where the First Meditation ends: amid the "inextricable darkness" (23) of this skepticism.

4.1.3 *The cogito*

We've explicated enough of the *Meditations* to articulate the Cartesian skeptical argument (§4.2), but I'd like to consider the second meditation briefly, and for one reason: to emphasize the severity of Descartes' method of doubt. In this meditation Descartes argues that he can be certain of at least one proposition, and by looking at his argument we'll be able to appreciate what he thinks is required to solve his skeptical problem.

Descartes continues to imagine that he is deceived by a demon, that the external world of buildings and trees does not exist, that his body does not exist, and then he wonders:

Does it follow that I too do not exist? No: if I convinced myself of something then I certainly existed. But there is a deceiver of supreme power and cunning who is deliberately and constantly deceiving me. In that case I too undoubtedly exist, if he is deceiving me; and let him deceive me as much as he can, he will never bring it about that I am nothing so long as I think that I am something. So after considering everything very thoroughly, I must finally conclude that this proposition, *I am, I exist*, is necessarily true whenever it is put forward by me or conceived in my mind. (26)

Before explaining Descartes' insight here, we need to get a misunderstanding out of the way.[8] Descartes' insight is sometimes explained by appeal to the slogan "I think, therefore I am", which is actually a line that occurs in the *Discourse* (32), and the standard name for his first certain item of knowledge (which I've stuck with), "cogito", is the Latin word for "I think" (while "sum" means "I exist"). But this misrepresents the insight of the *Meditations*, for if the proposition that I am were a conclusion based on the premise that I think, then this would just raise the question: how can I be certain that I think? We at least would need some account of why this is certain. But, in fact, we can explain why Descartes can be certain that he exists, without appealing to the premise that he thinks.

Consider the reason that, at least at the end of the First Meditation, I can't be certain that I have hands. The reason is that it's possible that I merely think that I have hands, while really I'm deceived about this proposition by the demon. The same, when it comes to the reason that I can't be certain that 2+3=5: it's possible that I merely think that 2+3=5, while really I'm deceived about this proposition by the demon. Now it might seem at first like the same could be said when it comes to the proposition that I exist: it's possible that I merely think that I exist, while really I'm deceived about this proposition by the demon. But that's actually impossible: it's impossible for me to believe that I exist and be deceived, since if *I* am being deceived, then I exist, and so I'm not actually being *deceived*. The proposition that I exist turns out to have an amazing property: I can't believe it and be wrong. That's what Descartes means when he says that the proposition that I exist is necessarily true whenever it is put forward by me or conceived in my mind. And, obviously, this applies not only to me, nor only to Descartes, but to anyone: it is impossible for someone to believe that she exists and for her belief to be false. This proposition cannot be falsely believed.

So this belief, that I exist, gets put back in the basket (§4.1.2). Eventually, so will many others. What I want to emphasize is what was required, for Descartes, to avoid universal suspension of judgment: a proposition that could not be falsely believed. Even while suspending judgment about whether 2+3=5, Descartes found something certain enough to believe—something more certain than that 2+3=5. Even if we conclude that Descartes' epistemological standards are too high (cf. §4.3), we should be awed by his discovery of a proposition that meets them. Regardless of the success of any other aspect of his project (cf. §4.4.3), it seems to me that Descartes was successful in showing that there is a species of self-knowledge that is "the most certain and evident of all possible objects of knowledge for the human intellect" (cf. §4.1.1).

4.2 The Cartesian skeptical argument

We turn now from Descartes' argument to the "Cartesian skeptical argument", the merits of which we'll consider below (Part II). We'll articulate the argument (§4.2.1), clarify the scope of its conclusion (§4.2.2), discuss whether the species of skepticism proposed is "radical" (§4.2.3), and motivate the argument's second premise (§4.2.4).

4.2.1 The argument

Call the following the **Cartesian skeptical argument**:

1   I know that I have hands only if I can know that I'm not deceived by a demon (about whether I have hands).

2   I can't know that I'm not deceived by a demon (about whether I have hands).

3   Therefore, I don't know that I have hands.

The second premise articulates the idea that there is no way to tell whether or not you are deceived by a demon (§4.1.2). The first articulates an assumption that was tacit in Descartes' reasoning: knowing whether p requires knowing that you're not deceived about whether p. Given these two premises, the conclusion obviously follows.

Perhaps we should accept this skeptical conclusion. But we should know what we're getting into. First, it seems like the argument generalizes on the content of the proposition known. Consider the following argument schema:

4   I know that p only if I can know that I'm not deceived by a demon (about whether p).

5   I can't know that I'm deceived by a demon (about whether p).

6   Therefore, I don't know that p.

What propositions could we substitute into this schema, to yield an argument as good as argument (1)–(3), above? I would suggest any and all of the following:

- That I am a human being.
- That there are any human beings.
- That I live in Edinburgh.
- That Edinburgh is a city in Scotland.
- That I own a pair of cufflinks.
- That I do not own a shotgun.
- That material or physical objects exist.
- That climate change is (partially) caused by human activity.
- That whales evolved from land mammals.
- That water is H_2O.
- That I spoke to Simon Feldman on the phone yesterday.
- That other people exist.
- That democracy is the worst form of government, except for all the others.
- That torture is immoral.
- That Rothko is better than Twombly.
- That unicorns do not exist.
- That all bachelors are unmarried.
- That 2+3=5.
- That there are infinitely many prime numbers.
- That for all propositions that p and that q, if p, and if p then q, then q.

Let's grant Descartes' point that I can know that I exist, and also his idea (*Meditations* 29) that I can know about my own mental life, i.e. about what sensations, experiences, thoughts, or emotions I am having. However good argument (1)–(3) is, there is an equally good instance of argument schema (4)–(6), when it comes to any proposition that p, other than those concerning my own existence and mental life.

Second, the argument obviously generalizes on the subject of knowledge. We appealed to nothing special about me, or about Descartes, that made argument (1)–(3) compelling.[9] Consider the following argument schema:

7 S knows that p only if S can know that she's not deceived by a demon (about whether p).

8 S can't know that she's not deceived by a demon (about whether p).

9 Therefore, S doesn't know that p.

However good argument (1)–(3) is, there is an equally good instance of argument schema (7)–(9), when it comes to any person and any proposition that p, other than those concerning her own existence and mental life.

This means that, if argument (1)–(3) is sound, then there is a sound argument for the following species of Academic skepticism (§1.3.3):

Cartesian skepticism: No one knows anything (except for propositions about her own existence and mental life).

An argument is **sound** if and only if it is valid and its premises are true. An argument is **valid** if and only if, necessarily, if its premises are true, then its conclusion is true. So when we ask after the soundness of the Cartesian skeptical argument, we are asking after the truth of Cartesian skepticism.

4.2.2 Beyond sense perception

The scope of Cartesian skepticism (§4.2.1) is broad, and includes the propositions of mathematics and logic. It can be argued that the skepticism Descartes imagines in his *Meditations* was of a narrower species: skepticism about sense perception in particular. Harry Frankfurt (1970, Chapters 7–8) makes the case for this interpretation: the narrator of the First Meditation is a "naïve empiricist" who thinks mathematics is based ultimately on sense perception, which is why the evil demon possibility threatens her beliefs about mathematics. This explains how the arguments of the First Meditation support Descartes' rationalist conclusion that *a priori* knowledge is more secure than *a posteriori* knowledge (cf. 4.1.1). If Frankfurt is right, then we misrepresented Descartes' argument, above (§4.1.2); we should have focused our attention only on perceptual beliefs.

However, if this interpretation is right, then Descartes was wrong. He should have included *a priori* knowledge in the scope of his skepticism. We cannot know whether a malicious demon of utmost power and cunning is manipulating our senses, causing us to have misleading perceptual experiences. But if that is plausible, then surely this is: we cannot know whether a malicious demon of utmost power and cunning is manipulating our rational faculties, causing us to have misleading *a priori* intuitions, or causing us to make mistakes when we reason. I don't have an account of the causes of our *a priori* beliefs, but whatever the correct account says, any demon that could cause us to have systematically misleading perceptual experiences could also interfere with the causes of our *a priori* beliefs, resulting in systematic error.[10] As Richard Popkin (1979) argues:

> Descartes was willing to consider the most radical and devastating of sceptical possibilities, that not only is our information deceptive, illusory, and misleading, but that our faculties, even under the best of conditions, may be erroneous. (p. 178)

I take Descartes' insight to be that we know that it is possible to go astray in cases where we think we have the most perfect knowledge (cf. §4.1.2). Just as we know that one-off cases of perceptual error are possible, indeed common, we know that one-off cases of *a priori* error are possible, indeed common. The demon hypothesis simply serves to generalize such possibilities: we imagine the demon causing such errors on a massive scale. On my own I am prone to one-off perceptual errors; in the clutches of the demon, I would be prone to systematic perceptual error. But if that's right, then the same can be said about *a priori* error.

I have also included moral and aesthetic propositions within the scope of Cartesian skepticism (§4.2.1), and the reason is the same: we know that one-off cases of moral and aesthetic error are possible, indeed common—so common that many not-especially-skeptical people already reject the possibility of moral and aesthetic knowledge. All I am suggesting here is that, if the possibility of demon deception means that our perceptual beliefs don't amount to knowledge, then the same possibility means that our moral and aesthetic beliefs don't amount to knowledge.

I find Mersenne's remarks on this point, in his objections to the *Meditations*, to be apt:

> Why should it not be in your nature to be subject to constant—or at least very frequent—deception? How can you establish with certainty that you are not deceived, or capable of being deceived, in matters which you think you know clearly and distinctly? Have we not often seen people turn out to have been deceived in matters where they thought their knowledge was as clear as the sunlight? (Second Objections, 126)

This thought, if it applies at all, applies not only to our perceptual beliefs, but to our mathematical, logical, moral and aesthetic beliefs as well.

4.2.3 "Radical"

Consider a species of urbane Academic skepticism on which you can never be absolutely certain about the fundamental nature of reality (§1.3.3). Compared to Cartesian skepticism (§4.2.1), this seems like a trifling and weak epistemological claim. Cartesian skepticism has more bite. It says we know next to nothing. For this reason, Cartesian skepticism is sometimes called "radical". Is this appellation apt? I have emphasized the severity of Descartes' method of doubt (§4.1.3), but it's unclear that the Cartesian skeptical argument inherits this "severity". I'll make three comments, each of which suggests a sense in which Cartesian skepticism is not "radical".

First, Cartesian skepticism has a relatively weak **modality** (§1.3.4). It doesn't say that knowledge is impossible; it just says that no one knows anything. Whether the Cartesian skeptical argument could be modified to support a modally stronger species of skepticism is an open question at this point. The key premise here is the second: is our inability to know that we're not deceived by a demon a contingent fact about actual human beings, or is it a fact about human nature, or is it a fact about knowledge itself? Is the modal weakness of our articulation a liability? I think not; let's proceed to investigate whether Cartesian skepticism is true, and set aside the question of whether some modally stronger species of skepticism is also true.

Second, note well that the Cartesian skeptical argument does not appeal to the premise that I do not have hands, nor to the premise that I am deceived by a demon. It does not even appeal to the premise that it is logically or metaphysically possible that I am deceived by a demon! Its second premise says that I cannot know that I am not deceived by a demon; if this is true, then there is a sense in which it is possible that I am deceived by a demon. (Philosophers call this "epistemic possibility".) This fact about the Cartesian skeptical argument makes for an important difference between the **Cartesian skeptic** (i.e. someone who defends the Cartesian skeptical argument and thus Cartesian skepticism) and the Pyrrhonian skeptic who employs, for example, the five modes (§1.2.2). The Cartesian skeptic grants, for the sake of argument, that your beliefs are true: she grants that you have hands (if you do), that you're not deceived by a demon, and she grants the truth of whatever scientific and philosophical theories you believe. Her conclusion is that none of these beliefs amount to knowledge: that you do not know that you have hands, nor that you're not deceived by a demon, nor that such-and-such scientific and philosophical theories are true. The Pyrrhonian refuses to grant that your beliefs are true: she challenges you at every turn, demanding reasons to back up your beliefs, and reasons for those reasons, and so on. In this respect, the Cartesian skeptic is **concessive**, by contrast with the Pyrrhonian.

Third, note well that Cartesian skepticism is consistent (cf. §9.1.2) with a species of **mitigated skepticism** (§1.3.3), on which people have many reasonable beliefs. The Cartesian skeptic's conclusion that I don't know that I have hands is consistent with the view that it is reasonable for me to believe that I have hands. As with the modality of Cartesian skepticism, it is an open question whether the Cartesian skeptical argument could be modified to support the view that no one has any reasonable beliefs about anything (except for propositions about her own existence and mental life).

Descartes appears to have accepted the knowledge-belief principle (§1.3.3). In the narrative of the *Meditations*, at least, one's options are certainty or suspension of judgment: there is no room for mere reasonable belief that does not amount to knowledge. As he puts it in the *Rules*:

[I]t is better never to study at all than to occupy ourselves with objects which are so difficult that we are unable to distinguish what is true from what is false, and are forced to take the doubtful as certain[.] So ... we reject all such merely probable cognition and resolve to believe only what is perfectly known and incapable of being doubted. (362; cf. *Discourse*, 18)

Some of the leading pro-science Catholics of his time (like Mersenne and Gassendi) had adopted mitigated skepticism as a way of conceding the force of skeptical arguments while leaving room for reasonable religious and scientific belief. Descartes wanted no part of this fashionable concession. At least when it came to science, for Descartes it was knowledge or nothing (cf. Popkin 1979, pp. 174–5; Williams 1983, pp. 342–3).

4.2.4 The second premise

Setting aside the first premise of the Cartesian skeptical argument (§4.2.1), to which we'll return below (Chapter 6), let's attend to the second premise: that I can't know that I'm not deceived by a demon. Is this true?

Before we get to looking at reasons in favor of thinking that the second premise is true, both here and later on (cf. especially Chapter 5), we should consider the following thought: the second premise of the Cartesian skeptical argument is *obviously* true. Let me get clear on what I mean here. I don't mean to suggest that the obviousness of the second premise is a good reason in favor of thinking that the second premises is true, as though one might try to convince someone that the second premise is true by pointing out how obvious it is. If someone doesn't think that the second premise is true, then she doesn't think that it's obviously true. The obviousness of the second premise isn't going to be part of a defense of the second premise. But if you think that the second premise is obviously true, then it doesn't need to be defended, in the sense that you don't need to hear the defense of it to be convinced that it is true.

I mention the idea that the second premise is obviously true for three reasons. First, I think it is obviously true: it seems obviously true, to me. Second, Robert Nozick, whose work we'll be discussing later (§6.2.2), thinks this too, and appreciating this is essential for understanding his views. He defends an account of knowledge that has the consequence that we don't know that we're not deceived by a demon, and, about the question of whether we know that we're not deceived, he says:

> [W]e do not know we're not being deceived by an evil demon[.] So says the skeptic, and so says our account. And also so we say—don't we? For how could we know that we're not being deceived that way, dreaming that dream? [...] It is a virtue of our account that it yields, and explains, this result. (1981, p. 201)

What I want to take away from this is the fact that Nozick treats the fact that his account has the consequence that we don't know that we're not deceived by a demon as evidence that favors his account. What this indicates is that he thinks that the second premise of the Cartesian skeptical argument, if not obvious, is intuitive, pre-theoretically plausible, or commonsensical. And this brings us to the third reason that we should consider the idea that the second premise is obviously true: if it is obviously true, then attempts to defend it could end up obscuring that fact. We might find a particular defense of the premise lacking, and think that that was a mark against the premise. But if the premise is obviously true, then the fact that some defense of it fails is no mark against it. More importantly, if the second premise is obviously true, then our failed attempts to explain why it is true should also not count against it.

You might not think that the second premise is obviously true, and, as I've been suggesting, obviousness is not something to be argued over.[11] Indeed, you might think that the second premise is obviously *false*. John Greco (2008) writes:

> Is that premise [that I cannot know that I am not a brain in a vat] initially (or pretheoretically) implausible? It seems to me that it is not. In fact, it seems to me that it is initially obvious that I *do* know that I am not a brain in a vat. (p. 111)

So there are very different intuitions among philosophers, when it comes to the obviousness of the second premise of the Cartesian skeptical argument. In any event, for the remainder of this section I'll sketch four defenses of the second premise. I'll present them in order of increasing convincingness, by my lights.

First, we might appeal to the following principle (cf. Brueckner 1994, p. 830; Vogel 2004, p. 427):

Underdetermination principle: If S's evidence for believing that p does not favor believing that p over believing some incompatible proposition that q, then S is not justified in believing that p.

And argue that our evidence does not favor believing that we are not deceived by a demon over believing that we are so deceived. This, along with the assumption that knowing that p requires being justified in believing that p, implies the second premise of the Cartesian skeptical argument.[12] The premise that our evidence does not favor believing that we are not deceived, however, has been challenged (cf. §4.5.4, §5.2.4).

A drawback of the appeal to the underdetermination principle is that the defender of Cartesian skepticism would be forced to adopt a species of unmitigated skepticism on which no one has justified beliefs about anything (except for propositions about their own existence and mental life). Below (Chapter 9), I will focus on mitigated Cartesian skepticism. This focus reflects my interest in examining the most plausible form of Cartesian skepticism. But you might think that unmitigated Cartesian skepticism is equally plausible. It is up to you to decide what species of skepticism to focus on in your own inquiries (see this chapter's "Readings").

Second, consider the fact that if you were deceived by a demon, you would still think that you were not. Here, again, is Nozick, on the possibility that we are deceived by a demon:

There is no way we can know it is not happening for there is no way we could tell if it were happening; and if it were happening we would believe exactly what we do now—in particular, we would still believe that it was not. (1981, p. 201)

As a defense of the second premise, this argument requires a controversial assumption called the "sensitivity principle", that we'll examine below (§6.2.2). But in advance of that examination, we can still appreciate the appeal of what Nozick is saying here.

Third, there is Descartes' point (§4.1.2): there is no "sign" by which you might distinguish being deceived from not being deceived. There is an excellent passage in Barry Stroud's book *The Significance of Philosophical Scepticism* (1984, pp. 20–3) in which he makes this point especially compelling. What we seek, Stroud suggests, is "some operation or test" that will tell us whether we're deceived by a demon. (Stroud talks about dreaming, but I'll adapt what he says to the case of demon deception.) Stroud argues that there are two distinct problems with the possibility of our ever knowing that we're not deceived, by using such a test. First (p. 21), supposing there is such a test, to use it you'd have to know about it. But to know that there's a test, one that can tell you whether you're deceived, you'd have to already have some way of knowing whether you're deceived—and this is what we were supposedly trying to establish. Think of how people sometimes say that you can pinch yourself to tell if you're dreaming (or of those nonsensical devices they use in the movie *Inception*). The idea is that if you pinch yourself and wake up, then you know that you were dreaming, but if you pinch yourself and don't wake up, then you know that you're not dreaming. But the only way the pinch test could ever work is if you had some way of knowing whether you're dreaming, other than the pinch test. For how do you know that the pinch test is reliable? "Well, in the past, whenever I've been dreaming and pinched myself, I woke up, and whenever I've not been dreaming and pinched myself, I didn't wake up". But this presupposes that you had some way of knowing whether you're dreaming, other than the pinch test. Second (pp. 21–3), even if you knew about a test that could tell you whether you're deceived, to know that you're not deceived you would have to know that you've performed the test and that it delivered a negative verdict. But "[a]nything one can experience in one's waking life can also be dreamt about; it is possible to dream that one has performed a certain test" (p. 22), and this obviously applies to the case of demon deception as well. Assuming that the first premise of the Cartesian skeptical argument is true, to know that you've performed the test and that it delivered a negative verdict, you must be able to know that you're not deceived by a demon (about whether you've performed the test and that it delivered a negative verdict). But this is what we were supposedly trying to establish.

Fourth, we might appeal to the principle that, if S knows that p, then there is some way that S knows whether p, along with the premise that there is no way for you to know whether you are deceived by a demon. Some version of the proposed principle seems right. Imagine that you know that there is a tree outside your window. How do you know? It is easy to imagine that the answer to this question is: by seeing the tree. Or imagine that you know that the Knicks lost last night. How do you know? It is easy to imagine that the answer is: by reading it in the newspaper. When you know something, there is some way that you know it. (Even when we are inclined to say that we "just know" something, when we really do know that thing, it later turns out that there was some way that we knew it.) And some version of the proposed premise seems right as well. Suppose for the moment that you do know that you're not deceived by a demon. Well, how do you know? Given the proposed principle, there is some way that you know that you're not deceived. What is it? And here I think we realize that *there is no way you could know that you're not deceived by a demon.*[13] It is not just that all the ways—methods, strategies, faculties, processes, mechanisms, whatever—that we can think of are all ways that could be manipulated by the demon. It is also that all the ways that we can think of—perception, memory, intuition, testimony, reasoning, whatever—are not ways of knowing whether you're deceived by a demon. You cannot, for example, *see* whether you are deceived by a demon, in the way that you can see whether there's a tree outside your window.

There is obviously much more to be said about the second premise of the Cartesian skeptical argument, but these are some of the reasons that its second premise is appealing. We will return to some of these issues below (Chapter 5).

4.3 Infallibilism

A natural reaction upon reading the *Meditations* (cf. §4.1.2) is to ask: why does Descartes insist on a proposition being certain before he will believe it? You might think that his conclusion at the end of the First Meditation—that nothing is certain—is completely right, but also completely uninteresting. Who cares if nothing is certain? Many things are probably true, and it is reasonable to believe those things. Indeed, even granting that nothing is certain, why conclude that we have no knowledge?

The reason some people are inclined to conclude that we have no knowledge, on the basis of the premise that nothing is certain, is that they endorse the following view about knowledge:

Infallibilism: If S knows that p, then S is certain that p.

"Certainty" is ambiguous (cf. Reed 2008); I mean here the "psychological" sense of "certainty" that refers to complete or absolute conviction or to the highest degree of belief. In short, to be certain is to be sure. Infallibilism says that certainty, in this sense, is a necessary condition on knowledge.

Descartes seems to have endorsed infallibilism, or something quite like it (cf. Williams 1978, Chapter 2). In the *Rules* he says that "[a]ll knowledge is certain and evident cognition" (362). However, Descartes' view is subtle. The Latin words that we are translating with "knowledge" and "cognition" are "scientia" and "cognitio", respectively. Scientia is contrasted with "merely probable cognition [cognitio]" (*ibid*.); and "no act of awareness [cognitio] that can be rendered doubtful seems fit to be called knowledge [scientia]" (*Meditations*, Second Replies, 141). So there are two species of cognitio: scientia, which requires certainty, and merely probable cognitio, which doesn't. If we were to translate "probabilis tantum cognitio" with "knowledge", then Descartes doesn't endorse infallibilism, but merely the view that scientia requires certainty. How then to translate "scientia"? As the Latin word suggests, Descartes has the sciences—physics, astronomy, chemistry—in mind here. (Recall that in the *Meditations* he wants to establish something firm and lasting "in the sciences", and that the *Discourse* concerns "seeking truth in the sciences".) He seems thus to hold (cf. Popkin 1979, pp. 172–80; Williams 1983, p. 344):

Scientific infallibilism: If theory T is the result of successful scientific theorizing, then we can be certain that T is true.

Since Descartes' time, this conception of science has fallen out of favor, and few would argue with the claim that it has been completely discredited (see e.g. Popper 1963, Chapter 1).

Infallibilism (i.e. that knowledge requires certainty) has also fallen out of favor. (For a contemporary defense, see Unger 1975.) But what is essential to recognize in this connection (cf. Greco 2008, p. 116) is the fact that the Cartesian skeptical argument (§4.2.1) does not presuppose, nor in any way assume or depend on, infallibilism. (Nor, for that matter, does it presuppose scientific infallibilism.) None of the motivations for the second premise (§4.2.4) presuppose infallibilism, and, as we'll see (Chapter 6), infallibilism is orthogonal to the first premise as well. The idea behind the Cartesian skeptical argument is very much *not* that you cannot be certain that you're not deceived by a demon, and therefore know very little. That argument would, indeed, presuppose infallibilism. The idea behind the Cartesian skeptical argument is that you've got no way of knowing whether you're deceived, and therefore know very little.

Note also that the Cartesian skeptical argument does not presuppose internalism (§2.1.1), and that it does not presuppose the argumentative constraint on knowledge (§3.2.2). (In connection with this, note that the skeptical arguments discussed in previous chapters did not presuppose infallibilism; cf. Frances 2005, p. 26.)

If infallibilism is orthogonal to the soundness of the Cartesian skeptical argument, why have I brought it up here? The reason is that the vast majority of discussions of Cartesian skepticism that you will encounter will dwell, perhaps exclusively, on Descartes' "obsession" with certainty. For many, a "quest for certainty" is synonymous with epistemology since Descartes. But infallibilism is a red herring, in connection with what we are calling the "Cartesian skeptical argument", even if not in connection with Descartes' own views.

Now you may be thinking that infallibilism is obviously true, and thus that it is neither here nor there that the Cartesian skeptical argument does not presuppose it. As I mentioned above, infallibilism has fallen out of favor, and you will find almost no contemporary epistemologists who defend it. Why not? One reason is that, as Peter Unger (1975) shows, there is short argument from infallibilism to a species of rustic Academic skepticism: knowledge requires certainty, but there's nothing we can be certain about, so knowledge is impossible.

As with internalism and the argumentative constraint on knowledge, some people think that infallibilism is obvious, and others think that it is obviously false. You will have to make up your own mind about it. But I shall warn you against one easy mistake. We should not say that infallibilism is true, but that everyday (or ordinary, or non-philosophical) knowledge doesn't require certainty. For everyday knowledge is a species of knowledge, and if S has everyday knowledge that p, then S knows that p. If S can have everyday knowledge that p without being certain that p, then knowledge does not require certainty. You might object that everyday knowledge is not a species of knowledge. But in that case, the phrase "everyday knowledge" is like the phrase "fake leather", and it would be misleading to use the phrase in epistemology. (It would be like bringing fake leather products to a leather market.) Alternatively, you might object that what requires certainty is absolute (or real, or true) knowledge. But unless knowledge requires certainty, infallibilism is false. (And there would be no objection to saying that absolute knowledge requires certainty, if "absolute" just means "certain", although it would be less misleading to simply say "certain".)

4.4 Between three rocks and a hard place

Recall the definitions of soundness and validity (§4.2.1). If an argument has two premises and a conclusion, then there are four, and only four, possibilities:

- The first premise is false.

- The second premise is false.

- The argument is invalid.

- The conclusion is true.

I shall repeat: these are the only four possibilities. This applies to the Cartesian skeptical argument (§4.2.1), which is an argument with two premises and a conclusion. Thus there are four, and only four, possibilities[14]:

- The first premise is false, i.e. it is false that I know that I have hands only if I can know that I'm not deceived by a demon (about whether I have hands).

- The second premise is false, i.e. it is false that I can't know that I'm not deceived by a demon (about whether I have hands).

- The Cartesian skeptical argument is invalid.

- The conclusion is true, i.e. I do not know that I have hands—and (given the fact that the argument generalizes) Cartesian skepticism is true.

As is characteristic of an interesting philosophical problem, none of these possibilities is plausible. One of them must be the case, but it is difficult to see how any of them could be the case. This is the **problem of Cartesian skepticism**. No one has an **answer** to the problem of Cartesian skepticism unless she can say which of the four possibilities is the case.

If this does not seem like a "problem" to you now, I hope it will seem like one after we've looked at the anti-skeptical possibilities (Part II). This is both because this will help reveal what is implausible about Cartesian skepticism, and because this will help reveal what is implausible about the anti-skeptical possibilities.

What is important to recognize now is that one of these four possibilities must be the case. This means that, if Cartesian skepticism is false, then one of the first three possibilities must be the case. And this means that, if you reject Cartesian skepticism, then you must think that either the first premise of the Cartesian skeptical argument is false, or the second premise is false, or the argument is invalid. Now another important point. You might reject Cartesian skepticism, and not know which of the three alternative possibilities is the case. You might think that either the first premise is false, or the second premise is false, or the argument is invalid, but not know which of these three is the case. But you do not have an answer to the problem of Cartesian skepticism unless you can say which of these three is the case.

4.5 Unpersuasive objections to the Cartesian skeptical argument

In the last section of this chapter, we'll look briefly at some objections to the Cartesian skeptical argument (§4.2.1) that, so I'll argue, are unpersuasive. More promising anti-skeptical objections will be discussed below (Part II). I'll deal with these objections briefly—too briefly, their defenders will object. Citations of relevant literature are provided for those who wish to explore these ideas further.

4.5.1 The self-refutation objection

We'll first consider the two objections we considered above (§1.4): the self-refutation objection (this section) and the apraxia objection (§4.5.2). Applied to the Cartesian skeptical argument (§4.2.1), the self-refutation objection points out that Cartesian skepticism implies that no one knows that Cartesian skepticism is true. But this is consistent with Cartesian skepticism. In general, everything we said about Academic skepticism and the self-refutation objection, above (§1.4.1), applies to Cartesian skepticism as well.

The self-undermining objection (§1.4.1) cannot be so easily dismissed. Cartesian skepticism implies that no one knows that the premises of the Cartesian skeptical argument are true. The Cartesian is thus forced to advance an argument, the premises of which she does not (by her lights) know to be true. Is this problematic?

We have already encountered the idea that good arguments must proceed from known premises—this was premise (e) of the Humean skeptical argument (§3.2.1). The defender of the Cartesian skeptical argument must reject the principle that one should not advance an argument unless one knows its premises are true. How plausible is such a move? It seems to me that it is plausible, given that the Cartesian can propose two alternative principles: that you should not advance an argument unless you believe its premises are true (a **principle of sincerity**), and that you should not advance an argument unless said beliefs are reasonable (a **principle of reasonableness**). Suppose the defender of the Cartesian skeptical argument believes, and reasonably believes, that the premises of the argument are true (cf. Curley 1978, p. 50): this is coherent, because Cartesian skepticism is consistent with mitigated skepticism (§4.2.3). And even if the defender of the argument does not know that its premises are true, she can give reasons in defense of those premises (cf. §4.2.4, Chapter 6). Her lack of knowledge, therefore, does not undermine her argument.

4.5.2 *The apraxia objection*

It is a truth universally acknowledged, that the mention of skepticism must invariably be met with the apraxia objection. Nearly two millennia after the Stoics first challenged the Academics with this objection, Thomas Reid, in his *Inquiry into the Human Mind on the Principles of Common Sense* (1764), thus challenged the skeptics of his day, who insisted that "you ought to resolve firmly to withhold assent, and to throw off this belief of external objects, which may be all delusion" (6.20). Reid replied:

> I think it would not be prudent to throw off this belief, if it were in my power. [Suppose] I resolve not to believe my senses. I break my nose against a post that comes in my way; I step into a dirty kennel; and, after twenty such wise and rational actions, I am taken up and clapped into a mad house. (*Ibid.*)

From what I have said about Descartes' project, this would not apply to the skepticism of the *Meditations* (cf. Williams 1978, pp. 32, 46). As Descartes notes in the *Discourse*, "in practical life it is sometimes necessary to act upon opinions which one knows to be quite uncertain just as if they were indubitable" (31; cf. 24–5). The project of the *Meditations*, since it involves devoting oneself "solely to the search for truth," (*ibid.*) involves a thoroughly impractical method, which is why it requires "a clear stretch of free time."

Neither does the apraxia objection threaten the Cartesian skeptical argument (§4.2.1). First, Cartesian skepticism is Academic, not Pyrrhonian (§1.3.3), and there is no recommendation of suspension of judgment (cf. §9.1). At most, there is the recommendation of hypothetical suspension of judgment (§4.1.1), by way of motivating the argument. Second, suppose it were the case that *believing* the conclusion of the Cartesian skeptical argument were to have the kinds of consequences Reid imagines will befall the skeptic. This would not threaten the argument. The Cartesian skeptic alleges, for example, that you do not know that you have hands. That it would be impractical to believe that you do not know that you have hands is orthogonal to the question of whether you know that you have hands. And so it is orthogonal to Cartesian skepticism. The defender of an argument is committed to the *truth* of its conclusion, not its practicality.[15] Students of skepticism sometimes say that Cartesian skepticism is logical, but impractical. (There are echoes of a Kirk/Spock dichotomy in this idea.) In epistemology, however, we are interested in whether Cartesian skepticism is *true*.

Another way of putting this is to point out that the apraxia objection does not provide an anti-skeptical answer to the problem of Cartesian skepticism

(§4.4). It does not allege that one of the premises of the Cartesian skeptical argument (§4.2.1) is false, or that the argument is invalid. It seems to me that any would-be objection that does neither of those things, i.e. that does not offer an anti-skeptical answer to the problem of Cartesian skepticism, is no objection at all.

4.5.3 Descartes' theological strategy

In the Third and Fourth Meditations, Descartes argues respectively for the existence of God and for the claim that God is not a deceiver. He would thus argue that we *can* know that we're not deceived by a demon, and thus reject the second premise of the Cartesian skeptical argument.

Students of skepticism sometimes complain that Descartes "appeals" to God in answering the problem of Cartesian skepticism. But this is a weak complaint. Descartes, in the Third Meditation, argues that God exists. If his argument is sound, then God exists, and his "appeal" is to something that exists. It is obscure why this would undermine his anti-skeptical strategy.

The most famous and influential objection to Descartes' strategy, first pressed by Mersenne (*Meditations*, Second Objections, 124–5) and Arnauld (see below), is that Descartes' argument is viciously circular. Descartes seems to invite this objection in the Third Meditation: he proposes "as a general rule that whatever I perceive very clearly and distinctly is true" (35), but then writes that "I do not yet even know for sure whether there is a God", and seems to concede that there remains a "slight reason for doubt" about the "general rule" just mentioned (36). In order to remove that doubt, he offers his arguments for the existence of God and for the claim that God is not a deceiver. But Descartes seems to (in some sense) use the admittedly slightly doubtful rule of clear and distinct perception in giving those arguments. For example, one premise in his argument for the existence of God is that "there must be at least much reality in the efficient and total cause and in the effect of that cause" (40). How does Descartes know this? The only way he could know it is by clearly and distinctly perceiving the truth of that proposition; as he puts it, this proposition "is manifest by the natural light" (*ibid.*). But it seems like Descartes' argument has gone in a circle. As Arnauld puts it, "we can be sure that God exists only because we clearly and distinctly perceive this. Hence, before we can be sure that God exists, we ought to be able to be sure that whatever we clearly and distinctly perceive is true" (Fourth Objections, 214).

However, it would be hasty to reject Descartes' anti-skeptical strategy on these grounds. For one thing, it is unclear that *any* anti-skeptical strategy can avoid something like this kind of circularity (cf. §3.2, §5.3.1). For another, there are sophisticated ways of making sense of Descartes' strategy, on which it is not viciously circular (Frankfurt 1970, chapter 15; Curley 1978, chapter 5; Williams 1978, chapter 7; 1983, pp. 438–50; Sosa 1997). Descartes' strategy does not obviously fall to the circularity objection.

The problem with Descartes' anti-skeptical strategy, it seems to me, is that his arguments, for the conclusions that God exists and that God is not a deceiver, are unsound. It's beyond the scope of our study of skepticism to go into the details, and you can draw your own conclusions about those arguments. They rely on controversial metaphysical, psychological, and ethical claims that, for my part, do not seem to be true.

4.5.4 *Skepticism about demons*

Here is a kind of objection to the Cartesian skeptical argument: "I am not religious and I don't believe in demons. Since the argument presupposes the existence of demons, I find it unconvincing". However, the argument does not presuppose the existence of demons. Its second premises says that we do not know that a certain kind of demon does not exist. It is consistent with this that there are no demons of any kind.[16]

But isn't it incredibly unlikely that I'm deceived by a demon? The skeptic has two options in responding to this. First, she might challenge the claim that demon deception is unlikely: my grounds for thinking that demon deception is unlikely include all sorts of things, my knowledge of which is called into question by the Cartesian skeptical argument. Second, she might concede that demon deception is unlikely, but insist that I cannot *know* that I am not deceived. Whether this strategy is plausible depends, at least in part, on *how* unlikely demon deception is. Can a case be made that demon deception is so unlikely that we know it is not the case?

In his book on *The Problems of Philosophy* (1912), **Bertrand Russell** (1872–1970) argued that:

> There is no logical impossibility in the supposition that the whole of life is a dream [, but] there is no reason whatever to suppose that it is true; and it is, in fact, a less simple hypothesis, viewed as a means of accounting for the facts of our own life, than the common-sense hypothesis that there really are objects independent of us, whose action on us causes our sensations. (Russell 1959, pp. 22–3)

More recently, Jonathan Vogel (1990a, 1993) has argued for a similar conclusion: the hypothesis that we are not deceived by a demon, and that most of our common-sense beliefs about the world are true, provides a better explanation of our sensory experiences than does the hypothesis that we are deceived by a demon. Now there are clearly many interesting issues to be discussed in connection with this idea. For our purposes, however, we should ask: does the fact that the hypothesis that we are not deceived, as opposed to the hypothesis that we are deceived, is a simpler and better explanation of our experiences provide a way of knowing that we are not deceived?

Imagine that we hear a rumbling in the attic and wonder what is causing the sound. I propose that it's squirrels, and you propose that there are gremlins bowling in the attic.[17] It seems like my squirrel hypothesis, as opposed to your gremlin hypothesis, is a simpler and better explanation of the rumbling. And it seems like it is very unlikely that there are gremlins bowling in the attic. And, finally, it seems like I can know that there are no gremlins bowling in the attic. But I don't think that we should think that this knowledge is based on the fact that the gremlin hypothesis is unlikely, or that it is a less simple and worse explanation than the squirrel hypothesis. Instead, if I know that there are no gremlins bowling in the attic, it is because I know that *there are no such things as gremlins*. And it is actually this fact that makes it the case that it is unlikely that there are gremlins bowling in the attic, and it is this fact that makes it the case that the gremlin hypothesis is a less simple and worse explanation than the squirrel hypothesis.

If this is right, then the fact that the hypothesis that we are not deceived by a demon, as opposed to the hypothesis that we are deceived, is a simpler and better explanation of our experiences does *not* provide a way of knowing that we are not deceived. If anything, our prior knowledge that there are no such things as demons makes it the case that it is unlikely that we are deceived, and that the hypothesis that we are deceived is a less simple and worse explanation than the hypothesis that we are not deceived. The considerations of likelihood, simplicity, and explanatory quality do not provide us with a way of knowing that we are not deceived by a demon.

4.5.5 Idealism

George Berkeley (1685–1753) is most famous for rejecting the existence of matter, where "matter" refers to something that can exist independently of being perceived or thought about. According to his **idealism**, nothing exists apart from minds and ideas. In his *Three Dialogues between Hylas and Philonous, in Opposition to Sceptics and Atheists* (1713), and in his *Treatise Concerning the Principles of Human Knowledge* (1710), he argues that idealism undermines skepticism (see *Dialogues*, pp. 61–4,[18] *Principles*, §§86–92; cf. Pappas 2008). But idealism *per se* does not provide an answer to the problem of Cartesian skepticism (§4.4), because the thesis that nothing exists apart from minds and ideas is orthogonal to the truth of the premises of the Cartesian skeptical argument. Consider, in particular, the second premise, and suppose that nothing exists apart from minds and ideas. This gives us no reason to think that the second premise is false.[19]

What the Berkeleyan idealist would need to do, to undermine the second premise of the Cartesian skeptical argument, is to adopt Descartes' theological strategy (§4.5.3). Berkeley, indeed, argues from idealism to the conclusion that God exists (*Principles*, §25), and if (as Descartes argues) the existence of God is incompatible with demon deception, then we can see how idealism undermines skepticism. However, this anti-skeptical strategy is only as good as the argument for theism (and the argument that God is not a deceiver) on which it rests.[20]

There is another reason why idealism's anti-skeptical credentials are doubtful. Idealism is sometimes articulated as the rejection of the distinction between appearance and reality. This idea would seem to somehow cut off the skeptic's line of reasoning, which appeals to the possibility of a systematic mismatch between appearance and reality. But this idea, at least, is no part of Berkeley's view: he accepts a distinction between veridical and non-veridical perception (*Dialogues*, p. 68, *Principles*, §§29–34). Once this distinction is granted, the possibility of systematic error can be articulated (cf. Greco 2008, pp. 117–18).

4.5.6 Cartesian dualism and indirect realism

Berkeley's anti-skeptical strategy (§4.5.5) understands the skeptic as making the *metaphysical* mistake of assuming the existence of matter. One of the most important and influential kinds of responses to skepticism understands the skeptic as making some kind of metaphysical mistake about the relationship between mind and world. For example, Richard Rorty (1979) argues that Descartes' **dualism**—his view that mind and matter are distinct substances—is the culprit. As he puts it, "[t]he Cartesian mind simultaneously made possible veil-of-ideas skepticism and a discipline devoted to circumventing such skepticism" (p. 140). Only by thinking of "the mind" and "the material world" as separate can the question of "whether what the Eye of the Mind sees is a mirror (or a distorted mirror—an enchanted glass) or a veil" (p. 46) even arise. A common theme, when it comes to this kind of response to skepticism, is the implication of **indirect realism**, on which we perceive material things only indirectly, by perceiving our sensations or experiences, as an essential presupposition of Cartesian skepticism. The thought is that Descartes had a flawed conception of perceptual experience, or of the mind in general, and that this flawed conception is what makes possible the problem of Cartesian skepticism.

I'd like to emphasize two things, when it comes to this kind of response to Cartesian skepticism. First thing: the issues here, including the mind-body problem and the metaphysics of perception, are deep and important, and any student of skepticism should study them carefully. The literature on the relationship between mind and world is full of wonderful philosophical ideas (see this chapter's "Readings"). Second thing: Cartesian dualism and indirect realism are orthogonal to the plausibility of Cartesian skepticism. This is because they are orthogonal to the soundness of the Cartesian skeptical argument (§4.2.1), and thus rejecting them does not provide an answer to the problem of Cartesian skepticism (§4.4). Cartesian dualism and indirect realism are not presupposed by the premises of the Cartesian skeptical argument. And as I have argued (§4.2.3), the argument targets not only our perceptual beliefs, but our mathematical, logical, moral, and aesthetic beliefs as well. It is possible, and perhaps right, to understand Descartes' project (§4.1) as that of closing the gap between the immaterial mind and the material world, which gap consisted of a "veil of ideas". But the Cartesian skeptical argument presupposes no such gap, and no such "veil". It merely presupposes (if anything) the possibility of systematic error in our beliefs.

What I have said in this section is *highly* controversial. It is important that you consult the relevant literature (see this chapter's "Readings") and make up your own mind.

4.5.7 *The impossibility of systematic error*

If the Cartesian skeptical argument (§4.2.1) presupposes the possibility of systematic error in our beliefs, then perhaps we should challenge that possibility. If systematic error is impossible, then it is impossible that I am deceived by a demon, since the description of demon deception included the idea that the deception was systematic (cf. §4.1.2), and *deception* implies false belief. If this is right, then it might be grounds for believing that I am not deceived, and if I have grounds for believing that I am not deceived, then I seem to be in a position to know that I am not deceived—which contradicts the second premise of the Cartesian skeptical argument (cf. Bouwsma 1949).

But why think that systematic error is impossible? You might appeal here to the work of **Donald Davidson** (1917–2003) (e.g. 2001, Essays 10–14; cf. Nagel 1999). Davidson argues that it is not possible to attribute beliefs to someone unless one attributes mostly true beliefs to that person; more plausible than the hypothesis that the person—or creature—has mostly false beliefs is that she—or it—does not have beliefs at all. Therefore, he argues, it is impossible for someone to have mostly false beliefs.

The defender of the Cartesian skeptical argument might meet this idea head on, and argue that the scenario Descartes describes is obviously possible, and so there must be some mistake in Davidson's argument. Were Davidson's argument sound, then it would be impossible for someone to be deceived in the way Descartes describes, but since that is obviously possible, Davidson's argument must be unsound. The next step would be to figure out where his argument goes wrong (cf. Lewis, 1984).

Alternatively, we might narrow the scope of Cartesian skepticism. In the scenario Descartes describes, I am and always have been the demon's victim. Imagine, instead, that I have only become the demon's victim last night (cf. Chalmers 2005, pp. 152–9), in such a way that my beliefs about the past are true, but my beliefs about what's going on now are mostly false. For reasons that we don't have to go into here, Davidson has no argument against the possibility of this scenario. So the impossibility of systematic error leaves unthreatened an alternative species of Academic skepticism, on which no one knows anything about what is going on in the present.

Davidson's conclusion can be made to look appealing by considering someone who is a "brain in a vat", hooked up to a computer all her life, that has caused her to have all the same experiences that you've had (cf. Putnam 1981, chapter 1; Chalmers 2005). She has the experience of looking out the window and seeing a tree, but there's no real tree, and no real window, because she's just a brain in a vat. But you might think that this is compatible with the belief she forms, on the basis of her experience, being true. She believes "that there's a tree outside the window", but what does she mean by a "tree"? Perhaps what she means by "tree" is something different from what we mean by "tree" (after all, she has never encountered what we call "trees"). A "tree", for her, is some electronic or virtual or computer-constituted thing. And so her belief "that there's a tree outside the window", along with most of her other beliefs, is true.

However, this doesn't get us the conclusion we would need, that it is impossible that I'm deceived by a demon, of the sort that Descartes describes. For in the case of the victim of a demon, of the sort Descartes describes, it is not plausible to say that what she means by "tree" is something different from what we—or the demon—mean by "tree". We imagined a malicious demon of utmost power and cunning, one who "has employed all his energies in order to deceive me". If the demon has the concept of a "tree", he can cause me to form beliefs using that concept. My concepts will inherit their meanings from those of the demon. It doesn't matter that I wouldn't know about the origin of these meanings. Imagine that a slightly malicious and moderately cunning Mandarin-speaking person tattoos characters on my arm that mean (in Mandarin) "I am a jackass", although I think the characters mean "I am a badass". My tattoo says that I'm a jackass, and not that I am a badass, regardless of whether I'm aware of its meaning. In the same way that the Mandarin speaker forces me to represent the proposition that I'm a jackass, whether I like it or not, the demon that Descartes describes forces me to believe a ton of false propositions, whether I like it or not.[21]

4.5.8 Naturalism

In his discussion of skepticism (cf. §4.5.2), Thomas Reid says that he will not suspend judgment about the deliverances of his senses

> because it is not in my power: why, then, should I make a vain attempt? It would be agreeable to fly to the moon, and to make a visit to Jupiter and Saturn; but, when I know that Nature has bound me down by the law of gravitation to this planet which I inhabit, I rest contented, and quietly suffer myself to be carried along in its orbit. My belief is carried along by perception, as irresistibly as my body by the earth. And the greatest sceptic will find himself to be in the same condition. (*Inquiry*, 6.20)

There are a number of views, concerning skepticism, that are grouped under the heading of **naturalism**; they have in common something like the idea that Reid articulates in this passage: human cognition is part of nature, and we are naturally non-skeptical creatures. Naturalism has a rich and varied philosophical history, from Hume and Reid's time (§3.1.2) to the present day (cf. Quine 1969, Wittgenstein 1969, Kornblith 2002). However—and many self-described naturalists would agree—it does not provide an answer to the problem of Cartesian skepticism (§4.4). Reid's claims, and other descriptive claims about human cognition, are perfectly compatible with Cartesian skepticism (§4.2.1).

4.6 Conclusion

The Cartesian skeptical argument has taken center stage in contemporary discussions of skepticism, and we'll turn now (Part II) to the anti-skeptical possibilities. It will emerge that the Cartesian skeptical argument presupposes an epistemological claim known as "the closure principle" (Chapter 6). We can thus remind ourselves of the various skeptical arguments that we have looked at, and identify their key presuppositions.

Skeptical argument	Controversial presupposition
The problem of the criterion (§1.2.2, §2.1.1)	Internalism (§2.1.1), or something like it
Agrippa's trilemma (§1.2.2) and the Humean skeptical argument (§3.2.1)	Argumentative constraint on knowledge (§3.2.2), or something like it
Descartes' skeptical argument (§4.1.2)	Infallibilism (§4.3), or something like it
The Cartesian skeptical argument (§4.2.1)	The closure principle (Chapter 6)

In any event, we turn now to contemporary anti-skepticism. We'll look first at an anti-skeptical strategy inspired by the philosophy of G. E. Moore.

Readings

The *Meditations* and the *Discourse* are essential for understanding Descartes' anti-skeptical project (§4.1); I've also included three interpretative discussions of that project.

- *Meditations on First Philosophy* (e.g. Descartes 1997).

- *Discourse on the Method* (e.g. in Descartes 1998).

- H. Frankfurt, *Demons, Dreamers, and Madmen* (Frankfurt 1970).

- E. M. Curley, *Descartes Against the Skeptics* (Curley 1978).

- B. Williams, *Descartes: The Project of Pure Inquiry* (Williams 1978).

I recommend the following, on the Cartesian skeptical argument (§4.2.1), and on how to formulate arguments for Cartesian skepticism.

- B. Stroud, *The Significance of Philosophical Scepticism* (Stroud 1984).

- M. Williams, *Unnatural Doubts* (Williams 1996).

- J. Greco, "Skepticism about the External World" (Greco 2008).

- A. Brueckner, "The Structure of the Skeptical Argument" (Brueckner 1994).

- J. Vogel, "Skeptical Arguments" (Vogel 2004).

Above, I set infallibilism aside (§4.3); the following will give you a start on that topic.

- P. Unger, *Ignorance: A Case for Scepticism* (Unger 1975).

- K. Popper, "Science: Conjectures and Refutations" (Popper 1963, chapter 1).

- B. Reed, "Certainty" (Reed 2008).

I also set aside indirect realism (§4.5.6); the following will give you a start on that topic.

- W. Sellars, "Empiricism and the Philosophy of Mind" (Sellars 1956).

- R. Chisholm, *Perceiving* (Chisholm 1957).

- J. L. Austin, *Sense and Sensibilia* (Austin 1962).

- H. Putnam, *Reason, Truth, and History* (Putnam 1981).

- J. McDowell, *Mind and World* (McDowell 1994).

PART TWO

Anti-Skepticism

5

The Moorean Persuasion

Recall the Cartesian skeptical argument (§4.2.1):

1   I know that I have hands only if I can know that I'm not deceived by a demon (about whether I have hands).

2   I can't know that I'm not deceived by a demon (about whether I have hands).

3   Therefore, I don't know that I have hands.

The Cartesian skeptic accepts the conclusion of the argument. The **anti-skeptic** rejects the conclusion. Given the four exhaustive possibilities when it comes to this argument (§4.4), there are three anti-skeptical possibilities:

● The first premise is false.

● The second premise is false.

● The argument is invalid.

We turn now (Part II) to a discussion of the three forms of anti-skepticism that have been most influential in the contemporary debate about Cartesian skepticism. The first (discussed in this chapter) maintains that the second premise of the Cartesian skeptical argument is false. The second (Chapter 6) maintains that the first premise is false. The third (Chapter 7) maintains (more or less) that the argument is invalid.

   The anti-skeptical ideas discussed in this chapter were inspired by the philosophy of **G. E. Moore** (1873–1958). Moore's work had a profound and lasting influence on philosophy in the English-speaking world, and he is responsible, in no small part, for the important role that "common sense" and "ordinary language" have played in contemporary "analytic" philosophy. Indeed, Moore—along with philosophers like Gottlob Frege and Bertrand

Russell—should be understood as initiating the practice known as "analytic philosophy". Moore's work is a paradigm of this practice: his writing is clear, his thinking is rigorous, and he pays meticulous attention to the details of argumentation and language.

5.1 Moore's anti-skeptical argument

Moore rejected Cartesian skepticism, and his anti-skeptical argument is best articulated in his papers "Hume's Theory Examined" (1953) and "Four Forms of Scepticism" (1959). The bulk of these papers is devoted to a careful articulation of skeptical arguments offered by Hume and Russell, respectively, and the details of Moore's interpretations are not relevant to our present concerns. In both papers, Moore asks us to imagine that we are looking at a pencil—"just an ordinary wooden pencil" (1953, p. 65)—and then articulates an argument for the conclusion that we do not know that it is a pencil. Both arguments appeal to the idea that we cannot directly or immediately perceive the pencil, and that what we can directly or immediately perceive are "sense data", distinct from the pencil. The argument in "Hume's Theory" combines this with the premise that we would need to have directly or immediately perceived a correlation between "sense data" (of this kind) and pencils, to have knowledge that this is a pencil. The argument in "Four Forms" combines the premise that we cannot directly or immediately perceive the pencil with the premise that the alternative sources for belief—"analogical or inductive arguments"—do not yield knowledge. Again, the details of these arguments aren't our concern here. What's important is that, in each case, Moore carefully explains the premises of the argument for the conclusion that he does not know, of the pencil, that it is a pencil. Moore's big contribution comes in his criticism of these skeptical arguments:

> If Hume's principles [i.e. the premises of his skeptical argument] are true, then, I have admitted, I do *not* know *now* that this pencil—the material object—exists. If ... I am to prove that I *do* know that this pencil exists, I must prove, somehow, that Hume's principles, one or both of them, are *not* true. In what sort of way, by what sort of argument, can I prove this? It seems to me that, in fact, there really is no stronger and better argument than the following. I *do* know that this pencil exists; but I could not know this, if Hume's principles were true; *therefore*, Hume's principles, one or both of them, are false. (1953, p. 71)

> Is it, in fact, as certain that all these four assumptions [of Russell's skeptical argument] are true, as that I *do* know that this is a pencil ...? I cannot help

answering: It seems to me *more* certain that I *do* know that this is a pencil … than that any single one of these four assumptions is true, let alone all four. (1959, p. 226)

We can anticipate what Moore would likely say about the Cartesian skeptical argument: I know that I have hands, therefore either the first premise or the second premise of the Cartesian skeptical argument is false. We can see what Moore is up to by considering the following three claims:

- I know that I have hands only if I can know that I'm not deceived by a demon (about whether I have hands).

- I can't know that I'm not deceived by a demon (about whether I have hands).

- I know that I have hands.

These three claims are jointly inconsistent; they cannot all be true. At least one of them must be given up. Which one should it be? One way of articulating Moore's point is that the third of these claims—that I know that I have hands—is the least plausible candidate for rejection. The third claim is more certain and more obvious than the first two. Given the inconsistency, one or both of the first two claims should be given up, and not the third.

Moore's argument is profound in its simplicity. The skeptic presents us with an argument for an incredible conclusion. But if the conclusion really is incredible, then we can appeal to its negation as a premise in an argument *against* the skeptic's premises. One of the things that fascinates us about Descartes' skeptical meditations (§4.1.2) is the way that a shocking skeptical conclusion is generated from seemingly innocuous premises. Moore exploits the fact that the conclusion is shocking—too shocking, he argues, to be believed. But if the conclusion of the argument is false, and the argument is valid, then one of the premises must be false as well.

We'll consider some objections to Moore's argument, below (§5.3). Philosophers sometimes have trouble taking Moore's anti-skeptical argument seriously,[1] so before proceeding it is worth considering the motivations for, and implications of, Moore's kind of response to skepticism.

One important point that is made vivid by Moore's argument is the fact that the Cartesian skeptical argument has premises. This sounds trivial and innocuous, but it's actually an important point. There is a temptation to want to say to Moore: "You're just *assuming* that you know that you have hands! You've not given any *reason* to think that your premise is true!" But if the success of an argument relies on the provision of reasons for its premises, then the Cartesian skeptic must also provide such reasons. Just as Moore's argument proceeds from the premise that he knows that he has hands, the Cartesian skeptical argument proceeds from its two premises. The charge that Moore's argument is based on an *assumption* can only be coherently maintained by the skeptic if her argument is *not* based on any assumptions. But it is hard to see how that could turn out to be the case: it seems like every argument is, in some sense, based on assumptions. For even when we defend the premises of our arguments, our defenses consist in the giving of additional arguments, which also have premises. So: just as skeptical arguments call Moore's premise into question, Moore's argument calls the skeptic's premises into question. And the significant upshot of all this is really just the fact that skeptical arguments have premises that can be called into question.

Moore is often understood as a "common sense philosopher". Articulating the notion of a "common sense philosopher" is no easy task. Part of the difficulty stems from our lack of a clear notion of "common sense". There seems to be some sense in which Moore's argument "appeals to common sense"; we at least want to say that his premise (that he has hands) is "commonsensical" and that Cartesian skepticism is not "commonsensical". And it is an important aspect of Moore's way of arguing against skepticism that he appeals to instances of knowledge that he implies he shares with his audience or reader.[2] Moore's argument is not based on the idea that he, and only he, has this item of knowledge that refutes the skeptic's premises. It is rather that he, and everyone else, including the skeptic, has such an item of knowledge. When Moore draws our attention to the pencil that he is holding, we come to know that it is a pencil just as well as he does. In this way, Moore's appeal is to an item of "common" knowledge—i.e. knowledge that is had by all the parties to the conversation.

Moore is sometimes credited with clarifying the role of **Moorean facts** in philosophy; these are, as David Armstrong (1980) puts it, "facts which even philosophers should not deny, whatever philosophical account or analysis they give of such facts" (p. 441), The idea of a privileged class of propositions, immune from philosophical revision, is suggested by Moore in his paper "A Defence of Common Sense" (1925), in which he offers a "list of truisms, every one of which (in my own opinion) I *know*, with certainty, to be true" (pp. 32–3). The list includes:

- There exists at present a living human body, which is *my* body.
- The earth has existed for many years before I was born.
- That mantelpiece is at present nearer to my body than that bookcase.

- In the case of very many of the other human bodies which have lived upon the earth, each has been the body of a different human being, who has, during the lifetime of that body, had many different experiences.

These, we can assume, are paradigm Moorean facts, along with (when thought by Moore):

- I have hands.

But here is an important point: the premise of Moore's anti-skeptical argument is *not* yet on our list of Moorean facts. For that premise was:

- I know that I have hands.

This is why, in his "Defence of Common Sense" (p. 34), Moore supplements his initial list of truisms (about his body, about his environment, about other people) with a "single truism" to the effect that the previous truisms on the list are all things that can be, and often are, known. As **David Lewis** (1941–2001) puts it, "[i]t is a Moorean fact that we know a lot" (1996, p. 549). Moore does think that his premise (that he knows that he has hands) is a Moorean fact, but it is extremely important to note that this thought does not follow from the premise that it is a Moorean fact that Moore has hands. The one proposition, that Moore has hands, is a claim about the existence of some hands; the other proposition, that Moore knows that he has hands, is a claim about Moore's cognitive relationship with the fact that he has hands. And it is one thing to say that the former proposition is a "common sense" truism, immune to philosophical revision, and another to say that the latter proposition is a "common sense" truism, immune to philosophical revision.[3] This is so, even if we agree with Moore that his truisms are known, with certainty, to be true. From the fact that the proposition that p is a truism, let us grant it follows that I know that p. It does not follow from this that the proposition that I know that p is a truism. For one thing, from that conclusion it would follow that I know that I know that p. And that does not obviously follow from the assumption that I know that p.

In this connection, it is important to note that Moore's premise is *not* that he is not deceived by a demon. That proposition is, perhaps, a Moorean fact, just as much as the proposition that Moore has hands. But the proposition that Moore is not deceived by a demon is different from the proposition that Moore knows that he has hands, and so it is one thing to say that the former proposition is a Moorean fact, and another to say that the latter proposition is a Moorean fact.

There is one more important thing to keep in mind about the idea that Moore's anti-skeptical argument involves an "appeal to common sense". It seems to me that if this is right, then Moore's argument is successful only if at least one premise of the Cartesian skeptical argument is *not* "commonsensical". For if the premises of the Cartesian skeptical argument are "commonsensical", along with Moore's premise, then it is unclear why we should favor Moore's argument, as opposed to the Cartesian skeptical argument. If we are inclined to understand Moore's argument as an "appeal to common sense", then we must address the question of whether, and to what extent, the premises of the Cartesian skeptical argument are "commonsensical". For my part, it is unclear that the premises of the Cartesian skeptical argument are any less "commonsensical" than Moore's premise (cf. §4.2.4, Chapter 6).

There is another way of understanding Moore's anti-skeptical argument, on which his appeal is to something more personal than "common sense". Suppose you believe, or are inclined to believe, that p_1, and that p_2, and that p_3, but that you come to realize that p_1, p_2, and p_3 are jointly inconsistent. What should you do? A natural answer is that you should reject whichever of those three propositions seems least obvious to you. You cannot go on believing all three, for you know that at least one of them is false. None of them individually seems false; that's what we meant by saying that you believe or are inclined to believe them all. But you must give one of them up. And what should settle that matter? Again, a natural answer is that you should reject whichever of the three propositions seems true to the least extent, i.e. whichever proposition is least obvious to you. That seems to be precisely what Moore is recommending: when you realize that the premises of the Cartesian skeptical argument and the proposition that you know that you have hands are jointly inconsistent, you must give up believing at least one of these propositions. But surely it should not be the proposition that you know that you have hands, since this surely seems more obvious than either of the premises of the Cartesian skeptical argument.

That last idea is one that you might challenge. Above (§4.2.4), I said that the second premise of the Cartesian skeptical argument seemed obvious to me. And, as we'll see (Chapter 6), the first premise of the Cartesian skeptical argument also has claims on being obvious. In a contest of obviousness, it may not be clear which of the three relevant propositions is least obvious. And the Cartesian skeptic, of course, finds the proposition that Moore knows that he has hands the least obvious of the three. (In this connection, it is important to keep in mind that the proposition in question is that Moore knows that he has hands, not the proposition that he has hands, nor the proposition that he is not deceived by a demon.)

A final comment on the motivations for, and implications of, Moore's anti-skeptical argument. In his articulation of the problem of the criterion, Roderick Chisholm (1982) draws a distinction between two approaches in epistemology, which he calls "methodism" and "particularism" (p. 66).

Methodists maintain that, in epistemology, we must first answer questions about the nature of knowledge—e.g. whether knowledge requires certainty, whether knowledge requires the ability to give a good argument—and then answer questions about the scope of our knowledge—i.e. questions about what propositions we know. The methodist will first formulate a theory of knowledge, and then apply it to draw conclusions about what we know. **Particularists**, by contrast, will first determine what propositions we know, and then formulate a theory of knowledge that explains the scope of our knowledge. Chisholm classifies Moore as a particularist (pp. 68–9). Moore begins by determining the scope of our knowledge, and in particular that he knows that he has hands, and he is prepared to reject claims about the nature of knowledge on the basis of his determinations concerning the scope of our knowledge. So the question of whether Moore's argument is successful may depend significantly on the question of whether epistemological particularism is true.

You might wonder whether the debate between methodists and particularists is relevant to the Cartesian skeptical argument: does the argument make any assumptions about the nature of knowledge, prior to drawing its conclusion about the scope of our knowledge?[4] The second premise is not a claim about the nature of knowledge, but is itself a claim about the scope of our knowledge. However, we'll see (Chapter 6) that the first premise is an instance of a more general principle, which is a claim about the nature of knowledge—although many would argue that it is an extremely modest claim.

5.2 Mooreanism in contemporary epistemology

In this section we'll look at how Moore's anti-skeptical strategy has been developed and elaborated by contemporary epistemologists.

5.2.1 Neo-Mooreanism

Recall Moore's objection to the Cartesian skeptical argument (§5.1): I know that I have hands, therefore either the first premise or the second premise of the Cartesian skeptical argument is false. The contemporary epistemologists that are inspired by Moore go one step further, by identifying the premise of the Cartesian skeptical argument that they think is false: the second premise. Here, then, is their **neo-Moorean argument:**

1   I know that I have hands only if I can know that I'm not deceived by a demon (about whether I have hands).

2 I know that I have hands.

3 Therefore, I can know that I'm not deceived by a demon.

Regardless of the plausibility of neo-Mooreanism, we now have an answer to the problem of Cartesian skepticism, in the sense of "answer" articulated above (§4.4). **Neo-Mooreans** base their rejection of the second premise of the Cartesian skeptical argument on the neo-Moorean argument.[5]

When it comes to Cartesian skepticism, the controversial premise of the neo-Moorean argument is the second premise: that I know that I have hands. To motivate her position, the neo-Moorean should have something to say in defense of this premise. As we'll see (§§5.2.2–5.2.4), this will require the neo-Moorean to say something about the nature of knowledge.

5.2.2 A non-argumentative conception of knowledge

How do I know that I have hands? What conception of knowledge would allow us to see how such knowledge is possible? Neo-Moorean typically reject the argumentative constraint on knowledge (§3.2.2). My knowledge that I have hands does not depend on my ability to give a good argument that I have hands. They thus follow Moore (1939) in this regard:

> How am I to prove now that 'Here is one hand, and here's another'? I do not think that I can do it. In order to do it, I should need to prove for one thing, as Descartes pointed out, that I am not now dreaming. But how can I prove that I am not? I have, no doubt, conclusive reasons for asserting that I am not now dreaming; I have conclusive evidence that I am awake: but that is a very different thing from being able to prove it. (p. 169)

To see what Moore is getting at, think about how you can recognize your friends by seeing their faces. Almost everyone has this ability, although certain types of brain damage can cause you to lose it. Imagine now that you recognize your friend Anne, you see that it is her by seeing her face, which you recognize. You now *know* that it is Anne; but you could not *prove*, or give any *good argument*, that it is her. The reason is that you are unable to articulate or describe the distinctive features of Anne's appearance, that you recognize, and which constitute your evidence that it is Anne whom you see.

'I can know things', Moore concludes, "that I cannot prove" (p. 170). So although Moore would argue that you can prove that you're not deceived by a demon, he would not argue that you can prove that you have hands. The Moorean thus articulates a **non-argumentative conception of knowledge**:

she offers an account of the nature of knowledge on which the argumentative constraint on knowledge is false.

5.2.3 Neo-Mooreanism I: reliabilism

Contemporary epistemologists understand (propositional) knowledge (cf. Chapter 8) as a species of true belief. But it is usually assumed that not all true beliefs amount to knowledge. So what distinguishes knowledge from true belief? Consider:

Argumentative conception of knowledge: S knows that p iff (i) p, (ii) S believes that p, and (iii) S can give a good argument that p.

The neo-Moorean rejects this account of the nature of knowledge (§5.2.2). What account can she offer in its place? Here is one prominent proposal:

Reliabilism: S knows that p iff (i) p, (ii) S believes that p, and (iii) S's belief that p was formed in a reliable way.

Knowledge, in other words, is reliably-formed true belief. This account of the nature of knowledge has received considerable discussion over the last 30 years, and defenders of reliabilism have offered numerous clarifications, amendments, and qualifications to their proposal.[6] These details need not concern us here.[7] We need only clarify two words in our definition: "reliable" and "way".

Let's begin with the latter. Although one can be more specific if one likes, we can remain relatively neutral on what a "way" of forming beliefs is: a **way**, for our purposes, is a method, a strategy, a process, or the use of a cognitive or intellectual faculty, or of a source of information or belief. Intuitively, we can categorize our beliefs in terms of the ways in which they were formed: my belief that the sun is shining right now is based on sense perception, my belief that the battle of Hastings was in 1066 is based on testimony, and some of my beliefs are based on biases and wishful thinking. Reliabilism maintains that whether a belief amounts to knowledge will depend crucially on the way in which that belief was formed.

What, then, is reliability? In one sense, "reliable" means the same as "to be relied upon". A reliable way of forming beliefs, then, would just be a way of forming beliefs that one ought to use. This is *not* the sense of "reliable" being employed in our definition of reliabilism. In our sense, a way of forming beliefs is **reliable** just in case beliefs formed in that way tend to be true. The reliability of a process that yields beliefs, or of a method of forming beliefs, or of a source of beliefs, is down entirely to the extent to which the resulting beliefs tend to be true.

So: reliabilism says that knowledge is reliably-formed true belief. What is essential to understand about reliabilism is how completely different it is from the following view:

Completely different view: S knows that p iff (i) p, (ii) S believes that p, and (iii) S knows that her belief that p was formed in a reliable way.

The difference comes out when we consider Fido, who believes that there is food in his dish, on the basis of sense perception (i.e. he sees the food in his dish), but does not know that his belief about the food was formed in a reliable way (because, being a dog, he does not think about his beliefs). Fido's true belief was formed in a reliable way, but he does not know that his belief was formed in a reliable way. Reliabilism implies that Fido knows that there is food in his dish; the completely different view implies that he does not know.

What has all of this to do with skepticism and neo-Mooreanism? The answer is that, if reliabilism is true, then it is possible for me to know that I have hands, prior to knowing that I am not deceived by a demon (about whether I have hands). Regardless of whether I know that I am not deceived by a demon, I meet the three conditions that, according to reliabilism, are jointly sufficient for knowing that I have hands: (i) I have hands, (ii) I believe that I have hands, and (iii) my belief that I have hands was formed in a reliable way. What reliable way? Although it is not easy to say exactly how I have come to believe that I have hands, it seems obvious that my belief is based on sense perception, in one way or another. I see my hands right here in front of me, and I can (in a rather difficult to articulate way) feel that they are there as well. (As I consider this, I move my fingers around—this feels like some kind of evidence that they are *my* hands.) In any event, my belief is based on sense perception. But sense perception is a reliable process or faculty; the way in which I formed my belief that I have hands is, indeed, a reliable way. And so reliabilism implies that I know that I have hands.

You might object: "But how do you *know* that sense perception is reliable?" This is where the difference between reliabilism and the completely different view comes into play. The completely different view implies that it is a necessary condition on knowing (that I have hands) that I *know* that my belief (that I have hands) was formed in a reliable way. If the completely different view were true, your question would be most apt, since I haven't suggested that I know that sense perception is reliable. But your question is a *non sequitur*, if reliabilism is true. If reliabilism is true, although it is a necessary condition on knowing (that I have hands) that my belief (that I have hands) was formed in a reliable way, it is *not* required that I *know* that my belief (that I have hands) was formed in a reliable way. If reliabilism is true, moreover, reliably-formed true belief is sufficient for knowledge, *regardless of whether you know that said belief is reliably-formed.*[8]

We can see again how the question of internalism (§2.1.1) is of central importance in connection with philosophical skepticism. Suppose that the reliabilist is right about the following claim:

S knows (that p) only if S's belief (that p) was formed in a reliable way.

And suppose that the internalist is right, i.e. that:

If S knows (that p) only if q, then S knows (that p) only if S knows that q.

These two premises entail that:

S knows (that p) only if S knows that S's belief (that p) was formed in a reliable way.

Which is maintained by the completely different view, and which is incompatible with reliabilism. Therefore, reliabilism is incompatible with internalism.

You might object: "The reliability of sense perception is exactly what the Cartesian skeptical argument calls into question. It is therefore illegitimate to appeal to the reliability of sense perception in giving a criticism of the Cartesian skeptical argument." However, while there is a sense in which it is true that the Cartesian skeptical argument "calls into question" the reliability of sense perception, there is an important sense in which this is not true. The premises and conclusion of the Cartesian skeptical argument are claims about what I *know,* and if the argument is sound, then I surely do not *know* that sense perception is reliable. But the argument is silent on the question of whether sense perception is, in fact, reliable. The argument is that I do not *know* whether I am deceived by a demon, not that I *am* deceived by a demon. The defender of the Cartesian argument can *grant* that I am not deceived by a demon (and that I have hands); her point is that I do not *know* that I am not deceived (and that therefore I do not know that I have hands). And the defender of the Cartesian argument should grant this, since there is absolutely no reason to think otherwise than that I am not deceived by a demon (and that I have hands); as Descartes would put it, no sane person has ever doubted these things.

Now you might think, at this point, that if the Cartesian skeptic is prepared to *grant* that sense perception is reliable, then we should dismiss Cartesian skepticism, and investigate a more "radical" kind of skeptic, who will not grant that sense perception is reliable (cf. §4.2.3). I disagree: Cartesian skepticism is interesting precisely because it is not so "radical" as to refuse to grant that sense perception is reliable. It seems to me that it is much easier to dismiss someone who refuses to grant that I have hands (where my hands are in plain view, and where there is no suspicion of their being artificial faux-hands, etc.), especially if she gives me no reason to doubt that I have hands, than it is to dismiss someone who sensibly grants that I have hands, but who offers an argument that I do not know that I have hands. Cartesian skepticism may be less "radical" than other species of skepticism, but it is much more difficult to dismiss.

The reliabilist's anti-skeptical strategy can be difficult to understand. We'll conclude this section by articulating one way of developing this strategy, with the goal of better understanding the nature of the reliabilist's answer to the problem of Cartesian skepticism. Ernest Sosa (1999) defends neo-Mooreanism by appeal to the idea that my belief that I have hands is "safe", where:

> S's belief (that p) is **safe** iff S would believe that p only if it were so that p. (p. 142)

What does it mean to say that someone would believe that p only if it were so that p? Sosa intends his definition of safety to imply that someone's belief (that p) is safe just in case she could not easily go wrong (i.e. she could not easily believe something false) in believing that p. And he proposes that S knows (that p) only if S's belief (that p) is safe.

We can combine this idea with reliabilism, to yield an account of the nature of knowledge:

> **Safety theory of knowledge:** S knows (that p) iff (i) p, (ii) S believes that p, and (iii) S's belief (that p) is safe.

Regardless of whether I know that I am not deceived by a demon, I meet the three conditions that, according to the safety theory of knowledge, are jointly sufficient for knowing that I have hands: (i) I have hands, (ii) I believe that I have hands, and (iii) my belief that I have hands is safe. Why think that my belief is safe? Because I could not easily go wrong in believing that I have hands. Compare an irrational gambler, who believes for no good reason that the next roll of the dice will yield an "8". Even if the next roll *will* yield an "8", she does not *know* that the next roll will yield an "8", because her belief is not safe: she could easily go wrong in believing that the next roll will yield an "8". So argues the defender of the safety theory of knowledge. My belief that I have hands is unlike the belief of the gambler. I could not easily go wrong in believing that I have hands.[9] And so the safety theory of knowledge implies that I know that I have hands.

To sum up: the defender of reliabilism has the resources to defend the controversial second premise of the neo-Moorean argument (§5.2.1).

5.2.4 Neo-Mooreanism II: perceptual dogmatism

Reliabilism is not the only view about the nature of knowledge to which we might appeal in defense of neo-Mooreanism. Consider what James Pryor (2000) calls **dogmatism about perceptual justification**:

> The dogmatist about perceptual justification says that when it perceptually seems to you as if p is the case, you have a kind of justification for believing p that does not presuppose or rest on your justification for anything else, which could be cited in an argument … for p. To have this justification for believing p, you need only have an experience that represents p as being the case. No further awareness or reflection or background beliefs are required. (p. 519)

So, for example, when I look at my hands, it perceptually seems to me as if I have hands. According to dogmatism, I now have justification for believing that I have hands, simply in virtue of the fact that it perceptually seems to me that I have hands.

Pryor's proposal depends, for its plausibility, on an assumption about the nature of perceptual experience, namely, that perceptual experience has representational content. When I look at my hands, the perceptual experience that I have represents the proposition that I have hands as true. This assumption is required for the plausibility of Pryor's claim that my perceptual experience alone provides justification for believing that I have hands. To see why, consider the fact that, for the dogmatist, my perceptual experience *alone* constitutes *evidence* that I have hands. Some pieces of evidence owe their status as evidence to various assumptions or, as Pryor puts it, background beliefs. Consider this pistol that detectives found in my apartment. The pistol constitutes evidence that I committed the murder, but only relative to a body of background beliefs: that this pistol is the murder weapon, for example. By contrast, for the dogmatist, my perceptual experience of my hands *alone* constitutes evidence that I have hands.

We must make an assumption to see the connection between this idea and neo-Mooreanism. What is the connection between the dogmatist's idea, that I have justification for believing that I have hands, and the second premise of the neo-Moorean argument, on which I know that I have hands? We might say that knowledge is true belief for which one possesses justification; then dogmatism implies that I know that I have hands, since I have hands, and I believe that I have hands, and I have justification for believing that I have hands. But this proposal is not quite right, given that such justification can be *defeated* in various ways, such that a true belief for which one possesses justification does not, intuitively, amount to knowledge. Suppose it perceptually seems to me that there are pink rats dancing on my coffee table, but that I also recall having just taken a large dose of some drug whose side-effects include hallucinations of pink rats. Even if I ignore this fact and irrationally come to believe that there are pink rats dancing on my coffee table, and even if there happen, improbably, to be pink rats dancing on my coffee table, intuitively I do not know that there are pink rats dancing on my coffee table, despite (as per dogmatism) my possession of justification for believing that there are. The reason is that my justification is defeated by my awareness of having taken the drug. But our proposal can be amended to avoid (at least) this problem; let's assume that knowledge is true belief for which one possesses undefeated justification. Given this assumption, dogmatism implies that I know that I have hands. Thus the defender of perceptual dogmatism has the resources to defend the controversial second premise of the neo-Moorean argument (§5.2.1).

5.3 Two objections to Mooreanism

We now turn to two objections to neo-Mooreanism (§5.2.1). The first (§5.3.1) articulates the most popular kind of resistance to Moore's anti-skeptical argument: that the argument is viciously circular or question-begging. I'll argue that this objection does not succeed. The second objection (§5.3.2) is that it remains obscure how we can know that we're not deceived by a demon; I think this objection succeeds.

5.3.1 The circularity objection

Moore (1953) was aware that many people would not be impressed by his anti-skeptical argument:

> I think that the fact that, if Hume's principles were true, I could not know of the existence of this pencil, is a *reductio ad absurdum* of those principles. But, of course, this is an argument that will not seem convincing to those who believe that the principles are true, nor yet to those who believe that I really do not know that this pencil exists. It seems like begging the question. (p. 72)

Moore goes on to argue that his argument "really is a good and conclusive argument" (*ibid.*). Let's try to articulate the sense in which Moore's argument involves "begging the question", and then examine whether this is a threat to neo-Mooreanism.

There is a sense of "begging the question" on which an argument begs the question iff its conclusion is among its premises. Such arguments have the virtue of validity, but seem to fall short as arguments; thus the idea that they "beg the question". This sense of "begging the question" reveals an apparent connection between the notion of "begging the question" and the notion of a "circular" argument: if you argue "p, therefore p", your argument has gone in a (very short) circle. In any event, the neo-Moorean argument does not "beg the question" in this sense (cf. Moore 1939, p. 166): its conclusion is not among its premises.

You might object that, although the conclusion of the neo-Moorean argument is not explicitly among its premises, there remains some sense in which the conclusion of the neo-Moorean argument is presupposed by its premises. For example, you might argue that you cannot know that you have hands unless you already know that you're not deceived by a demon (about whether you have hands), and that *that* provides a sense in which the conclusion of the neo-Moorean argument is presupposed by its premises. But if that is sufficient for "begging the question", then it seems that an argument "begs the question" if its premises entail its conclusion. But in that case "begging the question" does not seem like a bad thing, since it is equivalent to validity, which is a virtue for an argument, not a vice.

The burden is on the objector to articulate the sense in which the premises of the neo-Moorean argument "presuppose" its conclusion, in some problematic way, i.e. in some way that indicates that the neo-Moorean argument is a bad argument. One possibility is suggested by Moore in the quotation above: "begging the question" has something to do with an argument's persuasive power. Moore's argument would not seem convincing to Moore's opponents—perhaps that is all there is to the fact that it "begs the question". Crispin Wright (2000) develops this thought:

A *cogent* argument is one whereby someone could be moved to rational conviction of the truth of its conclusion. So a chain of valid inferences cannot be cogent if only someone who already took themselves to be rationally persuaded of the conclusion could rationally receive whatever grounds purportedly warranted its premises as doing just that. (p. 16)

To determine whether an argument is cogent, therefore, we must imagine someone who does not take herself to be rationally persuaded of the conclusion of the argument—e.g. someone who doubts the conclusion of the argument—and ask whether such a person could be rationally persuaded, by the argument, to believe its conclusion. Given Wright's notion of cogency, we could then argue: (1) an argument that is not cogent is thereby flawed,

(2) the neo-Moorean argument is not cogent, therefore (3) the neo-Moorean argument is flawed.

However, I do not think it is at all clear whether the neo-Moorean argument is, or is not, cogent, in Wright's sense. Could someone who doubts that she can know that she's not deceived by a demon be rationally persuaded, by the neo-Moorean argument, to believe that she can know that she's not deceived by a demon? It is unclear how we should answer this question. Things may be simpler when it comes to a different kind of Moorean argument. Consider the following, inspired by an argument of Moore's in his paper "Proof of an External World" (1939), which we'll call **Moore's proof**:

1   I have hands.

2   If I have hands, then I'm not deceived by a demon (about whether I have hands).

3   Therefore, I'm not deceived by a demon (about whether I have hands).

There is something quite plausible about the idea that someone who doubted the conclusion of Moore's proof could not be rationally persuaded, by the argument, to believe its conclusion. If this were not the case, Descartes' hypothetical doubt would have been easily overcome. What Descartes' thought experiment shows us is that it is extremely difficult, if not impossible, to come up with any argument that can overcome doubt about the proposition that you are not deceived by a demon. So Moore's proof indeed seems not to be cogent. But it's unclear how this bears on the status of the neo-Moorean argument.

So it is unclear whether the neo-Moorean argument is not cogent. It is also unclear whether the fact that an argument is not cogent always means that the argument is flawed. Thomas Reid makes the following observation:

> If a sceptic should build his scepticism on [the] foundation ... that all our reasoning and judging powers are fallacious in their nature, or should resolve to withhold assent until it be proved that they are not, it would be impossible by argument to beat him out of this stronghold; and he must even be left to enjoy his scepticism. (*Essays on the Intellectual Powers of Man*, 6.5)

At first glance, you might think that this fact about the skeptic's "stronghold" is a mark in favor of skepticism. But is it really? Compare Reid's skeptic to the conspiracy theorist, who likewise cannot be beaten out of her "stronghold". She maintains that Barack Obama was born in Indonesia and that there has been a massive cover-up to keep this secret. She cannot be convinced otherwise, for any piece of evidence that Obama was not born in Indonesia can be dismissed as a fabrication of the cover-up. But this apparent strength of her position is actually a kind of weakness: her absurd hypothesis has made her unable to appreciate some eminently reasonable arguments. Our best argument against the conspiracy theory ("Here is Obama's birth certificate; here are his childhood friends," etc.) is not a cogent argument. But this hardly seems to show that our argument is flawed. A cogent argument against the conspiracy theorist's hypothesis cannot be given. But this hardly supports the conspiracy theorist's position. Likewise, even if a cogent argument against Cartesian skepticism cannot be given, this does not suggest that Cartesian skepticism is true.[10]

In spite of this point, the intuition may remain that the neo-Moorean argument somehow "begs the question" against the skeptic, in a way that undermines the neo-Moorean's position. But, again, the burden is on us to articulate the relevant sense of "begging the question".[11]

5.3.2 The Nozickian objection

There is another way of challenging the neo-Moorean argument (§5.2.1). We reasonably doubt an argument's soundness when we cannot under-stand how the conclusion could be true. The conclusion of the neo-Moorean argument is that I can know that I'm not deceived by a demon (about whether I have hands). You might wonder: how could that be? And to the extent that this question remains unanswered, you might reasonably refrain from accepting the soundness of the neo-Moorean argument. This objection will have traction with those, like Robert Nozick, who think that there is something obvious about the second premise of the Cartesian skeptical argument (§4.2.4); that's why we can call it the "Nozickian objection". And it will have no traction with those who think that the second premise of the Cartesian skeptical argument is obviously false. However, in any event, the neo-Moorean argument prompts an obvious question: *how* can I know that I'm not deceived by a demon?

Perhaps you can know that you're not deceived by a demon on the basis of Moore's proof (§5.3.1). I assumed above that the argument isn't cogent, but we saw that lack of cogency isn't necessarily a flaw in an argument. At least it is not clear that one cannot know that p, on the basis of a non-cogent argument that p. However, considerations of cogency aside, it still does not seem plausible that you could know that you are not deceived by a demon, on the basis of Moore's proof. I seem to have no way of knowing whether I am deceived by a demon. But why doesn't Moore's proof provide a way of knowing? The same reasons we gave in defense of the second premise of the Cartesian skeptical argument (§4.2.3) seem like reasons to think that Moore's proof does not provide a way of knowing that I am not deceived by a demon.

The neo-Moorean does not need to say that we know that we're not deceived on the basis of Moore's proof. Her argument is the neo-Moorean argument, and that argument involves no commitment to Moore's proof as providing a way of knowing. But the neo-Moorean does maintain that I can know that I'm not deceived by a demon. The question remains: how can I know that? One of the attractive things about reliabilism (§5.2.3) is the idea that, when you know something, there is always some way that you know it. But this idea makes trouble for the idea that I can know that I'm not deceived by a demon. Consider the idea that my belief that the sun is shining right now is based on sense perception. I can *see* that the sun is shining. But I cannot *see* that I'm not deceived by a demon. But if I cannot see this, how indeed can I know whether I'm deceived by a demon? By deduction from premises already known? That was Moore's proof. What way—what method or faculty or process—do I have for knowing whether I am deceived by a demon? For a great many propositions that p, it seems quite right that I have a method or faculty or process that enables me to know whether p. But when it comes to the proposition that I am not deceived by a demon, it seems quite wrong that I have any such method or faculty or process at my disposal. Although I think that I am not deceived—indeed, I would say that I am absolutely sure that I am not deceived—it does not seem that I have any way of *knowing* that I am not deceived, and in virtue of this it does not seem that I know that I am not deceived.

5.4 Conclusion

The task for the neo-Moorean (§5.2) is to explain how it is possible to know that you are not deceived by a demon. I have not argued that this cannot be done, but it is unclear how this could be done. There is, of course, much more to be said about this, and about neo-Mooreanism in general. We have here considered the neo-Moorean's rejection of the second premise of the Cartesian skeptical argument (§4.2.1). We turn next to another anti-skeptical possibility: that the first premise of that argument is false.

Readings

A study of Moore's epistemology should begin with the three papers suggested below; I also recommend Barry Stroud's excellent and careful discussion of Moore's texts.

- "Hume's Theory Examined" (Moore 1953).

- "Four Forms of Scepticism" (Moore 1959).

- "Proof of an External World" (Moore 1939).

- B. Stroud, "G. E. Moore and Scepticism: 'Internal' and 'External'" (Stroud 1984, Chapter 3).

On methodism and particularism in epistemology (§5.1), consult the following texts.

- R. Chisholm, "The Problem of the Criterion" (Chisholm 1982, Chapter 5).

- R. Fumerton, "The Problem of the Criterion" (Fumerton 2008).

The following pieces comprise defenses and sympathetic discussions of Moorean anti-skepticism and related views.

- R. Chisholm, "The Skeptic's Challenge" (Chisholm 1989, Chapter 1).

- J. Greco, "How to Reid Moore" (Greco 2003).

- C. Hill, "Process Reliabilism and Cartesian Skepticism" (Hill 1996).

- E. Sosa, "How to Defeat Opposition to Moore" (Sosa 1999).

- J. Pryor, "The Skeptic and the Dogmatist" (Pryor 2000).

- T. Kelly, "Moorean Facts and Belief Revision, or Can the Skeptic Win?" (Kelly 2005).

Consult the following on the idea (§5.3.1) that Moorean anti-skepticism involves vicious circularity.

- E. Sosa, "Philosophical Skepticism and Epistemic Circularity" (Sosa 1994).

- B. Stroud, "Scepticism, 'Externalism', and the Goal of Epistemology" (Stroud 1994).

- R. Fumerton, "Externalism and Skepticism" (Fumerton 1995, Chapter 6)

- J. Vogel, "Reliabilism Leveled" (Vogel 2000).

- J. Van Cleve, "Is Knowledge Easy—or Impossible? Externalism as the Only Alternative to Skepticism" (Van Cleve 2003).

- J. Pryor, "What's Wrong With Moore's Argument?" (Pryor 2004).

- C. Wright, "Cogency and Question-Begging" (Wright 2000).

- C. Wright, "Anti-Sceptics Simple and Subtle: G. E. Moore and John McDowell" (Wright 2002).

- J. Brown, "Doubt, Circularity, and the Moorean Response to the Skeptic" (Brown 2005).

6

Nonclosure

Recall the first premise of the Cartesian skeptical argument (§4.2.1):

> I know that I have hands only if I can know that I'm not deceived by a demon (about whether I have hands).

In this chapter we'll consider the prospects for denying this premise. The premise is implied by the "closure principle", which some epistemologists have criticized. If the "closure principle" is false, and if it is false for the reasons that these epistemologists have given, then we should reject the first premise of the Cartesian skeptical argument.

6.1 Articulating the closure principle

Although it takes some work to get the precise formulation of the "closure principle" right, the basic idea behind it is easily grasped. Consider what Barry Stroud (1984) says in the following passage:

> Suppose that on looking out the window I announce casually that there is a goldfinch in the garden. If I am asked how I know it is a goldfinch and I reply that it is yellow, we all recognize that in the normal case that is not enough for knowledge. "For all you've said so far", it might be replied, "the thing could be a canary, so how do you know it's a goldfinch?" A certain possibility compatible with everything I have said so far has been raised, and if what I have said so far is all I have got to go on and I don't know that the thing in the garden is not a canary, then I do not know that there is a goldfinch in the garden. I must be able to rule out the possibility that it is a canary if I am to know that it is a goldfinch. Anyone who speaks about knowledge and understands what others say about it will recognize this fact or condition in particular cases. (pp. 24–5)

Let's focus on the idea that, if I don't know that it's not a canary, then I don't know that it's a goldfinch. That is equivalent to the idea that, if I know that it's a goldfinch, then I know that it's not a canary. Stroud is clearly onto something here. But what is the general "fact or condition" that we recognize in this particular case? Or, to put that another way, what explains the fact that, if I know that it's a goldfinch, then I know that it's not a canary?

As Stroud suggests, it has something to do with the fact that the proposition that it's a canary is incompatible with the proposition that it's a goldfinch. To put that another way, the proposition that it's a goldfinch entails the proposition that it's not a canary. (The proposition that p **entails** the proposition that q iff, necessarily, if p then q.) So what explains the fact that, if I know that it's a goldfinch, then I know that it's not a canary? It seems to have something to do with the fact that the proposition that it's a goldfinch entails the proposition that it's not a canary.

But for that fact to answer our question, we need to assume something like the following principle:

If S knows that p, and the proposition that p entails the proposition that q, then S knows that q.

Given that the proposition that it's a goldfinch entails the proposition that it's not a canary, this principle implies that, if I know that it's a goldfinch, then I know that it's not a canary.

For various reasons that needn't concern us here, the principle just formulated is not plausible.[1] We can avoid some of these problems by amending the principle to:

Closure principle: If S knows that p, and the proposition that p entails the proposition that q, then S can know that q.[2]

This formulation isn't perfect. You might wonder what it means to say that someone "can" know that q. In some cases, you know that p, and the proposition that p entails the proposition that q, and you already know that q. (In this sense, you "can" know that q—since you already know that q.) If you are an ornithologist, for example, and you know that there is a goldfinch in the garden by recognizing its distinctive beak, then you already know that the bird in the garden is not a canary. However, in other cases, you know that p, and the proposition that p entails the proposition that q, but you do not already know that q. In these cases, the closure principle implies that you are in a position to know that q. In what sense are you "in a position" to know? The idea is that, if you know that p, where the proposition that p entails the proposition that q, then you can come to know that q by (i) recognizing that the proposition that p entails the proposition that q, and (ii) deducing the proposition that q from the proposition that p.[3] Think here of someone who knows that such-and-such axioms (of some mathematical system) are true, but does not yet know some theorem (of that system), which the axioms entail. By working out a proof of the theorem, she is able to come to know that the theorem is true. But we should note the imperfection of this formulation. Consider the proposition that there is a jar of pickles in my kitchen cupboard. I don't know whether there are pickles in my cupboard: I don't remember one way or the other, and my partner often puts pickles there without my knowing about it, etc. Now: *can* I know that there are pickles in my cupboard? Supposing that there are pickles in my cupboard, in one sense I obviously can know this: I am capable of going home and looking in the cupboard and seeing the pickles. But this is not the sense of "can" relevant to our closure principle. In the relevant sense, I *cannot* know that there are pickles in my cupboard. I am not presently in a position to know that. My position could change—I could go home and look in the cupboard—but in my present position, this is something that I cannot know.

Above, I said that the first premise of the Cartesian skeptical argument (§4.2.1) is implied by the closure principle. The latter implies the former only if we make the following assumption:

The proposition that I have hands entails the proposition that I am not deceived by a demon (about whether I have hands).

But this assumption is certainty true. To be deceived about whether p, it must be the case both (i) that you believe that p, and (ii) that the proposition that p is false. However, necessarily, if I have hands, then the proposition that I have hands is not false, but true, and so I cannot be deceived about whether I have hands. Therefore, necessarily, if I have hands, then I am not deceived by a demon (about whether I have hands). And that is just to say that the proposition that I have hands entails the proposition that I am not deceived by a demon (about whether I have hands). And given this assumption, the closure principle implies the first premise of the Cartesian skeptical argument.

6.2 Against the closure principle

In this section we'll look at the two most influential criticisms of the closure principle, offered by Fred Dretske (§6.2.1) and Robert Nozick (§6.2.2).

6.2.1 Dretske against closure

In his paper "Epistemic Operators" (1971), Dretske offers the following as a counterexample to the closure principle:

> You take your son to the zoo, see several zebras, and, when questioned by your son, tell him they are zebras. Do you know they are zebras? Well, most of us would have little hesitation in saying that we did know this. We know what zebras look like, and, besides, this is the city zoo and the animals are in a pen clearly marked 'Zebras'. Yet, something's being a zebra implies that it is not a mule and, in particular, not a mule cleverly disguised by the zoo authorities to look like a zebra. Do you know that these animals are not mules cleverly disguised by the zoo authorities to look like zebras? (pp. 1015–16)

Dretske argues that you do not know that the animals in the pen are not disguised mules, since you do not have any good reason to believe that they are not disguised mules. If he's right, then (in the relevant sense) you cannot know that the animals in the pen are not disguised mules. (As above, you might check; but you cannot know, given your present position.) But if you do know that they are zebras, then we have a counterexample to the closure principle, since the proposition that the animals in the pen are zebras entails the proposition that the animals in the pen are not disguised mules.

It is easy to construct cases that, at least at first glance, have the same basic structure as Dretske's case:

- You know that you will not take a trip to Dubai this year. But you do not, and cannot, know that you will not win a free trip to Dubai in a raffle and subsequently take a trip to Dubai. And the proposition that you will not take a trip to Dubai entails the proposition that you will not win a free trip to Dubai in a raffle and subsequently take a trip to Dubai.

- You know that your car is parked on Christopher Street. But you do not, and cannot, know that your car has not been stolen and moved from Christopher Street. And the proposition that your car is parked on Christopher Street entails the proposition that your car has not been stolen and moved from Christopher Street.

On its own, these would-be counterexamples might not count for much, but their appeal can be strengthened by looking at Dretske's explanation of why the closure principle fails in these, and other, cases. I mentioned above that Dretske argues that you do not have any good reason to believe that the animals in the pen are not disguised mules. On the assumption that knowledge requires the possession of good reasons, he concludes that you do not know that the animals in the pen are not disguised mules. But if you know that the animals in the pen are zebras, then (according to Dretske's assumption) you must have some good reason to believe that the animals in the pen are zebras. If all this is right, we have discovered something interesting about good reasons: someone can have good reasons to believe that p, where the proposition that p entails the proposition that q, but lack good reasons to believe that q.

How can this happen? One way of seeing how it could happen is by thinking about evidence. What is your evidence that the animals in the pen are zebras, which evidence provides your reason for believing that they are zebras? It is something like: that they are striped equids, in a pen labeled "Zebras". This, indeed, is evidence that the animals are zebras. But it is no evidence at all that they are not disguised mules. The same, *mutatis mutandis*, in the other cases: your evidence that you won't visit Dubai is the fact that you can't afford the trip, but this is no evidence at all that you won't win the raffle; your evidence that your car is parked on Christopher Street is the fact that you remember parking it there, but this is no evidence at all that it hasn't been stolen. Knowledge, at least in cases like these, seems to require the possession of evidence, but you can have evidence that p, where the proposition that p entails the proposition that q, and lack evidence that q.

The "closure principle" gets its name from the idea that knowledge is "closed" under entailment, where a propositional attitude O(x) is **closed under entailment** iff, necessarily, if O(p) and the proposition that p entails the proposition that q, then O(q). Knowledge, Dretske argues, is not closed under entailment. It is worth considering the fact that not all propositional attitudes are closed under entailment (cf. Dretske 1970). Belief isn't closed under entailment: it is possible to believe that p, where the proposition that p entails the proposition that q, and fail to believe that q, as in the case of believing that the axioms are true without believing that some theorem is true (§6.1). Neither is regret: it is possible to regret that p, where the proposition that p entails the proposition that q, and fail to regret that q. For example, I regret that I was rude to my friend, and the proposition that I was rude to my friend entails the proposition that I have a friend, but I do not regret that I have a friend. So we are familiar with propositional attitudes that are not closed under entailment. On the present proposal, knowledge is simply one of these.

If Dretske's argument against the closure principle is sound, then we should reject the first premise of the Cartesian skeptical argument (§4.2.1). If my evidence that there are zebras in the pen is no evidence that they are not disguised mules, then we should surely say that my evidence that I have hands is no evidence that I am not deceived by a demon (about whether I have hands). If the zebra case is a counterexample to the closure principle, then so is the following:

- I know that I have hands, but cannot know that I am not deceived by a demon (about whether I have hands). And the proposition that I have hands entails the proposition that I am not deceived by a demon (about whether I have hands).

6.2.2 Nozick against closure

In his *Philosophical Explanations* (1981), **Robert Nozick** (1938–2002) offers an alternative argument against the closure principle. He proposes an account of the nature of knowledge that, if it is true, implies that the closure principle is false. Here is his account (pp. 172–8):

S knows that p iff (i) p, (ii) S believes that p, (iii) if it were false that p, S would not believe that p, and (iv) if it were true that p, S would believe that p.

Note well that, on Nozick's account, these four conditions are each necessary for knowledge, and that the satisfaction of all four is sufficient for knowledge. As Nozick puts it, this account says that knowledge is true belief that "tracks the truth". What is most important for our purposes here is condition (iii) in Nozick's account. Although Nozick uses the word "sensitivity" differently, this condition has come to be known as the "sensitivity" condition. Here is a definition:

S's belief (that p) is **sensitive** iff, if it were false that p, S would not believe that p.

Nozick's account therefore commits him to the following:

Sensitivity principle: S knows (that p) only if S's belief (that p) is sensitive.[4]

Nozick's account of knowledge, and the sensitivity principle, are controversial, and the formulation above requires clarification and amendment.[5] But it will suffice for our purpose of understanding Nozick's anti-skeptical strategy. Let's look at why Nozick's account implies that the closure principle is false, and at Nozick's reasons for adopting his account.

First, Nozick's account implies that I know that I have hands, since all four conditions for knowledge are met: (i) I have hands, (ii) I believe that I have hands, (iii) if it were false that I have hands, I would not believe that I have hands, and (iv) if it were true that I have hands, I would believe that I have hands. Are (iii) and (iv) really true? Take (iv) first. The idea here is that I am disposed to believe that I have hands, when indeed I do. My having hands is not something that I would fail to notice. Now consider (iii). The idea here is that I would notice if I didn't have hands. If I didn't have hands—if they had been amputated, for example—I would know about it, and not believe that I had hands. Therefore, since all four conditions are met, Nozick's account implies that I know that I have hands.

You might object: "You said you would notice if you didn't have hands. But this is false, since if you were deceived by a demon about whether you have hands, you would not notice." However, this objection is sound only if, if I didn't have hands, it would be because I was deceived by a demon. But is that true? To employ a spatial metaphor, the possible scenario in which I am deceived by a demon is a "remote" possibility, by comparison with other scenarios in which I do not have hands, e.g. the scenario in which my hands have been amputated. To put this another way, condition (iii) asks us to consider what *would* be the case, *were* it false that I have hands. What would things be like, in other words, if I did not have hands? To answer this question, we should not consider "remote" possibilities, but "nearby" possibilities. But in scenarios that are "nearby" possibilities, I would notice if I did not have hands.

You might object: "But how do you know that the demon possibility is 'remote'?" We considered an analogous objection to the reliabilist's anti-skeptical strategy (§5.2.3), and the reply to this objection is the same as the one given above: if Nozick's account of the nature of knowledge is true, the objection is a *non sequitur*. What the sensitivity principle requires, for knowledge that p, is that, were it false that p, you would not believe that p. It does not require that you *know* that, were it false that p, you would not believe that p. Moreover, the Cartesian skeptic should grant that the demon possibility is "remote." Her argument (§4.2.1) is that, even though the possibility is "remote," since you do not know that it does not obtain, you do not know much of anything. So in taking the demon possibility to be "remote," Nozick is not "begging the question" against the skeptic.

Second, Nozick's account implies that I do not know that I am not deceived by a demon (about whether I have hands). The reason is that my belief (that I am not deceived) is not sensitive, and so the sensitivity principle is not satisfied. What that principle requires, if I am to know that I am not deceived by a demon, is that, were it false that I am not deceived by a demon, I would not believe that I am not deceived by a demon. Now the question of what would be the case, were it false that I am not deceived by a demon, is just the question of what would be the case, were I deceived. So what the sensitivity principle requires is that, were I deceived by a demon, I would not believe that

I am not deceived by a demon. But this is false: were I deceived by a demon, I would still think that I was not deceived. Condition (iii) is not satisfied, and therefore I do not know that I am not deceived by a demon. Moreover, if this is right, it seems clear that I cannot (in the relevant sense) know that I am not deceived by a demon. There is nothing I can do, in my present position, to acquire a sensitive belief that I am not deceived.

If Nozick's account of knowledge is true, we have a counterexample to the closure principle. For the proposition that I have hands entails the proposition that I am not deceived by a demon (about whether I have hands), and Nozick's account implies that I know the former proposition, but cannot know the latter proposition.

Our conclusion at this point is conditional: if Nozick's account of knowledge is true, then the closure principle is false. So why accept Nozick's account of knowledge? For his part, Nozick defends his account on the grounds that it has the implications just described. Intuitively, I know that I have hands. And, intuitively, I don't know that I am not deceived by a demon (about whether I have hands)—for how could I know that? Nozick's account explains why both these intuitions are true, and that is a mark in favor of his account of the nature of knowledge (cf. §4.2.4).

The implications for the Cartesian skeptical argument (§4.2.1) are clear: the first premise of the argument is false, if Nozick's account of knowledge is true. Given that Nozick defends his account by appeal to the two intuitions just described, we can articulate **Nozick's argument** as follows:

1 I can't know that I'm not deceived by a demon (about whether I have hands).

2 I know that I have hands.

3 Therefore, it is not the case that I know that I have hands only if I can know that I'm not deceived by a demon (about whether I have hands).

Nozick's conclusion is incompatible with the closure principle, but more importantly (for our purposes), it is the negation of the first premise of the Cartesian skeptical argument. If Nozick's argument is sound, the Cartesian skeptical argument is not.

6.3 In defense of closure

Dretske (§6.2.1) and Nozick (§6.2.2) reject the closure principle; they defend (what Nozick calls) **nonclosure**. Some critics of nonclosure find the view so incredible that they are inclined to ridicule it. Richard Feldman (1995), for example, writes that "the idea that no version of this principle is true strikes me, and many other philosophers, as one of the least plausible ideas to come down the philosophical pike in recent years" (p. 487). This kind of remark—the argument *ad populum*, and the suggestion that one's interlocutors are especially unreasonable, compared to other philosophers—is a rhetorical device, and it provides little support for the closure principle.

In this section we'll look at ways of defending the closure principle. It seems to me that the closure principle can be defended against Dretske and Nozick's objections. We'll first look at some reasons for doubting the would-be counterexamples to the closure principle (§6.3.1), and then articulate some arguments in favor of the closure principle (§6.3.2).

The closure principle, which we are considering in this chapter, is what is sometimes called "single-premise closure", to distinguish it from the following principle:

> **Multi-premise closure:** If S knows that p_1, and knows that p_2, ... and knows that p_n, and p_1 ... p_n together entail q, then S can know that q. (cf. Hawthorne 2004, p. 33)

Multi-premise closure is controversial.[6] One of the main reasons is that the probability of a conjunction can be less than the probability of its conjuncts, and when there are many conjuncts, the probability of their conjunction can be a lot less than the probability of its conjuncts. But this problem, which threatens multi-premise closure, is not a problem for "single-premise closure", i.e. the closure principle (§6.1).

6.3.1 Rethinking the zebra case

Above (§6.2.1), I said that, in Dretske's zebra case, you have evidence that the animal in the pen is a zebra but no evidence that the animal in the pen is not a disguised mule. But you might wonder whether this shows that, or explains how, you could know that the animal in the pen is a zebra, but be unable to know that the animal in the pen is a disguised mule.

The Cartesian skeptic, for example, will object that, while perhaps you have some evidence that the animal in the pen is a zebra, you lack evidence sufficient for knowledge: you do not know that the animal in the pen is a zebra, since this entails that you are not deceived by a demon (about whether the animal in the pen is a zebra), and you cannot know that you are not so deceived. In the same way, the Cartesian skeptic will dismiss our other would-be counterexamples: on her view, you do not know that you have hands, much less where you will or will not take a trip, or where your car is or is not parked.

However, there is an alternative way of avoiding Dretske's conclusion.[7] Perhaps Dretske goes wrong not in assuming that you know that the animal in the pen is a zebra, but in assuming that you do not know that the animal in the pen is not a disguised mule. Dretske has an argument in defense of that assumption: you do not know that the animals in the pen are not disguised mules, since you do not have any good reason to believe that they are not disguised mules. But is this really the case? Let's grant that my evidence that the animals are zebras does not constitute evidence that they are not disguised mules. You might think that, in the case described, I have *other* evidence that the animals in the pen are not disguised mules. For example, zoo hoaxes are not particularly common; on the contrary: they are exceptionally rare, if they even happen at all. This background knowledge is evidence that the animals in the pen are not disguised mules. And so, perhaps, I know that they are not disguised mules, after all. We might think of the zebra case, on the present proposal, as akin to the case in which an ornithologist knows that there is a goldfinch outside my window—knowing that the bird is a goldfinch requires already knowing that it is not a canary. But the ornithologist already knows this, since she has recognized the bird's distinctive beak. Likewise, knowing that the animals in the pen are zebras requires already knowing that they are not disguised mules. But we know this, since we know that the zoo would not perpetrate a hoax.

We might be able to say something similar about our two other would-be counterexamples. It will depend on the details of the cases. Is it really the case that I do not know that I will not win a free trip to Dubai in a raffle? This seems to depend on whether I plan to enter such a raffle. If I have no such plans, don't I plausibly know that I will not win? Alternatively, suppose that I have already purchased a ticket in such a raffle, where the odds of my winning are ten-thousand to one. Many contemporary epistemologists are inclined to say that I cannot know that I will not win the raffle, but you might wonder whether this is really so. It does not strike me as implausible to maintain that you know that you will not win the raffle. This is something that it would not be strange to say, in some contexts: "Should I start saving money for a trip to Dubai? Perhaps not, for I might win that raffle. No, no, I know I won't win that silly raffle. I should start saving now". This seems like a coherent and sensible reflection.[8] If so, then we have no counterexample to closure. Alternatively, if we imagine that the odds are shorter, say ten to one, then it seems wrong to say that you know that you will not win the raffle. But if the odds are short enough so that *that* seems wrong, then it may also seem wrong to say that you know you will not take a trip to Dubai—and so there is again no counterexample to closure.[9] And the same point applies, *mutatis mutandis*, to the car theft case. If Christopher Street is a quiet suburban lane where crime is unheard-of, then it is not plausible that you do not know that your car has not been stolen. On the other hand, if Christopher Street is a crime-infested hellhole where no sane person would leave their car for ten minutes, then it is not plausible that you know your car is still parked there.

So it seems that there are plausible ways of understanding our would-be counterexamples, on which the closure principle is preserved. But we can do more: we can offer positive reasons for thinking that the closure principle is true.

6.3.2 Arguments for the closure principle

For many philosophers, the closure principle is obviously true. As above (§4.2.4), we should neither underestimate nor overestimate the importance of obviousness. If you find the closure principle obvious, then the project of giving an argument in its defense might strike you as unnecessary. But without some reason for thinking that the closure principle is true, we shall have nothing to say to the defenders of nonclosure. So while it would not necessarily be problematic to proceed on the assumption that the closure principle is true, if it seems to you that the principle is obviously true—for what else are you supposed to do, proceed on assumptions that don't seem to you to be obviously true?—it would be better if we could say something in its defense.

Some philosophers argue that the closure principle is the best explanation of the fact that deduction from known premises is a way of knowing. This is sometimes put by saying that deduction is a way of "extending" our knowledge (Williamson 2000, p. 117): we start by knowing that p, and by deducing the proposition that q, from the proposition that p, we come to know that q. Even the Cartesian skeptic can advance this argument; perhaps what little knowledge we have can be extended through deduction, or perhaps the idea that deduction from known premises is a way of knowing is best understood, for the skeptic, as a hypothetical proposition: if there were any known premises, we could get more knowledge by deduction from them. In any event, so the argument goes, the closure principle explains why deduction from known premises is a way of knowing.

This argument is an inference to the best explanation, so it leaves open the possibility that the defender of nonclosure might come up with a better explanation of the phenomenon in question. Saying (or explaining the fact) that deduction from known premises is a way of knowing does not commit you to the closure principle. The closure principle, in effect, says that deduction can always be used to extend one's knowledge. But that X is a way of knowing does not imply that X can always be used to acquire knowledge. Perhaps deduction can sometimes, or even most of the time, be used to extend one's knowledge. This would be sufficient to explain deduction's status as a way of knowing. But this argument puts the burden on the defender of nonclosure, to articulate a better explanation for this fact, than that the closure principle is true.

There is another argument for the closure principle that I think is harder to resist. Entailment (§6.1) is necessarily truth-preserving: if the proposition that p entails the proposition that q, then the proposition that p cannot be true unless the proposition that q is true. To put that another way, if the proposition that p entails the proposition that q, it is necessarily true that, if it is true that p, then it is true that q. Suppose then that I know that p, and that the proposition that p entails the proposition that q. The proposition that p is true, and so the proposition that q is also true. This follows as a matter of necessity from the fact that the proposition that p is true. Suppose, further, that I recognize all of this, and on that basis believe that q. It is hard to understand how this true belief could fail to amount to knowledge. The truth of this belief is necessitated by the fact that I know that p. So there is no possibility of error in forming this belief: given that I know that p, and that the proposition that p entails the proposition that q, I could not possibly go wrong in believing that q. In general, if you know that p, and the proposition that p entails the proposition that q, then you could not possibly go wrong in believing that q.

Believing that q, in such a situation, is therefore akin to believing that you exist. Recall Descartes' cogito (§4.1.3): what struck us as so important about the cogito was the fact that one could not possibly go wrong in believing it. Propositions entailed by what you know seem to have the same property: you could not possibly go wrong in believing them.

There is a wrinkle here, for someone might believe some proposition entailed by what she knows, but for no good reason: she believes that there are infinitely many primes not because this is entailed by the axioms of number theory, but because she loves primes and wants there to be lots of them. Intuitively, she does not know that there are infinitely many primes. (In the same way, someone might believe the cogito, but for no good reason.) But in the good case, in which a person believes something entailed by what she knows *because* it is entailed by what she knows, it is hard to understand how her true belief could fall short of knowledge. Her belief has the cogito-like property: she could not possibly go wrong in forming a belief with this property. And her belief is responsive to this fact; she is not believing for no good reason, as in the case of the lover of primes. How could the belief fall short of knowledge? It does not seem that it could. But nonclosure says that it could. Therefore, nonclosure is false.

6.4 Conclusion

In connection with the problem of Cartesian skepticism (§4.4), we have considered three arguments:

The Cartesian skeptical argument (§4.2.1)	The neo-Moorean argument (§5.2.1)	Nozick's argument (§6.2.1)
1 I know that I have hands only if I can know that I'm not deceived by a demon (about whether I have hands).	1 I know that I have hands only if I can know that I'm not deceived by a demon (about whether I have hands).	1 I can't know that I'm not deceived by a demon (about whether I have hands).
2 I can't know that I'm not deceived by a demon (about whether I have hands).	2 I know that I have hands.	2 I know that I have hands.
3 Therefore, I don't know that I have hands.	3 Therefore, I can know that I'm not deceived by a demon (about whether I have hands).	3 Therefore, it is not the case that I know that I have hands only if I can know that I'm not deceived by a demon (about whether I have hands).

What is most interesting about these three arguments is that (i) each shares a premise with each of the other two and (ii) the conclusion of each is the negation of a premise of each of the other two. To see what I mean, let's adopt some symbols:

- M = I know that I have hands.

- S = I can know that I'm not deceived by a demon (about whether I have hands).

And "~" as the sign for negation, so, for example, "~M" means "I don't know that I have hands". We can re-formulate our arguments, using this symbolism:

The Cartesian skeptical argument	The neo-Moorean argument	Nozick's argument
1 M only if S.	1 M only if S.	1 ~S.
2 ~S.	2 M.	2 M.
3 Therefore, ~M.	3 Therefore, S.	3 Therefore, ~(M only if S)

Each argument calls into question a premise of each of the other two arguments. To put that another way, each argument appeals to a premise that is the negation of the conclusion of each of the other two. At most one of these arguments is sound (and, if "M only if S" is understood as a material conditional, at least one of them is sound); which (if any) is it? It seems to me that our discussion so far reveals that none of these arguments is *obviously* sound.

Readings

The following comprise discussions of the closure principle and would-be counterexamples to it.

- F. Dretske, "Epistemic Operators" (Dretske 1970).

- R. Nozick, "Knowledge and Skepticism" (Nozick 1981, Chapter 3).

- J. Vogel, "Are There Counterexamples to the Closure Principle?" (Vogel 1990b).

- R. Feldman, "In Defence of Closure" (Feldman 1995).

- J. Hawthorne, "Denying Single-Premise Closure" (Hawthorne 2004, pp. 36–46).

7

Skepticism and Language

Recall the four possibilities (§4.4), when it comes to the Cartesian skeptical argument (§4.2.1): either the first premise is false, or the second premise is false, or the argument is invalid, or the conclusion is true. We have considered the possibility that the first premise is false (Chapter 6) and the possibility that the second premise is false (Chapter 5). Two possibilities remain: that the argument is invalid, and that the conclusion is true (cf. Chapter 9). This chapter aims to explore that third possibility; this will require a discussion of a popular anti-skeptical strategy known as "contextualism".

An argument is valid if and only if, necessarily, if its premises are true, then its conclusion is true (§4.2.1). Isn't the Cartesian skeptical argument *obviously* valid? It seems like an instance of the argument form known as "*modus ponens*", all instances of which are valid.[1] Here is that form:

p only if q
p
Therefore, q.

However, an argument can seem valid, even when it really isn't, if an ambiguous word—a word that can have two different meanings—is used to state the argument. For example:

1 All banks in the UK are required to separate retail operations from investment banking.

2 The bank of the river Clyde is a bank in the UK.

3 Therefore, the bank of the river Clyde is required to separate retail operations from investment banking.

But this "bank argument" is obviously invalid: both of the premises are true, but the conclusion is false. It superficially looks like an instance of the following valid argument form:

All Fs are G
X is F
Therefore, X is G.

But the argument is invalid, because "bank" is ambiguous, and has a different meaning in the first and in the second premise. At least, the bank argument is invalid *if its premises are true*. For to understand the first premise as true, we must understand "bank" to refer to a kind of financial institution, but to understand the second premise as true, we must understand "bank" to refer to the edge of a river. The flaw manifested by this bank argument is sometimes called the "fallacy of equivocation". So we must consider the possibility that the Cartesian skeptical argument also commits this fallacy.

7.1 The linguistic turn

Moore's anti-skeptical strategy (§5.1) was sympathetically challenged by his colleagues **Norman Malcolm** (1911–90) and **Ludwig Wittgenstein** (1889–1951). In their writings on Moore's anti-skeptical strategy, Malcolm and Wittgenstein challenge Moore's premise that he knows that he has hands. What is notable about their objection is that they do not suggest that Moore does not know that he has hands (although see Wittgenstein 1969, §151), but that there is something wrong with his *saying* that he knows that he has hands. They do not object to the proposition that Moore knows that he has hands, but rather to his use of the sentence "I know that I have hands". Their ideas initiated a "linguistic turn" in epistemology that remains influential in contemporary discussions of knowledge and skepticism.

The essence of Malcolm and Wittgenstein's objection is that Moore is misusing the sentence "I know that I have hands". In his paper "Defending Common Sense" (1949), Malcolm argues that the sentence <I know that p> can only be meaningfully uttered in a context in which doubt about the proposition that p has been expressed or suggested. An utterance of <I know that p>, in a context in which no such doubt has been expressed or suggested, is "senseless", so you cannot utter <I know that p>, in a particular context, unless there is some doubt about whether p, in that context; otherwise, your utterance is "senseless". But in the context in which Moore utters "I know that I have hands", there is no doubt about whether Moore has hands—indeed, that's another way of putting the idea that it's a piece of common knowledge that he has hands. But if it really is common knowledge that Moore has hands, then, so the argument goes, his utterance of "I know that I have hands" is "senseless".

Wittgenstein offers a similar take on Moore's anti-skeptical strategy in his posthumous notebooks *On Certainty* (1969), agreeing with Malcolm that claims to knowledge can only be understood in a context of doubt. In a context of certainty that p, my utterance of <I know that p> could only function as an expression of the fact that the proposition that p "stands fast" for me (§116). But such an utterance would be misleading, since "[o]ne says 'I know' when one is ready to give compelling grounds" (§243). But this is precisely what Moore is not ready to do: he admits that he cannot prove that he has hands (cf. §5.2.2). This leads Wittgenstein to the same conclusion as Malcolm: that Moore's utterances of <I know that p> are, in some sense, without meaning. He writes:

> "I know that that's a tree." Why does it strike me as if I did not understand the sentence? though it is after all an extremely simple sentence of the most ordinary kind? It is as if I could not focus my mind on any meaning. (§347)

But, in any event, the upshot of Malcolm and Wittgenstein's discussion of Moore's anti-skeptical strategy is the idea that Moore's utterances of <I know that p> are, in one way or another, linguistically improper—they are misuses of the word "know".

In response to Malcolm's (1949) paper, Moore wrote a letter to Malcolm, which includes the following reply to the charge that his uses of <I know that p> are "senseless":

> If a person, under circumstances in which everybody would see quite clearly that a certain object was a tree, were to keep repeatedly pointing at it and saying "That's a tree" or "I know that's a tree," we might well say that that was a senseless thing for him to do, and therefore, in a sense, a senseless thing for him to say, [since] it could serve no useful purpose to say those words. (Moore 1993, p. 215)

But, Moore points out, there is another sense of "senseless", where it means that the word or sentence that has been uttered is meaningless or ungrammatical. An utterance of "Knowest arts treesing" is "senseless", in this sense. So "senseless" can mean either purposeless or meaningless. And while an utterance of "I know that's a tree", in the context Moore describes, may indeed be purposeless, it is obviously not meaningless. Now the important thing about this conclusion is that the fact that an utterance is purposeless is compatible with its being true. Indeed, in this case, the reason that an utterance of "I know that's a tree" would be purposeless is that it is so obviously true.

Moore's utterance of "I know that I have hands", you might think, is purposeless. But it is not meaningless. And even if Moore's utterance of "I know that I have hands" is purposeless, this is compatible with its being true. The truth of Moore's utterance is what we need, since that is sufficient for the truth of the first premise of the neo-Moorean argument.

So it does not seem that Malcolm and Wittgenstein's linguistic challenge undermines Moore's anti-skeptical strategy.[2] However, more recently there has been a revival of the idea that consideration of language can help us solve the problem of Cartesian skepticism.

7.2 Contextualism

In contemporary epistemology, **contextualism** is (roughly) the view that "know" is context-sensitive and thus that the truth-conditions of utterances of <S knows that p> depend on the context of utterance. Another way of putting this is to say that (the truth-conditions of) knowledge attributions are context-sensitive. As we look at various species of contextualism, this rough formulation will give way to more precise articulations of the contextualist idea.

7.2.1 Context-sensitivity

Lots of words and sentences are context-sensitive. To see what it means to say that a word is context-sensitive, consider the word "here". A distinctive thing about context-sensitive words is that apparently contradictory utterances can both be true, if they use a context-sensitive word. Imagine that Terry, in Tucson, says, "It's 95 degrees here", and Mindy, in Minneapolis, says, "It's not 95 degrees here". It is easy to imagine that both of their utterances are true—it really is 95 degrees in Tucson, and it really isn't 95 degrees in Minneapolis. The reason that these two utterances, which superficially look contradictory, can both be true is that they use the context-sensitive word "here". When Terry says "here", she refers to Tucson, and when Mindy says "here", she refers to Minneapolis. It seems that, at least in general, when someone says "here" she refers to her own location. This exemplifies what is distinctive of context-sensitive words (or sentences): their meaning is different depending on the context of conversation in which the word (or sentence) is uttered. And this explains why the truth-conditions of sentences, like "It's 95 degrees here", can depend on the context of utterance. The utterance of that sentence by Terry (as described above) is true iff it is 95 degrees in Tucson. But an utterance of that sentence by Mindy (as described above) would be true iff it were 95 degrees in Minneapolis.

There are a number of words that seem to share these features with "here", including "now", "this", "that", "you", and "I". But there are other ways for words (or sentences) to be context-sensitive. We'll look at three examples. Each of these, some contextualists would argue, is a useful analogue for understanding the word "knows".

First, consider the word "nearby". In some ways, "nearby" resembles "here". So Terry might truly say, "There are cactus nearby", while Mindy might truly say, "There are no cactus nearby". But when someone says "nearby", she does not always refer to her own location. Imagine that Terry and Mindy are talking on the phone, and Terry says that she would like to see some cactus. Mindy might truly say, "There are cactus nearby", using "nearby" to refer to Tucson. While it seems like when someone says "here" she refers to her own location, it seems like when someone says "nearby" she refers to whatever location is relevant in the context of conversation. The truth-conditions of sentences that use "nearby" can depend on the relevant location that is referred to by "nearby", in the context of conversation.

Second, consider the word "tall". As with "here" and "nearby", differences in context can result in utterances that superficially look contradictory, but which are both true. Imagine that Lucy is an NBA general manager. Her assistant suggests drafting Wyman, an undersized forward at 6'2". Lucy reminds her assistant that the team needs to draft a tall player, and says, "Wyman is not tall". Compare the situation of Sarah, human resources manager at a biscuit factory. Of all the applicants for a position in the factory, only Wyman can reach the controls on the top of the biscuit-making machine. Justifying her decision to her assistant, she points out that the job can only be performed by someone tall, and says, "Wyman is tall". Both Lucy and Sarah are speaking truly. How can this be? It is natural to account for the context-sensitivity of "tall" by appeal to the notion of standards. Lucy and Sarah are employing different standards for what counts as a "tall" person: when Lucy (in her context) says "tall", she means "tall enough to compete as a forward in the NBA", but when Sarah (in her context) says "tall", she means "tall enough to work the biscuit-making machine". Wyman is not tall, in the first sense, but he is tall, in the second sense. The truth-conditions of sentences that use "tall" can depend on the standards, for what counts as a "tall" person, employed in the context of conversation.

Finally, consider words like "all", "every", "some", and "none", which philosophers of language call our "idioms of quantification". Again, differences in context can result in utterances that superficially look contradictory, but which are both true. If Agnes says that she is thirsty and asks Anne whether there is any beer in the fridge, which is completely empty apart from a tiny puddle of spilled beer in the vegetable crisper, Anne speaks the truth when she says, "There's no beer in the fridge". But if April asks the same question, in advance of looking in the fridge, having just mentioned her deadly beer allergy that can be triggered by even the slightest contact with beer, Anne speaks the truth when she says, "There's some beer in the fridge". Philosophers of language explain this by saying there are different "domains of quantification" in the two contexts. In the context of Agnes and Anne's conversation, "some" and "none" refer only to drinkable portions of beer, whereas in the context of April and Anne's conversation, "some" and "none" refer to any beer whatsoever, or at least any amount of beer sufficiently large to potentially trigger April's allergy. Again, it is natural to explain what goes on in this case in terms of relevance: whether some beer counts as "some" beer depends on what is relevant in the context of conversation. In the context of Agnes and Anne's conversation, the tiny spill is irrelevant, but it is relevant in the context of April and Anne's conversation. So, again, the truth-conditions for sentences using the "idioms of quantification" depend on what is relevant in the context of conversation.

So we have an idea of what it means for a word or sentence to be "context-sensitive". What does this have to do with epistemology?

7.2.2 The context-sensitivity of "knows"

Many epistemologists argue that "knows" is context-sensitive.[3] For our purposes here, we'll consider a fairly rough and generic articulation of contextualism (again, the view that the truth-conditions for utterances of <S knows that p> depend on the context of utterance). Here's the idea. The standards for what counts as "knowing" depend on the context of conversation. In some contexts, the standards are relatively "high", and in other contexts, they are relatively "low". One influential way of thinking about high and low standards for "knowing" appeals to the idea of "relevant alternatives". Think of the case of the ornithologist identifying a bird as a goldfinch (§6.1). Whether she can be said to know that the bird is a goldfinch, so the argument goes, depends on whether she can rule out or eliminate various alternatives to its being a goldfinch. It seemed natural, above, to require for knowledge that the ornithologist rule out the possibility that the bird is a canary—and we imagined that she did this by recognizing the distinctive beak of a goldfinch. That possibility, that the bird is a canary, seemed like a relevant alternative. But what about the following possibility: the bird is a canary wearing a false beak, designed to look like the beak of a goldfinch? Or what about this possibility: the "bird" is not really a bird at all, but a realistic robot? Or what about: the "bird" is not really a bird, because the ornithologist is a victim of a deceptive demon, of the sort described by Descartes? Contextualism, of the rough and generic sort we're considering here, says that whether an alternative is relevant is down to facts about the context of conversation, and that attributing knowledge requires that the relevant person be able to rule out all relevant alternatives. In a low-standards context, the false-beak possibility, and the robot possibility, and the demon possibility, will not count as relevant alternatives. But in a high-standards context, the set of relevant alternatives expands, to include those possibilities. And if someone were to say, in a low-standards context, "The ornithologist knows that it's a goldfinch", then she would speak the truth; but if someone were to say, in a high-standards context, "The ornithologist doesn't know that it's a goldfinch", she would speak the truth as well. Contextualism maintains that, just as in other cases of context-sensitivity (§2.1), the truth-conditions for sentences using "knows" depend on the context of conversation. The ornithologist can rule out the possibility that the bird is a canary (or, at least, that it is a mere canary, i.e. not one wearing a false beak). Whether she can be said, by someone S, to know that the bird is a goldfinch, however, depends on the alternatives that are relevant in the context of S's conversation.

Is contextualism plausible? Is it plausible that "knows" is context-sensitive? There is some compelling evidence that is suggestive of contextualism: utterances that look superficially contradictory, but which both seem to be true. Here is a much-discussed pair of cases (cf. DeRose 1992, p. 913).

- It's Friday, and Keith and Jason are driving to the bank to deposit Keith's paycheck. When they arrive there is an annoyingly long line. But since nothing important rides on Keith's depositing the check anytime soon, he decides to return to the bank on Saturday. "Do you know that it'll be open tomorrow," Jason asks, "since not all banks are open on the weekend." "I know it'll be open tomorrow," Keith says, "because I was here last Saturday, and the bank was open." And so they leave without confirming the bank's hours.

- It's Friday, and Keith and Jason are driving to the bank to deposit Keith's paycheck. When they arrive there is an annoyingly long line. It's very important that Keith deposit the check before Monday, as he himself wrote a check to a dangerous gangster earlier in the day, who is expected to cash Keith's check Monday morning. But he suggests that they should leave, and that he'll return to the bank on Saturday. "Do you know that it'll be open tomorrow," Jason asks, "since not all banks are open on the weekend." "I guess you're right; I don't know that the bank will be open tomorrow. Although I was here last Saturday, and the bank was open, banks sometimes change their hours." And so he enters the bank to confirm its hours.

So the argument goes, Keith speaks truly in both cases. But his utterances look contradictory—"I know that the bank will be open tomorrow" in the first case; "I don't know that the bank will be open tomorrow" in the second case. Contextualism would provide a natural explanation of how this is possible: the standards are higher in the second case than in the first case; there is a difference in relevant alternatives. In particular, the possibility that the bank has (improbably) changed its hours is relevant in the second case, but not in the first. Since Keith can't rule out that possibility, and since knowledge requires ruling out all relevant alternatives, the sentence "I know that the bank will be open tomorrow", spoken by Keith, would not be true in the second context. But since that possibility is not a relevant alternative in the first case, we can easily imagine that the sentence "I know that the bank will be open tomorrow", spoken by Keith, is true in the first context.

There are alternative accounts of these, and related, cases.[4] But the contextualist account provides an appealing explanation of the linguistic phenomena. Let's grant that contextualism is true. What has this to do with the problem of Cartesian skepticism?

7.2.3 Contextualism and skepticism

Having argued for contextualism, Stewart Cohen (1988) writes:

> We can now gain some insight into how skeptical arguments work. In effect, skeptical arguments make alternatives relevant by forcing us to view the reasons in a way that makes the chance of error salient. Skeptical standards of relevance thereby take effect, creating a context where attributions of knowledge are incorrect. (p. 108)

Consider, for example, the possibility that I am deceived by a demon (about whether I have hands). So the argument goes, the skeptic changes the context of conversation and raises the standards, so that this becomes a relevant alternative. Since I can't rule out this possibility, the sentence "I know that I have hands", uttered in that context, would be false, and thus the sentence "I don't know that I have hands", uttered in that context, is true. But isn't that just to say that the skeptic's conclusion is true? Isn't that just to say that Cartesian skepticism is, after all, true? Is contextualism just a linguistically-motivated form of skepticism?

Keith DeRose (1995) explains the sense in which contextualism is an anti-skeptical position:

> [A]ccording to the contextualist ... the skeptic's present denials that we know various things are perfectly compatible with our ordinary claims

to know those very propositions. Once we realize this, we can
both the skeptic's denials of knowledge and our ordinary attribution
knowledge can be correct. (p. 5)

> [T]he skeptic gets to truthfully state her conclusion only by raising the
> standards for knowledge, [so the skeptical argument] doesn't threaten
> the truth of our ordinary claims to know ... which the skeptic attacks. For
> the fact that the skeptic can install very high standards that we don't live
> up to has no tendency to show that we don't satisfy the more relaxed
> standards that are in place in more ordinary conversations and debates. (p.
> 38; see also DeRose 1992, p. 917)

Imagine a conversation between two ornithologists, about whether the bird
in the garden is a goldfinch. "I know that it's a goldfinch", one says, "because
of the distinctive beak". She can thus rule out the possibility that the bird is a
canary. But can she rule out the possibility that she's deceived by a demon
(about whether the bird is a goldfinch)? Presumably, she cannot. But this
does not falsify her claim to knowledge, because the possibility that she's
deceived by a demon is not relevant in the context of her conversation with
her fellow ornithologist. Things might be different were she discussing the
matter with a Cartesian skeptic, who might "install very high standards", and
thus make it the case that the ornithologist could truly say, "I don't know that
it's a goldfinch". But this is compatible with her previous, "ordinary" claim.
The truth of the skeptic's conclusion is compatible with the truth of most of
our "ordinary" knowledge attributions. This allows us to understand Cohen's
(1988) diagnosis of the appeal of skeptical arguments:

> Skeptical arguments exploit the fact that certain considerations can lead to
> a shift in the standards of relevance. Failure to recognize the shift can lead
> us into paradox. (p. 110)

Paradox requires a set of claims that strike us as true, but which are
mutually inconsistent. The skeptic says: "You don't know whether you're
deceived by a demon, and thus you don't know much of anything, including
that you have hands". The defender of common sense says: "I, and other
people, do know many things, including that I have hands". These claims
appear incompatible, and it is hard to see which of them is false; they both
have a lot going for them. The contextualist argues that these claims are
not really incompatible: both are, or could easily be, true. There thus is no
paradox to be solved.

7.3 A problem for contextualism as an anti-skeptical strategy

Contextualism in epistemology has evolved from an anti-skeptical strategy, the interest of which derives from our interest in the problem of Cartesian skepticism, into an account of the semantics and pragmatics of knowledge attributions, the interest of which is independent of any such interest. Giving an account of the semantics and pragmatics of knowledge attributions has become a philosophical project of its own, distinct from the project of answering the problem of Cartesian skepticism. And this new project intersects with other projects in contemporary epistemology, such as that of explaining the value of knowledge and the "function" of knowledge attributions. Here we are interested in contextualism *as an anti-skeptical strategy*, and will not be specifically concerned with its credentials as an independently plausible account of the semantics and pragmatics of knowledge attributions. If contextualism provides a plausible answer to the problem of Cartesian skepticism, that would be a large mark in its favor, regardless of any other flaws that it may or may not have.

7.3.1 The (ir)relevance of language

Contextualism is a claim about the truth-conditions for utterances of <S knows that p>, rather than a claim about knowledge itself. Contextualism and, say, reliabilism (§5.2.3) are claims about different subject matters: the former is a linguistic claim about the meaning and application of the word "knows"; the latter is an epistemological claim about the nature of knowledge. This much is uncontroversial, and is common ground between defenders and critics of contextualism.

However, this point forms the basis of an objection to contextualism, as an anti-skeptical strategy. As Ernest Sosa (2000, pp. 3–4) argues, questions about language are sometimes irrelevant to superficially similar non-linguistic questions. If you wonder whether anyone at all loves you, it will be of no interest to learn that sometimes people speak the truth when they say, "I love you". The reason is that "you" is context-sensitive: people may speak the truth when they say, "I love you", but unless "you" refers to *you*, this fact is irrelevant to your original question of whether anyone at all loves you. The linguistic claim about the application of the word "love" is irrelevant to the romantic question of whether anyone at all loves you. But this casts doubt on the contextualist's strategy. Above (e.g. §4.1), I wondered whether I know much of anything, e.g. whether I know that I have hands. Contextualism tells me that people, perhaps including me, often speak the truth when they say, "I know that I have hands". But since "know" is context-sensitive, it is entirely obscure whether this linguistic claim is relevant at all to my original epistemological question. Linguistic claims about the application of context-sensitive words do not generally bear on superficially similar non-linguistic questions. Why think then that contextualism bears on my non-linguistic question about the extent of my knowledge?

DeRose (2009) calls this objection an "outburst" (p. 18), but this rhetoric is useless to our philosophical purpose. Does the contextualist have any reply to Sosa's objection? What can we say in the contextualist's defense? One possibility is that the context-sensitivity of "knows", because we are unaware of it, has led epistemologists into error. Now the idea that "knows" is secretly context-sensitive seems, itself, like a liability for contextualism (see e.g. Feldman 1999, p. 107; Hawthorne 2004, pp. 98–111), but let's grant it for the sake of argument. This is the idea behind Cohen's suggestion (§7.2.3) that the illusion of a skeptical paradox is the result of failing to appreciate a contextual "shift", and DeRose (2009) concurs: "all sorts of problems and mistakes in epistemology … will arise from a failure to recognize such shifts in meaning" (p. 19). Contextualism is relevant to epistemology, therefore, to the extent that it enables us to diagnose "problems and mistakes" that people make, as a result of their ignorance of the context-sensitivity of "knows". Let's consider, again, the problem of Cartesian skepticism (§4.4), and the question of whether there are any problems or mistakes that people make, when it comes to this epistemological problem, that the contextualist can diagnose.

7.3.2 The problem of Cartesian skepticism

Here, again, is the Cartesian skeptical argument (§4.2.1):

1 I know that I have hands only if I can know that I'm not deceived by a demon (about whether I have hands).

2 I can't know that I'm not deceived by a demon (about whether I have hands).

3 Therefore, I don't know that I have hands.

What has the contextualist to say about this argument? Does she provide an answer to the problem of Cartesian skepticism (§4.4)? I have suggested that the contextualist will say that the Cartesian skeptical argument is invalid, because it commits the fallacy of equivocation. Indeed, the contextualist seems in a good position to say that: the context-sensitivity of "knows" would provide for different meanings for the different uses of "knows" in the argument.

Very roughly, contextualism says that "knows" has a low-standards meaning and a high-standards meaning. So let's use "knows-L" to refer unambiguously to the low-standards meaning and "knows-H" to refer unambiguously to the high-standards meaning. We should now be able to re-state the argument so that its invalidity is obvious. How shall we do it? Perhaps:

1a I know-L that I have hands only if I can know-L that I'm not deceived by a demon (about whether I have hands).

1b I can't know-H that I'm not deceived by a demon (about whether I have hands).

1c Therefore, I don't know-L that I have hands.

That argument is, indeed, invalid. But why couldn't the skeptic respond by offering the following argument:

1d I know-L that I have hands only if I can know-L that I'm not deceived by a demon (about whether I have hands).

1e I can't know-L that I'm not deceived by a demon (about whether I have hands).

1f Therefore, I don't know-L that I have hands.

This argument is valid. The difference is between (1b) and (1e). (1b) says (roughly) that I can't have high-standards knowledge that I'm not deceived by a demon. (1e) says (roughly) that I can't have low-standards knowledge that I'm not deceived by a demon. If the contextualist is to avoid the skeptic's conclusion, she must reject (1e).[5] But is this at all plausible? The contextualist's idea was that the skeptic's conclusion, which is true in her context, is compatible with our ordinary knowledge attributions, which are true in ordinary contexts. Is "I know that I'm not deceived by a demon (about whether I have hands)" among those ordinary knowledge attributions, which are true in ordinary contexts? According to some species of contextualism (see e.g. Cohen 1988, Lewis 1996), once the possibility of demon deception is made salient in a conversation, that possibility becomes a relevant alternative. If that were true, then (1e) cannot plausibly be rejected: I can't have low-standards knowledge that I'm not deceived by a demon, because once that possibility is made salient, high-standards knowledge is the only game in town. The issues that arise here for the contextualist are complex (cf. DeRose 2009, Chapter 4), and I have given them only a very rough treatment here. But it remains obscure how the contextualist can defend the charge of invalidity, against the Cartesian skeptical argument.

Here is another possibility, which, as we'll see in a moment, is suggested by some contextualists. Perhaps the contextualist should offer the following re-statement of the Cartesian skeptical argument:

1g I know-H that I have hands only if I can know-H that I'm not deceived by a demon (about whether I have hands).

1h I can't know-H that I'm not deceived by a demon (about whether I have hands).

1i Therefore, I don't know-L that I have hands.

This argument is invalid: it illicitly draws a conclusion about low-standards knowledge from premises about high-standards knowledge. We might say, following DeRose and Cohen, that there is a contextual "shift" between the premises and the conclusion. Even though the premises are true, the conclusion may very well be false. Cartesian skepticism is thus avoided.

Or is it? The skeptic might respond by offering the following:

1j I know-H that I have hands only if I can know-H that I'm not deceived by a demon (about whether I have hands).

1k I can't know-H that I'm not deceived by a demon (about whether I have hands).

1l Therefore, I don't know-H that I have hands.

This argument is valid, so if its premises are true, then its conclusion is true as well. Perhaps we should accept that: recall the contextualist's idea (§7.2.3) that the skeptic's conclusion is true, in her high-standards context. But how then is Cartesian skepticism avoided? Here's what Cohen and DeRose say:

> What is truly startling about skepticism, is the claim that all along, in our day to day lives, when we have claimed to know things, we have been wrong[.] (Cohen 1988, p. 117)

> [S]keptical arguments ... threaten to ... establish the startling result that we never, or almost never, truthfully ascribe knowledge to ourselves or to other mere mortals. (DeRose 1995, p. 4)

Skepticism is thus understood as a linguistic claim, to the effect that our ordinary knowledge attributions are mistaken. But (1l) does not threaten our ordinary knowledge attributions; only (1i) does. So the skeptic must be understood as arguing for (1i).

In this respect, Cohen and DeRose inherit a theme from Malcolm (1977), on which skepticism is understood as a member of a family of "philosophical arguments and views which imply that innumerable observations of everyday life ... are really incorrect ways of speaking" (p. 170). It is this theme that represents the essence of what I called the "linguistic turn" in epistemology (§7.1): skepticism is understood not as an attack on our knowledge, but on our claims to knowledge, and the problem of skepticism is considered solved if we can provide an adequate defense of those claims.

One of the silliest mistakes in philosophy is getting into an argument about what the "real" issue or problem or question is, when it comes to some named philosophical topic, like "skepticism", or "free will", or "the mind-body problem". So although there is a temptation to say that the "real" problem of skepticism has nothing to do with defending ordinary language, we won't say that. But we should compare the skepticism refuted by contextualism—the skepticism that says that ordinary knowledge attributions are mistaken—and the skepticism contemplated by Descartes (§4.1). It is obvious that the skepticism Descartes engages with, if it were true, would have no implications for ordinary language. Descartes never considers the idea that, if we cannot prove that we're not victims of a deceptive demon, then ordinary knowledge attributions are mistaken. The idea he considers is that, if we cannot prove that we're not victims of a deceptive demon, then we know very little, and (as he would put it) there will be nothing in the sciences that is firm and likely to last. This conclusion, which Descartes seeks to avoid, would have absolutely no implications for ordinary language—or, indeed, for ordinary life in general (cf. §9.2).

Cohen (1988) writes that, "[i]f the skeptic's position is interesting, it is because he challenges our everyday knowledge attributions" (p. 117). In philosophy, the accusation that one's interlocutor's position is "uninteresting" is almost always a desperate measure, introduced when one has run out of objections. But suppose we understand skepticism as the following view:

> No one knows anything (except for propositions about their own existence and mental life), although many ordinary knowledge attributions are true, because "knows", in ordinary contexts, does not refer to genuine knowledge, but to some more easily acquired state.

Uninteresting? For my part, it sounds pretty interesting. DeRose (1995) calls this position "timid" (p. 5), but that seems like name-calling and not an objection. However, you might argue that this position is "uninteresting" because it presupposes infallibilism. DeRose (1995) argues that skeptical arguments aim to show "not only that we fail to meet very high requirements for knowledge, of interest only to misguided philosophers seeking absolute certainty, but that we don't meet even the truth conditions of ordinary, out-on-the-street knowledge attributions" (p. 4). But there are two problems with this thought. The first is that the Cartesian skeptical argument does not presuppose infallibilism (§4.3). The second (cf. Sosa 2000, pp. 7–10) is that, even if the standards employed by the Cartesian skeptic are different from those employed in ordinary life, it is obscure whether the skeptic is "misguided" in employing those standards. Let's suppose (although see Feldman 1999, pp. 107–11) that the skeptic's standards are indeed higher than those employed in ordinary life. Should we employ such high standards? That question is unanswered by contextualism: we can grant that "knows" is context-sensitive, and that skeptical denials of knowledge are compatible with ordinary knowledge attributions, and still wonder: which standards ought we to employ, the low or the high? Compare the NBA general manager: she can recognize that "tall" is context-sensitive, and that a "high standards" assessment of Wyman's tallness will have no bearing on whether he would pass a "low standards" assessment, and still conclude that the "high standards" are the ones that she ought to employ. So, even granting that the Cartesian skeptic employs extraordinary, high standards, it is obscure whether this threatens her position. And even if it does threaten her position, the reason is not that contextualism is true—once she disavows any critique of ordinary language. The argument that the skeptic ought not to adopt her high standards will be a normative or evaluative one, not a claim about the semantics and pragmatics of knowledge attributions.

7.4 Conclusion

In our discussion of anti-skepticism (Part II), we have considered three popular anti-skeptical strategies: neo-Mooreanism (Chapter 5), nonclosure (Chapter 6), and contextualism (this chapter). I have argued against all three; after studying the relevant literature, you may now be in a position to make up your mind about the problem of Cartesian skepticism (§4.4). More than anything else, I have urged (cf. §4.4) that an answer to that problem must defend one of four possibilities: that the conclusion of the Cartesian skeptical argument is true, that its first premise is false, that its second premise is false, or that the argument is invalid. Of these four, I have not said much about the possibility that Cartesian skepticism is true. We'll consider that possibility below (Chapter 9).

Readings

Here are three essential defenses of contextualism as an anti-skeptical strategy.

- S. Cohen, "How to Be a Fallibilist" (Cohen 1988).
- K. DeRose, "Solving the Skeptical Problem" (DeRose 1995).
- D. K. Lewis, "Elusive Knowledge" (Lewis 1996).

And here are some criticisms of contextualism as an anti-skeptical strategy.

- R. Feldman, "Contextualism and Skepticism" (Feldman 1999).
- E. Sosa, "Skepticism and Contextualism" (Sosa 2000).

The following discussions are highly recommended, on the question of whether skepticism is based on an illegitimately "high standard" for knowledge.

- B. Stroud, "Philosophical Scepticism and Everyday Life" (Stroud 1984, Chapter II).
- J. Vogel, "Skeptical Arguments" (Vogel 2004).

Finally, here are some discussions, both sympathetic and critical, of contextualism as an account of the semantics and pragmatics of knowledge attributions.

- K. DeRose, "Contextualism and Knowledge Attributions" (DeRose 1992).
- J. Stanley, "On the Linguistic Basis for Contextualism" (Stanley 2004).
- J. Hawthorne, "Contextualism and the Puzzle" (Hawthorne 2004, Chapter 2).
- J. Schaffer, "From Contextualism to Contrastivism" (Schaffer 2004a).
- K. DeRose, *The Case for Contextualism: Knowledge, Skepticism, and Context*, volume 1 (DeRose 2009).
- P. Rysiew, "The Context-Sensitivity of Knowledge Attributions" (Rysiew 2001).
- J. Brown, "Contextualism and Warranted Assertibility Manoeuvres" (Brown 2006).

PART THREE

New Directions

8

Beyond Propositional Knowledge

The problem of Cartesian skepticism (§4.4) is concerned with the extent of our knowledge: the skeptic says that we know nothing, except for propositions about our own existence and mental life, while the anti-skeptic says that we know more than that. But "knowledge" is ambiguous; there seem to be several species of knowledge. The species of knowledge that we discussed above (Chapters 1–7) is known to epistemologists as **propositional knowledge**. We refer to propositions with clauses that begin with "that", and another name for propositional knowledge is "knowledge-that". Knowledge that you have hands, knowledge that the sun will rise tomorrow, knowledge that 2+2=4, and knowledge that the cat is on the mat—these are all examples of propositional knowledge. But there seem to be other species of knowledge. Consider **practical knowledge**, or (in one sense of the words) "knowledge-how". Knowing how to ride a bicycle, knowing how to cook a stew, and knowing how to live well—these are all examples of practical knowledge.

There also seems to be a difference between propositional knowledge and **acquaintance knowledge**, or (in one sense of the words) "knowledge-of". Compare two situations. In the first, you inform me that, in the other room, the cat is on the mat. It is easy to imagine that I now know that the cat is on the mat, and that I am (indirectly) aware of the fact that the cat is on the mat. I have this item of propositional knowledge. Now, in the second situation, I come to know that the cat is on the mat by seeing the cat on the mat. Here I have the same item of propositional knowledge as I had in the first situation, but I am *also* directly aware of the cat, and so I have acquaintance with the cat. But in the first situation, I was not so acquainted. This notion of acquaintance knowledge, and the contrast with propositional knowledge, can be illuminated by considering the distinction between knowing someone and merely knowing who she is. I know a lot about Bill Clinton—I know that he was the 42nd President of the United States, that he has a daughter named Chelsea, that he recently adopted a vegan diet—and in virtue of this I can be said to know who he is. But I have never met Clinton, he and I are not (in a related but different sense) acquainted, and because of this I cannot be said to know Clinton.

Propositional knowledge, practical knowledge, acquaintance knowledge: these all seem like species of knowledge. In his *Metaphysics* (I.1–2), Aristotle suggests two additional species: **understanding** (ἐπιστήμη) and wisdom (σοφία). Understanding, Aristotle argues, is explanatory knowledge or "knowledge-why". It is one thing to know that fire is hot, which would be a case of mere propositional knowledge, and another to know why fire is hot, which would be a case of understanding. Wisdom, he goes on to argue, is a species of understanding: it is knowledge of *fundamental* explanations. There is a lively debate in contemporary epistemology about the relationship between knowledge and understanding. Most argue that understanding is not a species of propositional knowledge; some argue that understanding is not a species of knowledge at all; others argue that understanding is a species of non-propositional knowledge. But even if understanding is a species of propositional knowledge, it is distinct from propositional knowledge: not all instances of knowledge are instances of understanding.

Some epistemologists complain that contemporary epistemology has concerned itself primarily with propositional knowledge. In this chapter we'll do better than complaining: we'll take a look beyond propositional knowledge at some alternative species of skepticism. In particular, we'll consider doubts about our capacity for perceptual acquaintance (§8.1), knowledge of intrinsic properties (§8.2), and understanding (§8.3).

Although our interest here is in contemporary epistemology, it is worth noting that all three forms of skepticism to be considered in this chapter might serve as illuminating interpretations of the Ancient skeptics (§1.1). They are all species of non-rustic skepticism, akin to (or perhaps the same as) urbane or essential skepticism (§1.3.2).

8.1 Perceptual acquaintance

Let's call acquaintance in virtue of perceiving something **perceptual acquaintance**. We spoke above of perceptual acquaintance with something, but it makes just as much sense to speak of perceptual acquaintance with something's *properties*. Imagine that the cat on the mat is orange. It seems that, when I see the cat on the mat, I am not only acquainted with the cat (as I suggested above) but also with its color, i.e. its orange-ness. But there is a long and influential philosophical tradition that denies that I could be perceptually acquainted with the color of the cat. One way of motivating this thought is by denying that the cat really has a color with which one might be acquainted, which is a view that became popular in the Early Modern period. Here is what **Galileo Galilei** (1564–1642) says in *The Assayer* (1623):

> When I think of a physical material or substance, I immediately have to conceive of it as bounded, as having this or that shape, as being large or small in relation to other things, and in some specific place and at any given time, as moving or at rest, as touching or not touching another physical body, and as being one in number, or few or many. [...] But whether it is white or red, bitter or sweet, noisy or silent, and of a pleasing or unpleasant odor, my mind does not feel compelled to bring this in order to apprehend it; in fact, without our senses as a guide reason or imagination unaided would probably never arrive at qualities such as these. So it seems to me that taste, odor, color, and so on ... exist only in the mind that perceives them, so that if living creatures were removed, all these qualities would be wiped away and no longer exist.[1]

This position—that colors, sounds, tastes, and smells are not real properties of external things, but exist only in the perceiver's mind—found numerous adherents in Galileo's day, including John Locke (*Essay concerning Human Understanding*, II.21), René Descartes (*Meditations on First Philosophy*, Meditation Six), and Pierre Bayle (*Historical and Critical Dictionary*, "Pyrrho", Note B), and has had considerable popularity since then.

Galileo would suggest that, although I may enjoy acquaintance with "the orange-ness of the cat", this is not a real property of the cat, and, for this reason, perceptual acquaintance with the real properties of external things, corresponding to their colors, sounds, tastes, and smells, is not possible. Bertrand Russell articulates a version of this position in his *Analysis of Matter* (1927):

> We assume that different percepts imply difference in stimuli—i.e. if a person hears two sounds at once, or sees two colors at once, two physically different stimuli have reached his ear or eye. This principle ... suffices to give a great deal of knowledge as to the *structure* of stimuli. Their intrinsic characters, it is true, must remain unknown[.] (Russell 1954, p. 227; see also p. 197; 1959, pp. 46–7)

This position, applied to the possibility of acquaintance with the colors of external things, is implied by many contemporary views about the nature of the colors. It is most obviously implied by eliminativism or projectivism (e.g. Averill 1985), on which physical objects are not colored. But it is also implied by dispositionalism or relationalism (e.g. Cohen 2004), on which colors are dispositions to appear a certain way to perceivers. For while we are perceptually acquainted with how physical objects appear to us, we are not acquainted with their relevant dispositional or relational properties, and these are (on the present view) their colors. Finally, it is implied by physicalism or objectivism (e.g. Byrne and Hilbert 2003), on which colors are microphysical properties, for we are not perceptually acquainted with these properties of physical objects, and these are (on the present view) their colors.

We have been articulating the view that we are incapable of perceptual acquaintance with certain properties of external things. Which properties, exactly? This is a question about the scope (§1.3.2) of Galileo's skeptical claim. Galileo, as I have indicated, suggests colors, sounds, tastes, and smells, and in the passage cited above, he suggests properties which, at least, can lay claim to being real properties of external things: shapes and sizes, locations, and the properties of being in motion or at rest. Because these are real properties of external things, on Galileo's view, perhaps perceptual acquaintance with these is possible. The question of what distinguishes properties of the first type (e.g. colors) from properties of the second type (e.g. shapes) is a long-standing issue in the philosophy of perception: it is the question of what (if anything) distinguishes "secondary qualities" and "primary qualities". We won't discuss that question here. Nor will we discuss a related but distinct issue that arises in connection with our question about scope. In *The Problems of Philosophy* (1905, Chapter 5), Russell argues that we are only perceptually acquainted with "sense-data", and never with external things or their properties. If this is true, we are acquainted with neither the colors *nor* the shapes of external things.

For our purposes, let's consider a modest formulation of the implication of Galileo's claim, keeping in mind that a more ambitious formulation might very well be true.

Galilean humility: We are not capable of perceptual acquaintance with the colors, sounds, tastes, and smells of external things.

As I suggested in connection with contemporary views about the nature of colors, there are (roughly) two ways to motivate Galilean humility. Let's again focus on the case of color. The first way to motivate Galilean humility is to deny that colors are properties of external things, for example, by arguing that colors are properties of our minds or mental states. Since external things have no colors, perceptual acquaintance with their colors is impossible. The second way is to conceive of the colors as properties of external things with which, as it turns out, we are not capable of perceptual acquaintance, for example, by arguing that colors are microphysical properties. Either way, perceptual acquaintance with the colors of external things is ruled out.

As the foregoing suggests, the question of whether Galilean humility is true (and the question of scope, see above), depends on some big metaphysical questions about the nature of the colors and other properties. It is beyond the scope of this book to explore those questions. I'll conclude this section with two observations.

First, it is important to appreciate the sense in which Galilean humility is a species of skepticism. This classification rests on two assumptions: that the essence of skepticism is the denial of knowledge, and that perceptual acquaintance is a species of knowledge. Why make this second assumption? Mark Johnston (1996) makes a compelling case that perceptual acquaintance is a valuable kind of "cognitive contact" (p. 189) with external things. He writes that:

> An important part of what seems to make perception intrinsically valuable is that as well as providing us with propositional knowledge about just which properties objects have, perception also acquaints us with the nature of the properties had by those objects. It reveals or purports to reveal what those properties are like. As well as providing a map of our environment which helps us steer our way through the world, perception also seems to do something that no ordinary map could do, acquaint us with or reveal the natures of the perceptible properties of the things mapped. (p. 185)

And this leads straightaway to my second observation. As Johnston points out, perceptual acquaintance with external things and propositional knowledge of the external world are two different things. Descartes' story of the malicious demon (§4.1) threatens our would-be propositional knowledge, by providing a key idea for the Cartesian skeptical argument (§4.2.1). But it also threatens our would-be perceptual acquaintance: the victim of Descartes' demon not only lacks propositional knowledge, much less true propositional belief, she also has no "cognitive contact" with the world around her: she lacks perceptual acquaintance with external things. This, Johnston argues, "illustrate[s] a deeper epistemic anxiety about our own condition" (p. 187), namely, the problem of whether perceptual acquaintance with external things is possible. A solution to the problem of Cartesian skepticism (§4.4) will not necessarily provide us with any objection to Galilean humility. You might be satisfied that you know that the cat is on the mat, but still wonder whether you are acquainted with the cat, or with its properties. You might even be satisfied that you know that the cat is orange, but still wonder whether you are acquainted with the cat's orange-ness (cf. Averill and Hazlett

2012). Even if our propositional knowledge of the external world is secured (cf. Part II), the question of our perceptual acquaintance with the external world remains open.

8.2 Knowledge of intrinsic properties

It is characteristic of electrons that they have negative elementary electric charge, or "negative charge", for short. But what exactly is negative charge? A physics textbook would tell you that a substance with negative charge will repel (and be repelled by) other negatively charged substances and attract (and be attracted by) substances with positive charge. Does this answer our question? We know how a negatively charged substance will causally interact with other substances. However, you might think that we remain to some extent ignorant about negative charge. Although we know about the relational properties of negatively charged substances, we do not know what negative charge is like "in itself": we do not know the intrinsic nature of negative charge, which grounds the causal powers of negatively charged substances. But if we lack this knowledge, then no one will ever have it. The only thing we can ever know about properties like negative charge is how substances that have those properties causally interact with other substances. We can never know what such properties are like "in themselves"; we can never know their intrinsic natures.

Arguments like this have been advanced by Russell, who argues that physics can only discover the structure of the external world (1954, chapter XXIV and *passim*), by David Lewis (2009), who argues that we cannot know what the fundamental (and many other) properties of external things are, and by Kant, according to Rae Langton (2001), who argues that, on Kant's view, we are incapable of knowing the intrinsic properties of external things. Although the notion of an **intrinsic property**—roughly, a property that something has in virtue of the way it is, and not in virtue of how it is related to other things— is controversial, progress has been made in articulating it (Kim 1982; Lewis 1983; Langton and Lewis 1998; cf. Weatherson and Marshall 2012). If Langton is right, this was Kant's idea first, so let's follow her articulation:

> **Kantian humility:** We are not capable of knowing the intrinsic properties of external things.

Think again of our example of negative charge. Kantian humility implies that, while we may know the non-intrinsic properties of negatively charged substances, e.g. how they will interact with other charged substances, we cannot know their intrinsic properties. We cannot know what negatively charged substances are like "in themselves"; we can only know how they are related to other substances. Compared to Galilean humility (§8.1), this is more drastic stuff: Kantian humility applies to any intrinsic properties of external things, and maintains not only the impossibility of perceptual acquaintance, but of knowledge more generally (although we'll need to clarify this below). Galileo drew attention to our perceptual inadequacies by way of motivating scientific inquiry: while naïve perception fails to provide knowledge, physics will succeed. Kantian humility suggests that, as far as knowing the intrinsic properties of things, naïve perception and physics are in the same boat.

Why think that Kantian humility, or something like it, is true? Here is a rough sketch of the kind of argument that motivates Russell, Lewis, and Langton's Kant. First premise (cf. Russell, pp. 197–8; Langton 2001, p. 23; Lewis 2009, p. 204, p. 207): everything we know about external things is based on our knowledge of their causal powers (or dispositions, tendencies, etc.). We know how negatively charged substances causally interact with other substances; and we know about such interactions, ourselves, by causally interacting with negatively charged (and other) substances. Our knowledge of external things is ultimately based on perception, and perception gives us knowledge of the causal powers of external things. It is on this basis that we know what we know about them. Second premise (cf. Russell, pp. 287–9; Langton 2001, pp. 172–7; Lewis 2009, p. 209): there is never a necessary connection between the intrinsic properties of a thing and its causal powers. You can't deduce the intrinsic properties of a thing from its causal powers. Conclusion: we are not capable of knowing the intrinsic properties of external things.

This articulation of the argument is, as I said, rough. We can draw no firm conclusion about the plausibility of Kantian humility on the basis of this formulation. (For one thing, this formulation seems to uncharitably require a commitment to the view that only deduction can extend knowledge.) We have the basic idea, however, of another form of skepticism, distinct from Cartesian skepticism. For it is compatible with our knowing a great deal about the external world that we are ignorant of the intrinsic properties of external things. I can know that the cat is on the mat, that domestic cats are mammals descended from the African wildcat, that the mat was bought last year at IKEA, and so on, without knowing the intrinsic properties of any of the external things that I know very much about. For this reason, among defenders of Kantian humility there is a disagreement about whether the truth of the thesis is "cause for mourning", in virtue of our "inextinguishable desire" for knowledge of intrinsic properties (Langton 2001, p. 14), or whether it is no big deal (Lewis 2009, p. 204).

Kantian humility, as articulated, is ambiguous. Does the defender of Kantian humility reject the possibility of a species of acquaintance knowledge, or a species of propositional knowledge? "Knowing X" is ambiguous; it could mean acquaintance with X, or it could mean propositional knowledge about X. Langton (2001) suggests the former disambiguation when she writes that (on Kant's view) "there are intrinsic features of the world with which we can never become acquainted" (p. 176). So we might understand Kantian humility as the view that we are not capable of acquaintance with the intrinsic properties of external things. Kantian humility would be a variant on Galilean humility (§8.1), substituting intrinsic properties for Galileo's more limited list of colors and their kin. But Langton also suggests that Kantian humility implies propositional ignorance; Kant, on her view, maintains that:

> There exist things in themselves, there exist things that have an intrinsic nature. But we do not know them as they are in themselves: we do not know how they are intrinsically constituted, we do not know what their intrinsic nature is. (p. 22)

The "propositional" disambiguation is explicitly defended by Lewis (2009): the best and most complete fundamental theory we could come up with could be "realized" by a plurality of possible worlds. "There is indeed a true contingent proposition about which of the possible realizations is actual", he argues, "but we can never gain evidence for this proposition, and so can never know it" (p. 207). Think of the situation like this. We know that something plays the "negative charge role" (cf. p. 204) in our world: there's some intrinsic property had by negatively charged substances, which grounds their causal powers. But other intrinsic properties could have played the same role. How do we know which of this plurality of intrinsic properties actually plays the "negative charge role"? By hypothesis, these differences in intrinsic properties do not make for a difference in causal powers; that's just what we mean when we say that a plurality of intrinsic properties could have played the "negative charge role". But causal powers are all we know. So there is a true proposition about which intrinsic property plays the "negative charge role", but we can't know what it is; we can only know that something plays the "negative charge role". We could even give it a name—e.g. "negative charge"—but this won't amount to knowing which property it is; we can give the name "Jack the Ripper" to whomever committed such-and-such crimes, but we still don't know who committed such-and-such crimes (cf. p. 216).

Whether Kantian humility is plausible, on this disambiguation, depends on some metaphysical issues about properties and propositions that are beyond the scope of this book.[2] It seems to me that it is also worth inquiring further as to whether this knowledge, that the Kantian says is impossible, is especially valuable. This seems important given that defenders of Kantian humility suggest that the thesis is contingent on our human nature (Langton 2001,

p. 32; Lewis 2009, p. 218). For there may be many things that we contingently cannot know—the number of moons orbiting some distant planet, beyond the reach of our technology—where such ignorance is of no particular disvalue. (Of course, this raises the question of whether the knowledge denied by the Cartesian skeptic is of any particular value.) Finally, it is worth pointing out that, just as we say that there are two ways to motivate Galilean humility (§8.1), there are analogously two ways to motivate Kantian humility.

We have considered the second already: it is to argue that external things have intrinsic properties of which, as it turns out, we are incapable of knowledge. The first is to deny that external things have intrinsic properties; if external things have no intrinsic properties, then there is no possibility of knowing said properties. Whether that idea is plausible depends on whether we are prepared to posit causal powers without categorical grounds, which metaphysical question is beyond the scope of our discussion here.[3]

8.3 Understanding

The word "understanding" is ambiguous, but there is a species of understanding that is of particular interest to epistemologists (and philosophers of science): **explanatory understanding**, as when you understand why something is the case. Suppose you prepare a stew according to your favorite recipe, but the result tastes terrible. The reason is that you mistakenly added a handful of catnip when you should have added a handful of thyme. At first, you do not understand why the stew tastes terrible, but once you realize that it has catnip in place of thyme, you understand why.

Although there are other interesting species of understanding, we'll focus here on explanatory understanding, which exhibits most of the important features that the various species of understanding seem to share. As I mentioned above, the relationship between understanding and knowledge is controversial in contemporary epistemology,[4] but it is uncontroversial that knowledge that p because q is insufficient for understanding why p. This is because someone might know that p because q, without grasping the explanatory connection between q and p.[5] Consider, again, the case of the nasty stew. Suppose that you think catnip is a delicious herb that tastes very much like thyme. You might realize your mistake, in using catnip in place of thyme, but still not understand why the stew tastes terrible—you have no idea why substituting catnip for thyme would have any significant effect on the stew's flavor. Suppose, however, that you come to know that the stew tastes terrible because catnip was substituted for thyme: you've ruled out any other error in the recipe, or perhaps you're told by an expert chef that the catnip is the culprit. You might still not understand why the stew tastes terrible, even though you know that it tastes terrible because catnip was substituted for thyme. And the reason, so the thought goes, is that you fail to grasp the explanatory connection between the substitution of catnip for thyme and the terrible taste of the stew.

Now this might suggest that what would suffice for understanding, in this case, would be something like knowledge that catnip is not a delicious herb that tastes very much like thyme, or perhaps knowledge that catnip tastes bad, or perhaps knowledge of (acquaintance with) catnip's flavor. But it seems like someone could have all this, and still fail to understand why the stew tastes terrible. For she might not yet "put it all together"; she might have all this knowledge, but not yet have synthesized it into an explanation of the fact that the stew tastes terrible. This is what is meant by saying that understanding requires a grasp of explanatory connections. So: understanding why p requires more than (or perhaps does not even require) knowing that p because q; understanding why p requires grasping the explanation of the fact that p.

Knowledge of the proposition that p because q is insufficient for such a grasp. And, so you might think, no item or items of propositional knowledge will suffice for such a grasp. The grasp of explanatory connections, required for understanding, is a non-propositional attitude, or mental state, or mental action.[6]

Now there is also a contemporary debate over whether understanding is, in some sense, "factive."[7] Knowledge (of the sort epistemologists study) is "factive" in the sense that, necessarily, S knows that p only if it is true that p. Since the grasp required for understanding is non-propositional, the sense in which understanding could be understood as "factive" or "non-factive" is obscure. But we can get a grip on the question of whether understanding is "factive" by considering the case of would-be understanding on the basis of a false theory. Again, imagine that the stew tastes terrible because catnip was substituted for thyme. Suppose, however, that you believe that the stew tastes terrible because your enemy, whom you believe to be a wizard, put a hex on the stew, and you "grasp" how your magical nemesis brought the hex about, using such-and-such spell, whose workings make perfect sense to you.[8] Do you understand why the stew tastes terrible? It seems to me that you do not understand why the stew tastes terrible. You do not enjoy understanding of the flavor of your stew, but rather have a profound misunderstanding of your stew and its history. You do not grasp the explanation of the fact that the stew tastes terrible. What you "grasp" is no explanation at all of that fact. The explanation of some fact is something real, something that exists or obtains, something that in reality explains the relevant fact. ("The explanation," in this respect, is different from "an explanation"—"the explanation" means "the real explanation".) When you "grasp" your wizard enemy's hex, as an explanation of the flavor of your stew, you do not grasp the explanation of the stew's flavor: for what you grasp does not in reality explain the flavor of your stew.

If what I have said above is right, then we can draw an important conclusion about understanding: it has correctness conditions. When I understand why p, my attitude is correct (right, accurate), and when I misunderstand why p, my attitude is incorrect (wrong, inaccurate, mistaken, in error). And if this is right, we can appreciate an important corollary about understanding's object: the object of understanding is not (in general) a representation or body of information or set of beliefs or instances of knowledge, but rather the world (in a broad sense). Understanding represents explanatory connections; those explanatory connects are its object, not (in general) any representation of those explanatory connections. In some cases, representations are the object of understanding, as when I study some theory with an aim to understanding it: think about how a sociologist might study an astrological theory, and come to understand why the theory says what it says. In this case, the object of understanding is a representation, namely, the astrological theory. But this is not generally the case. Take an astronomer who understands why the stars appear as they do: the object of her understanding is the stars, and not any representation of them. Take an astrologer who misunderstands why people act the way they do: the object of her misunderstanding is human behavior, and not any representation of it.

I have sympathetically presented an argument that understanding is a species of non-propositional attitude, requiring a grasp of explanatory connections. And I have argued that a grasp of explanatory connections requires that said connections be real: to understand why p, you must grasp what in reality explains the fact that p. That understanding is "factive", in this sense, opens up the possibility of misunderstanding.

Misunderstanding is a species of error, and with the possibility of error comes the possibility of skepticism. We can distinguish at least three species of skepticism about understanding.

First, we might argue that we understand very little (or nothing) in Cartesian fashion, by appeal to the possibility of systematic misunderstanding. In connection with Cartesian skepticism (§4.2.1) we imagined a demon whose deception consisted in causing me to believe falsehoods. But we can imagine an alternative demon whose deception consists in causing me to misunderstand. (And we can imagine that such a demon leaves at least much of my propositional knowledge intact.) What would such a scenario be like? Imagine a demon who re-creates the world at every instant, so that his creative agency is a completely sufficient explanation for every fact that occurs. It seems to me that this would falsify, at least, the main of our ordinary causal explanations. We are inclined to say that the window broke because it was struck by the baseball; but on the present hypothesis, this is not so: the window broke because the demon caused it to break. In the world we are imagining, there is a systematic illusion of explanatory connections: there is an appearance of such-and-such explanatory connections (e.g. the usual physical explanations we would ordinarily give), but the real explanatory connections are completely different (because they all involve the demon's creative agency). So we might appeal to such a scenario in defense of skepticism about understanding. First premise: you understand why the window broke, by grasping the struck-by-a-baseball explanation, only if you can rule out alternative explanations of the fact that the window broke. Second premise: you cannot rule out the demon scenario just described. Conclusion: you do not understand why the window broke.

Second: we might wonder whether human beings are capable of understanding, or of certain species of understanding, such as understanding the fundamental nature of reality. Here we might appeal to the history of misunderstanding, in support of our skeptical conclusion: we have a lousy track-record when it comes to our attempts to understand, indicative of a contingent inability to do so.

Third: we might articulate a species of skepticism about understanding, akin to Galileo's view that physical objects are not colored (§8.1) and to the view that external things have no intrinsic properties (cf. §8.2). Just as knowledge is possible only if there are truths to be known, understanding is possible (given what I said about it, above) only if there are explanatory connections to be grasped. Consider again causal explanations in particular, and consider the view that causation is not a real relation between events, but rather something "subjective" or "projected". This metaphysical view does not sit well with the possibility of causal understanding, given the assumption that understanding requires grasping real explanatory connections. It is akin to the view that truth is "subjective", which does not sit well with the possibility of propositional knowledge, given the assumption that knowledge is "factive". Some philosophers would reject the view that knowledge is "factive", in defense of the possibility of knowledge of "subjective" truths—think here of the idea that ancient people knew that the earth was flat. The same move could be made when it comes to understanding, in defense of the possibility of understanding through the grasp of "subjective" or "projected" explanatory connections—think here of the idea that you might understand why the stew tastes terrible, by grasping the connection between the wizard's hex and the stew's flavor.

These arguments for skepticism about understanding require further study, but they strike me as promising lines of reasoning. Skepticism about understanding, it seems to me, cannot easily be dismissed (e.g. through a Moorean response). Linda Zagzebski (2001, §V) disagrees. Although she agrees that "[s]kepticism threatens whenever there is a goal that is such that we cannot tell for sure whether we have attained it even after we think we have done so" (p. 245), and that understanding is such a goal, she argues that "[u]nderstanding has internalist conditions for success, whereas knowledge does not" (p. 246). Thus:

> [U]nderstanding skepticism has never had a significant hold on the philo-sophical imagination. That is because the test for success is largely within the practice, the *techne*, itself. Reliably carrying out the goals of a *techne* can be verified within the *techne*. One's understanding of an art work can be proven by successfully giving that understanding to others by teaching it in an art history class, and success in teaching is defined within the practice of teaching. (*Ibid.*)

Now, on the one hand, if understanding has "internalist conditions for success" in the sense that the attitude, of which understanding is a species, cannot be correct or incorrect, then it seems right that skepticism about understanding cannot take hold. Zagzebski suggests such a "non-factive" conception of understanding at one point (p. 244). But if the relevant attitude can be correct or incorrect, then Zagzebski's contrast between understanding and knowledge is implausible. Think of a creationist biology teacher who offers an incorrect explanation of the origin of species, and who manages to pass this explanation on to her students. If "success is defined within the practice of teaching", then this teacher has succeeded, but this is no evidence that she understands the origin of species. The case is analogous to the teacher who teaches her students falsehoods. The fact that I can pass on my would-be understanding seems like no evidence that I really understand, just as the fact that I can pass on my would-be knowledge seems like no evidence that I really know. I conclude, given the possibility of misunderstanding, that skepticism about understanding cannot be dismissed.

8.4 Conclusion

We have considered three alternative species of skepticism, the truth of which is orthogonal to the truth of Cartesian skepticism (§4.2.1). All three deserve further study. In our final chapter, we'll return to Cartesian skepticism and the question of whether it is, in some sense, "impractical".

Readings

The following concern the question of perceptual acquaintance (§8.1).

- B. Russell, "Knowledge by Acquaintance and Knowledge by Description" (Russell 1959, Chapter V).

- M. Johnston, "Is the External World Invisible?" (Johnston 1996).

- B. Stroud, *The Quest for Reality: Subjectivism and the Metaphysics of Colour* (Stroud 2000b).

- A. Byrne and D. Hilbert, *Readings on Color, Volume 1: The Philosophy of Color* (Byrne and Hilbert 1997).

The following concern the thesis of Kantian humility (§8.2), and in particular the thesis as a form of skepticism.

- R. Langton, *Kantian Humility: Our Ignorance of Things in Themselves* (Langton 2001).

- D. Lewis, "Ramseyan Humility" (Lewis 2009).

- R. Langton, "Elusive Knowledge of Things in Themselves" (Langton 2004).

- J. Schaffer, "Quiddistic Knowledge" (Schaffer 2005b).

The following concern the nature of understanding (§8.3).

- L. Zagzebski, "Recovering Understanding" (Zagzebski 2001).

- S. Grimm, "Understanding" (Grimm 2010).

- S. Grimm, "Understanding as Knowledge of Causes" (Grimm forthcoming).

9

Skepsis and Praxis

We have considered (Part II) the three anti-skeptical possibilities, when it comes to the Cartesian skeptical argument (§4.4): that the first premise is false (Chapter 6), that the second premise is false (Chapter 5), and that the argument is invalid (Chapter 7). This chapter explores the remaining possibility: that the conclusion of the argument is true. So we shall here consider the plausibility of Cartesian skepticism. Our discussion will focus on the "practicality" of Cartesian skepticism, and will suggest a number of avenues for future research.

9.1 Mitigated Cartesian skepticism

Recall the distinction between mitigated and unmitigated skepticism, and the knowledge-belief principle (§1.3.3). We can contrast two species of Cartesian skepticism that are distinguished by their corresponding acceptance and rejection of the knowledge-belief principle (cf. §4.2.3):

Unmitigated Cartesian skepticism: No one knows anything (except for propositions about their own existence and mental life), and therefore (because the knowledge-belief principle is true), no one's beliefs about anything (except for propositions about their own existence and mental life) are reasonable.

Mitigated Cartesian skepticism: No one knows anything (except for propositions about their own existence and mental life), but at least some people's beliefs (about propositions other than those about their own existence and mental life) are reasonable. The knowledge-belief principle is (therefore) false.

You might argue that unmitigated Cartesian skepticism implies that we ought to suspend judgment about any proposition other than those about our own existence and mental life. But it is clear that mitigated Cartesian skepticism has no such implication.

In this chapter we'll be looking at the plausibility of mitigated Cartesian skepticism. A question that immediately arises for the mitigated Cartesian skeptic is whether her view can coherently be defended, as against unmitigated Cartesian skepticism: is there a plausible way to argue for mitigated Cartesian skepticism that does not also support unmitigated Cartesian skepticism?

9.1.2 Knowledge vs. reasonable belief

Mitigated Cartesian skepticism jibes with infallibilism (§4.3). Suppose you were to defend Cartesian skepticism by appeal to the following argument (cf. Unger 1975):

> Knowledge requires (reasonable) certainty, (reasonable) certainty is impossible (because it is never reasonable to be absolutely sure of anything), therefore, knowledge is impossible.

While this argument could be appealed to in defense of Cartesian skepticism, you could not plausibly appeal to this argument in defense of *unmitigated* Cartesian skepticism. The reason is that the analogue of this argument, when it comes to reasonable belief, is unconvincing:

> Reasonable belief requires (reasonable) certainty, (reasonable) certainty is impossible (because it is never reasonable to be absolutely sure of anything), therefore, reasonable belief is impossible.

This is unconvincing because the first premise, that reasonable belief requires (reasonable) certainty, is unconvincing. It seems completely reasonable to believe some things, even though you are not certain of those things. For example, I believe that my scheduled flight to Phoenix tomorrow will not be cancelled, but I am not certain of this. My belief, despite my lack of certainty, is reasonable.

Above (§4.3), I set infallibilism aside as orthogonal to the Cartesian skeptical argument (§4.2.1). So let us consider the question of whether we might appeal to the Cartesian skeptical argument in defense of unmitigated Cartesian skepticism. It seems that the plausibility of mitigated Cartesian skepticism depends on the answer to this question, for if an analogue of the Cartesian skeptical argument supports unmitigated Cartesian skepticism, then mitigated Cartesian skepticism cannot be defended by appeal to the

Cartesian skeptical argument. Here, then, is what that analogous argument would look like:

1   I reasonably believe that I have hands only if I can reasonably believe that I'm not deceived by a demon (about whether I have hands).

2   I can't reasonably believe that I'm not deceived by a demon (about whether I have hands).

3   Therefore, I don't reasonably believe that I have hands.

I think this argument is unconvincing as well. The reason is that, so it seems to me, the second premise is false. I believe that I'm not deceived by a demon, and this belief of mine is perfectly reasonable. (Does this belief amount to knowledge? Do I *know* that I'm not deceived by a demon? Here Nozick (§4.2.4) seems right: this is something I do not know. This is something I have no way of knowing.) But if I reasonably believe that I'm not deceived by a demon, then the argument just presented is unsound. Mitigated Cartesian skepticism, as opposed to unmitigated Cartesian skepticism, can therefore be defended by appeal to the Cartesian skeptical argument.

Why should you think that my belief that I'm not deceived by a demon is reasonable? There are a number of different ways you might defend this idea, and a satisfactory examination of them would take us beyond the scope of our study of Cartesian skepticism, which has often touched on the nature of knowledge, and towards a study of the nature of reasonable belief. I'll mention three promising possibilities here. First, you might appeal to Reid's idea (§4.5.2) that not trusting your faculties would get you into a lot of trouble. Not believing that you're not deceived by a demon, so the argument goes, would lead to such lack of trust; such lack of trust would have bad consequences for you; therefore, it is reasonable for you to believe that you're not deceived by a demon. Using terminology recently articulated by Crispin Wright (2004b), you have **strategic entitlement** to believe that you're not deceived by a demon. Second, you might appeal to the idea (Williams 1995, pp. 121–5; Wright 2004b) that not trusting your faculties would undermine the possibility of rational inquiry for you. Not believing that you're not deceived by a demon, so the argument goes, would lead to such lack of trust; such lack of trust would have bad consequences for you; therefore, it is reasonable for you to believe that you're not deceived by a demon. Again using Wright's terminology, you have **entitlement of cognitive project** to believe that you're not deceived by a demon. Third, you might appeal to the idea that demon deception is highly unlikely (§4.5.4). Since it is highly unlikely that you are deceived by a demon, so the argument goes, it is reasonable for you to believe that you are not deceived by a demon.

In any event, what is important about all three of these ideas is that none of them, so I am suggesting, implies that you have any way of knowing that you are not deceived by a demon. They are all at least consistent with mitigated Cartesian skepticism. More would need to be said, about the reasonableness of believing that you are not deceived by a demon, to provide a satisfying defense of mitigated Cartesian skepticism. But we will now move on to considering some objections to (mitigated) Cartesian skepticism.

9.1.2 "Crazy"

Many contemporary epistemologists would say that Cartesian skepticism is, in some sense, a "crazy" view. Some would say that skepticism is a silly idea that ought not to be given serious consideration by academics, except perhaps historians of ideas. But many defenders of the "craziness" of skepticism would assert something more modest: that while skepticism is an interesting view, and one that ought to be studied, it is not something that anyone actually believes or considers a "live" option. Even someone who were to defend skepticism, they would argue, would be doing something like playing "the Devil's advocate"—giving an argumentative defense of a position that she does not actually endorse.[1] The idea that skepticism is not a "live" option is further suggested by the fact that even those philosophers who are relatively sympathetic with skepticism rarely argue that skepticism is *true*, but rather that it cannot be refuted, or that the problem of skepticism cannot be solved, or that skepticism constitutes a paradox, or that the problem of skepticism is a significant problem that has yet to be solved. Barry Stroud (1984), for example, says that the consequences of Cartesian skepticism are "truly disastrous", but that the skeptical problem is none the less "significant" (p. 38).

Is skepticism "crazy", in the sense of not being a "live" option? On the assumption that it is a piece of common sense that we know a lot (beyond propositions about our own existence and mental life), Cartesian skepticism is a **revisionist** position: it denies a piece of common sense. Perhaps that is enough to ensure that Cartesian skepticism is not a "live" option (cf. §5.1). But we should consider the consequences of adopting such an anti-revisionist stance in other areas of philosophy. Consider the view that much of what we do in our ordinary lives is morally wrong, in virtue of our systematic failure to contribute to the alleviation of other people's suffering that results from poverty, famine, and war. Or consider the view that much of what we do in our ordinary lives is morally wrong, in virtue of our systematic harming of non-human animals. Or consider abolitionism (anti-slavery) in the eighteenth century. All three of these views, in what seems like the relevant sense, are (or were) revisionist positions in moral philosophy. They maintain (or maintained) that our common sense moral views are (or were) wrong. Can we dismiss (or could we have dismissed) these views as "crazy", simply in virtue of their conflict with common sense? It seems to me that to consistently adopt the anti-revisionist stance just sketched would be to adopt a thoroughgoing and particularly extreme form of **conservativism**. The best argument against such conservativism resembles Descartes' initial meditations on error: common sense has been wrong in the past, so it is possible that contemporary common sense is wrong. This supports thinking that revisionist philosophical positions, in general, can be "live" options. But if that is true, then there seems no reason not to treat Cartesian skepticism as a "live" option as well.[2]

Let me make two more observations in defense of the "sanity" of mitigated Cartesian skepticism. First, recall that the self-refutation and self-undermining objections do not threaten Cartesian skepticism (§4.5.1). This is especially clear when it comes to mitigated Cartesian skepticism, for the mitigated Cartesian skeptic can coherently and sincerely say that she reasonably believes both the premises and the conclusion of the Cartesian skeptical argument. Second, there is an interesting problem that arises for some species of skepticism that does not arise for Cartesian skepticism. Recall Sextus' distinction between two kinds of skepticism: the Academic skeptic is one who asserts that things cannot be apprehended, whereas the Pyrrhonian skeptic is still investigating (§1.3.3). Sextus implies that the Academic skeptic will not be able to engage in inquiry. As Socrates suggests (§1.4.2), someone who thinks knowledge is impossible will not be inclined to seek it. But if reasonable belief, but not knowledge, is possible, then there is no threat to inquiry, so long as we understand that what we seek, in inquiry, is reasonable belief, and not knowledge.[3]

9.1.3 *The contemporary apraxia objection*

Cartesian skepticism is a species of Academic skepticism, and so it is not threatened by the apraxia objection (§4.5.2). However, it is threatened by a related objection. While the apraxia objection says that suspension of judgment is incompatible with action, this related objection says that, if skepticism were true, our actions would not be rational. Let's take a look at this worry.

Many contemporary philosophers argue that there is a necessary connection between knowledge and rational action. More precisely, they argue that there is a necessary connection between knowing that p and the rationality of treating the proposition that p as a reason for action. Some (Fantl and McGrath 2002, 2007, 2009, Chapter 3) argue that knowing that p is *sufficient* for rationally treating the proposition that p as a reason for action: if you know that p, then it is rational to treat the proposition that p as a reason for action. Imagine that you know that the French will attack at noon. You want to defeat the French, and you know that, if they will attack at noon, you will defeat them if you move your armada into the harbor. It is rational for you to treat the proposition that the French will attack at noon as a reason for action, and to move your armada into the harbor on that basis.

Although it is controversial, the view that knowing that p is sufficient for rationally treating the proposition that p as a reason for action is not in any kind of conflict with Cartesian skepticism. However, others (Hawthorne 2004, pp. 29–30 and *passim*; Stanley 2005, pp. 9–11 and *passim*; Hawthorne and Stanley 2008) defend a different view that is in conflict with Cartesian skepticism.[4] On this other view, knowing that p is *necessary* for rationally treating the proposition that p as a reason for action: if it is rational to treat the proposition that p as a reason for action, then you know that p.[5] Call this the **knowledge requirement view**. Suppose that Cartesian skepticism is true. I do not know that I have hands, I do not know that 2+2=4, I do not know that the French will attack at noon. If the knowledge requirement view is true, then it would not be rational for me to treat any of these propositions—that I have hands, that 2+2=4, that the French will attack at noon—as reasons for action. But it seems like we treat propositions like these as reasons for action all the time. Yesterday I wanted to buy some bagels, but remembered that the bagel shop closes at 2 p.m. and so stayed home, since it was after 2 p.m. I treated the proposition that the bagel shop was closed as a reason for action; that the bagel shop was closed was my reason for staying home. If Cartesian skepticism is true, I did not know that the bagel shop was closed. And if the knowledge requirement view is true, it was not rational for me to stay home, on that basis. If the knowledge requirement view is true, then Cartesian skepticism implies that most of our everyday actions are not rational.

The Cartesian skeptic might be inclined to accept this consequence. (Recall our discussion of the perils of anti-revisionism, §9.1.2.) But this strikes me as implausible. The idea that the scope of our knowledge is limited does not, on its face, suggest that we suffer from any deficit of rationality. If the knowledge requirement view is true, Cartesian skepticism is transformed from a humble concession of our intellectual limitations into a distressing negative evaluation of our practical lives. Better for the Cartesian skeptic to reject the knowledge requirement view—if she can plausibly do so.

The Cartesian skeptic will have two tasks here. The first will be to articulate what is wrong with the arguments that have been put forward in defense of the knowledge requirement view. One argument of this kind appeals to the fact that we often criticize people for acting in ignorance. It seems to me that Jessica Brown (2008b, §4) has successfully refuted this argument: that we often criticize people for Φing without Ψing does not in general support the view that Ψing is necessary for rational Φing. The second task for the skeptic is to argue against the knowledge requirement view, by offering counter-examples. Here's a sketch of how that argument would go.[6] Imagine that you suspect, on the basis of inconclusive evidence, but do not know, that the French will attack at noon. A decision about the movement of the armada is called for, and you are in command. And so you make a command decision: on the assumption that the French will attack at noon, you move your armada into the harbor. You treat the proposition that the French will attack at noon as a reason for action, your action seems rational, but you do not know that the French will attack at noon. If so, the knowledge requirement view is false.[7]

There is much more that could be said about this case, about cases like it, and about the question of whether the knowledge requirement view is true.[8] We are back to Sextus' question about the "standard of action" (§1.4.2): is knowledge required for action, or can we act on the basis of some other standard? From the perspective of mitigated Cartesian skepticism, the answer is obvious: reasonable belief is sufficient for rational action.

9.2 The value of skepticism

The fact that some belief is valuable—e.g. that it would be beneficial for you to have that belief—never suggests that said belief is true. The value of believing that p is no evidence that p. However, one of the main sources of resistance to skepticism, both Ancient, Modern, and contemporary, has been some form of the apraxia objection (§1.4.2). Throughout the history of philosophy, anti-skeptics have consistently appealed to the dangers implicit in skepticism, and the skeptic has been variously depicted as impious, as immoral, or as imprudent (and sometimes as all three of these things). So it is legitimate, if not necessary, to consider here the value of believing mitigated Cartesian skepticism.

9.2.1 *The dangers of skepticism*

Hume's fiercest contemporary critic, **James Beattie** (1735–1803), in his *Essay on the Immutability of Truth, in Opposition to Sophistry and Scepticism* (1770), lamented the fact that skepticism "hath been extended to practical truths of the highest importance, even to the principles of morality and religion". This association of skepticism with immorality and atheism is a common theme in Early Modern discussions. Let's consider the question: is there any important connection between Cartesian skepticism and moral virtue?

Here is a relatively promising line of reasoning: moral virtue requires moral knowledge; the Cartesian skeptic lacks moral knowledge; therefore, the Cartesian skeptic lacks moral virtue. Call this the **virtue argument**.

The second premise of the virtue argument is not obviously true. It seems right that the Cartesian skeptic believes that she lacks moral knowledge, but it is controversial whether someone can know that p while believing that she does not know that p. However, let's grant the second premise for the sake of argument. The first premise has a rich tradition of defenders in the history of philosophy, tracing back to Plato and other non-skeptical Ancient philosophers. Above (§1.1), I suggested that the most important thing about the Ancient skeptics was their opposition to this view that knowledge is required for the good life. They would certainly have opposed the view that knowledge is required for moral virtue. What can be said in their defense?

There are at least two ways in which the first premise of the virtue argument might turn out to be false. First, it might turn out that moral virtue is less a matter of cognition and more a matter of emotion. There is a rich tradition in the history of philosophy that understands the essence of moral virtue in terms of certain emotions (like love, sympathy, concern for the welfare of others), and which downplays the role of moral knowledge. You might think that moral virtue is not a matter of knowing the truth about morality—e.g. knowing that it is your duty to help the poor—but rather a matter of being disposed towards moral emotions—e.g. caring about the welfare of the poor. If so, the first premise of the virtue argument is false.

Second, it might turn out that (reasonable) moral belief can play the same role, vis-à-vis moral virtue, that knowledge would play. Consider a case in which moral knowledge seems conducive to moral action: you are tempted to steal from the cookie jar, but you know that it's wrong to steal, and so you refrain from stealing. You might think that (reasonable) moral belief would do just as well here as moral knowledge. You do not need to know that it is wrong to steal, to resist the temptation to steal. If you believe that it is wrong to steal, you have a reason to resist temptation. If (reasonable) moral belief can play the same role, vis-à-vis moral virtue, that knowledge would play, we may have reason for suspicion about the first premise of the virtue argument.[9]

The virtue argument might be motivated by the thought that, if you do not know what the right thing to do is, then you will not be able to do the right thing (except perhaps by luck)—that you will be indecisive or unable to act (except perhaps randomly). If we again assume that the Cartesian skeptic never knows what the right thing to do is, then it follows from this thought that she will be indecisive. But this line of reasoning trades on an ambiguity in the notion of "knowing what the right thing to do is". In one sense, if you say that someone does not know what the right thing to do is, you are saying that she has no idea what the right thing to do is: she is unable to come to any conclusion about the matter. Such a person would be indecisive (let's assume), but there is no reason to think that the (mitigated) Cartesian skeptic lacks knowledge of the right thing to do, in *that* sense. Now, in another sense, if you say that someone does not know what the right thing to do is, you are saying that she lacks *knowledge* of the right thing to do, but may very well have come to a conclusion about the matter. But there is no reason to think that such a person would be indecisive.

To appreciate this point, imagine that you are waiting in line to vote in a referendum. The issue is complex and there is widespread disagreement among intelligent people about the right way to vote. You have given the issue some thought, although not as much as you might have given it, and have come to the tentative conclusion that voting "No" is the right thing to do, and so have decided to vote "No". You do not know, and do not take yourself to know, that voting "No" is the right thing to do, but this is what you believe is the right thing to do, and so you do it. You do not suffer from indecision—you do not freak out at the last minute and not vote, on account of not *knowing* what the right thing to do is. A certain kind of neurotic cannot bring herself to do anything, unless she knows that it is the right thing to do. But the non-neurotic is happy to base her actions on (reasonable) belief that falls short of knowledge.

Will there be any important practical difference between the person who thinks she knows that p and the person who thinks that she merely reasonably believes that p? This question deserves further study. You might think that the person who thinks that she knows will enjoy *some* kind of decisiveness that the person who thinks that she merely reasonably believes will not enjoy. But it is obscure whether this kind of decisiveness is something desirable or admirable. It is characteristic of violent fanatics that they take themselves to know the truth about morality (or politics, or religion, or whatever). You will not find a terrorist bomber who says: "I don't *know* that blowing up the embassy is the right thing to do, but after careful consideration I *think* that it is". A certain kind of decisiveness in moral matters may be unavailable to the Cartesian skeptic, but it is obscure whether this is any kind of mark against her position.

9.2.2 *Hume and Franklin on the value of skepticism*

In the final section of his *Enquiry concerning Human Understanding* (1748), having conceded that "no durable good can ever result from … *excessive* scepticism," (§XII.2, p. 159) and that such skepticism would not be "beneficial to society," (p. 160) David Hume describes two species of "*mitigated* scepticism or *academical* philosophy" that, he argues, are "both durable and useful" (§XII.3, p. 161) and "which may be of advantage to mankind" (p. 162). The second species of skepticism that Hume discusses is a kind of empiricism, which leads to "the limitation of our enquiries to such subjects as are best adapted to the narrow capacity of human understanding" (*ibid.*). This results in a negative outlook for "Divinity or Theology", "[m]orals and criticism", and to Hume's famous rejection of metaphysics as "sophistry and illusion" (p. 165) But Hume does not here have in mind Cartesian skepticism. Cartesian skepticism implies that we have no knowledge in theology, criticism, and metaphysics, but it also implies that we have no knowledge in physics, biology, and history. The Cartesian skeptic might propose limiting our inquiries to questions about our own existence and mental life, but that seems neither "useful" nor "advantageous" to anyone. And, as I argued above (§9.1.2), mitigated Cartesian skepticism is perfectly compatible with inquiry.

The first species of skepticism Hume considers, however, has more in common with mitigated Cartesian skepticism. Hume writes that:

> The greater part of mankind are naturally apt to be affirmative and dogmatical in their opinions; and while they see objects only on one side, and have no idea of any counterpoising argument, they throw themselves precipitously into the principle, to which they are inclined; nor have they any indulgence for those who entertain opposite sentiments. [...] But could such dogmatical reasoners become sensible of the strange infirmities of human understanding ... such a reflection would naturally inspire them with more modesty and reserve, and diminish their fond opinion of themselves, and their prejudice against their antagonists. [...] [A] small tincture of Pyrrhonism might abate their pride, by showing them, that the few advantages, which they may have attained over their fellows, are but inconsiderable, if compared with the universal perplexity and confusion, which is inherent in human nature. (p. 161)

What Hume says here about "a small tincture of Pyrrhonism" applies, I would like to suggest, to mitigated Cartesian skepticism. There is an important difference between someone who takes herself to know that p, on the one hand, and someone who believes that p, and who takes her belief to be reasonable, but who believes that she does not know that p, on the other. These two believers have different attitudes toward their beliefs, and we should expect these differences in attitude to be accompanied by differences in the believers' attitudes toward themselves and toward others. First, there is a sense in which knowledge, but not reasonable belief, brings inquiry to an end. A person who believes (that p), but who does not think that she yet knows (that p), is capable of further inquiry (about whether p), in a way that a person who takes herself to know (that p) is not. For example, as

Hume argues, the person who takes herself to know will be less disposed to discover the "counterpoising argument" to her own position. Second, whether we take ourselves to know can influence how we interact with people with whom we disagree. A person who believes (that p), but who does not think that she knows (that p), is capable of engaging with the views and arguments of someone who believes that ~p, in a way that a person who takes herself to know (that p) is not. For example (cf. §2.2), it seems coherent to regard someone else's belief (that p) as reasonable, even though you disagree with that person about whether p. But it does not seem coherent to think that someone else knows (that p), when you disagree with that person about whether p.

As David Fate Norton (2002) puts it, Hume recommends philosophical doubt, where "doubt" does not mean suspension of judgment (as in Descartes' hypothetical doubt, §4.1.1), but rather a certain "cognitive activity or philosophical method" (p. 384). We are to doubt our beliefs, that is "we are to attend to the counter-evidence and counter-arguments; we are to avoid precipitate decisions on the issues before us; we are to take note of the inherent limitations of our faculties" (*ibid.*). On my view, mitigated Cartesian skepticism has the same implications: in the absence of knowledge, this species of doubt is inevitable.

We might put it like this: the mitigated Cartesian skeptic adopts a modest or humble attitude toward the status of her beliefs. Does this show that mitigated Cartesian skepticism is "useful" or "advantageous"? It seems to me that it does. The mitigated Cartesian skeptic will be disposed toward sincere inquiry and respectful dialogue with other inquirers. On the assumption that these dispositions are both individually and socially valuable, mitigated Cartesian skepticism is both individually and socially valuable as well.

In his *Autobiography*, **Benjamin Franklin** (1706–90) suggests a related argument in defense of the value of skepticism, which appeals to the value of employing skeptical language. In Philadelphia, around 1727, Franklin and some friends formed a debating society called the "Junto". Given that all discussion was "to be conducted in the sincere Spirit of Enquiry after Truth ... all Expressions of Positiveness in Opinion, or of direct Contradiction, were after some time made contraband & prohibited under very small pecuniary Penalties" (p. 61).[10] Franklin later describes the specifics of these prohibitions in his discussion of the virtue of humility:

I ... forbid myself ... the Use of every Word or Expression in the Language that imported fix'd Opinion; such as *certainly*, *undoubtedly*, &c. and I adopted instead of them, *I conceive*, *I apprehend*, or *I imagine* a thing to be so and so, or it appears to be at present. (p. 94; see also p. 18)

Franklin would say the same thing about claims to knowledge that he says here about claims to certainty and indubitableness: they should be replaced with humbler language, such as claims to belief or opinion. The point of all this is to further "the chief Ends of Conversation", namely, "to *inform*, or to be *informed*, to *please* or to *persuade*" (p. 18). Humble language ("I believe", "In my opinion", etc.) is conductive to the flow of information between conversational participants, makes conversation more pleasant, and provides for the possibility of rational persuasion. Dogmatic language ("I know", "It is certain", etc.) results in entrenchment, unpleasant conflict and divisiveness, and dialectical standoffs. But humble language is skeptical language: the Cartesian skeptic, so long as she is sincere, will not claim knowledge or certainty on any topic (apart from the topics of her own existence and mental life). Franklin's humility might be achieved without being a Cartesian skeptic, of course. But the Cartesian skeptic is well-positioned to acquire the virtue: she need only be sincere in what she says about the status of her beliefs. Compare the person who takes herself to know: she will need to say or suggest that she does not know, while taking herself to know, i.e. she will need to be insincere in what she says about the status of her beliefs.

If Franklin is right, there is a species of virtuous humility that the mitigated Cartesian skeptic will easily acquire. On the assumption that possessing such humility is both individually and socially valuable, mitigated Cartesian skepticism is both individually and socially valuable as well.

9.3 Conclusion

The skepticism that I have sympathetically described here is inspired by Descartes' skeptical meditations (§4.1), but assumes no form of infallibilism (§4.3). Unlike Pyrrhonian skepticism (§1.3.3), it is not a way of life, but it has practical implications. Unlike Pyrrhonian fideism (§1.5), it lacks conservative and religious implications. Like all species of Academic skepticism (§1.3.3), it is a philosophical position—and one that, I have argued (§9.1.2), should be taken as seriously as its competitors (cf. Part II).

Descartes' story of the malicious demon (§4.1) seems far removed from everyday life. It seems like an absurd fantasy, cooked up in isolation from worldly concerns, designed to serve a project of pure inquiry, and one that lacks practical, social, or political implications. In this chapter I have tried to suggest otherwise: far from being "impractical", Cartesian skepticism can be understood to have individual and social benefits. The reason for this, I think, is that Descartes' story is not so far removed from everyday life as it seems. Perhaps no one has ever been deceived as thoroughly as Descartes imagines himself being deceived, but human beings have been deceived in deep and systematic ways—and in ways that have had profound ethical implications. The false testimony of political and religious authorities has successfully kept millions of people in the dark about the rapes and murders of millions of other people. And worse: it has persuaded millions to believe that those rapes and murders were justified. And worse still: it has persuaded millions to participate in those rapes and murders. This stuff wasn't cooked up in the philosopher's study—it happened at Auschwitz, in Rwanda, at My Lai, at Abu Ghraib. Propaganda and ideology are just the most blunt examples of what we might call everyday demons: the deceptions that we human beings have always, and will always, be prone to. These include hatred on the basis of sexual orientation, race, and countless other properties, as well as benign forms of wishful thinking and bias. Considered in this context, Descartes' surprising project—the general demolition of one's opinions—looks less absurd, and more like what it is: a way of coping with our all-too-human ability to err. And whether or not there would be a way to keep Descartes' demon from imposing on you (as Descartes suggests), there does seem to be hope for keeping our everyday demons at bay: the humility of mitigated skepticism.

Readings

Consult the following, on the view that "knowledge is the norm of practical reasoning" (§9.1).

- J. Fantl and M. McGrath, "Evidence, Pragmatics, and Justification" (Fantl and McGrath 2002).

- J. Hawthorne and J. Stanley, "Knowledge and Action" (Hawthorne and Stanley 2008).

- J. Brown, "Knowledge and Practical Reason" (Brown 2008b)

The following were discussed above, in connection with the value of skepticism (§9.2).

- D. Hume, *Enquiry concerning Human Understanding*, §XII (e.g. in Hume 1975).

- B. Franklin, *Autobiography* (e.g. in Franklin 2008).

Notes

Epistle to the Reader

1   In his book *Scepticism Comes Alive* (2005), p. 77.
2   I mean this in a different, but not altogether different, sense than that employed by Pablo Neruda: "Anyone who doesn't read Cortázar is doomed. Not to read him is a grave invisible disease which in time can have terrible consequences. Something similar to a man who had never tasted peaches. He would be quietly getting sadder, noticeably paler, and probably little by little, he would lose his hair."
3   *The Search for Truth by means of the Natural Light* (1701), 512.

Chapter 1

1   By "Ancient", I mean the period often called "classical antiquity", i.e. the period spanning the eighth century BC through the sixth century AD; by "Early Modern", I mean the period spanning the sixteenth century AD through the eighteenth century AD; by "contemporary", I mean the present, including the last 50 years or so.
2   On the distinction between skepticism and these earlier philosophies, see Sextus, *Outlines*, I 210–19.
3   On the relationship between skepticism and medical empiricism see Sextus, *Outlines*, I 236–41; Annas and Barnes 1985, Introduction; Barnes 1990, pp. 5–7. The positions of the two schools were, at least, consistent.
4   For English quotations from Plato I am using G. M. A. Grube's translations of *Apology* and *Meno*, both in Plato 1997.
5   I mean "rejection" to cover suspension of judgment (cf. §1.3.3).
6   For English quotations from Diogenes I am using R. D. Hicks' translation of the *Lives* (Diogenes Laertius 1925).
7   Cf. Montaigne's critique of the value of knowledge (§1.6). See also Frede 1979, p. 24.
8   For English quotations from Sextus I am using Julia Annas and Jonathan Barnes' translation of *Outlines of Scepticism* (Sextus Empiricus 2000) and Richard Bett's translation of *Against the Logicians* (Sextus Empiricus 2005).

9 For English quotations from Cicero I am using Charles Brittain's translation of *On Academic Scepticism* (Cicero 2006).

10 In this respect, like the ten modes, the five modes are not five distinct skeptical arguments (cf. Hankinson 1995, p. 186; Barnes 1990, chapter 5).

11 I follow Annas and Barnes here in using "standard"; "standard" and "criterion" are interchangeable and both translate "κριτήριον". For more on the meaning of "κριτήριον", see Striker 1996, Essay 2.

12 Compare, for example, the idea that skepticism involves refraining from "claims", "knowledge-claims", or "truth-claims" (Burnyeat 1980, p. 27, p. 51; Barnes 1990, pp. 142–3; Vogt 2010a).

13 This terminology is from Barnes 1982, p. 61.

14 'Iff' means "if and only if".

15 On this interpretation, see Striker 1996, pp. 138–40; cf. Williams 2010, pp. 298–300.

16 On this interpretation, which follows Cicero's in *On Academic Scepticism*, see Burnyeat 1980, pp. 32–6; Striker 2010. See also Hume, *Enquiry concerning Human Understanding*, §XII.

17 Cicero, for his part, says that both Arcesilaus (*Scepticism*, 1.45) and Carneades (2.28) recommended suspension of judgment about whether knowledge is possible, although Cicero himself is sympathetic with maintaining that knowledge is impossible (2.28; see also Striker 2010, p. 196). Against Cicero's interpretation, see Annas and Barnes 1985, p. 14; Striker 1996, p. 136.

18 This will raise an urgent question of why the propositions expressed by (4*) can legitimately be exempted from suspension of judgment. How, for example, can (4*) avoid Agrippa's trilemma (§1.2.2)? Myles Burnyeat (1980) argues that "[s]tatements which merely record how things appear … are not called true or false", in the debate between the skeptic and the dogmatist (p. 30). On the assumption that propositions are essentially entities which are true or false, it follows that (4*) does not express a proposition—and thus there is no question of belief, disbelief, or suspension of judgment here. As Burnyeat puts it, "belief is the accepting of something as true", and so "[t]here can be no question of belief about appearance" (p. 31).

19 What follows applies, *mutatis mutandis*, to the species of non-rustic Pyrrhonian we imagined above, who believes that the skeptical phrases are true.

20 Sextus writes that "many things are said that allow for an exception, and just as we say that Zeus is the father of the gods and humans, allowing for the exception of himself …, so too, when we say that there is no demonstration, we say this allowing for the exception of this argument showing that there is no demonstration" (*Against the Logicians* 2.479).

21 From W. D. Ross' translation in Aristotle 1984.

22 Burnyeat (1980) writes that the skeptic has no beliefs. However, he employs an unorthodox conception of belief, on which there are no beliefs save those about "real existence". The spirit of his view jibes with the interpretation of Pyrrhonian skepticism as urbane or essential skepticism.

23 On this understanding, Pyrrhonian skepticism is second-order (§1.3.1).

24 Historically, the appeal to appearances and natural feelings is associated with Arcesilaus. His reply to the apraxia objection prompted the Stoic charge that the skeptic had reduced herself to the state of an irrational animal. In response to this, Carneades proposed "reasonable" or "persuasive" appearances as the skeptic's standard of action. In this way, the Academy moved toward mitigated skepticism (cf. §1.3.3).

25 However, compare the fact that medical empiricists and their competitors prescribed different courses of treatment (Annas and Barnes 1985, p. 16).

26 Here (and in what follows) I follow Richard Popkin's (1979) influential account. See also Schmitt 1983.

27 It is controversial whether Montaigne was, in fact, a religious believer. As Popkin points out (1979, p. 55), fideism has been eloquently articulated both by atheists—either ironically, or out of fear of censorship (or worse), or both—and by true believers. I follow Popkin in treating Montaigne's expressions of fideism as sincere.

28 For English quotations from Montaigne I am using M. A. Screech's translation of "An Apology for Raymond Sebond", in Montaigne 2003, to which I refer with page numbers.

29 For English quotations from Bayle I am using Richard Popkin's translation of the *Historical and Critical Dictionary* (Bayle 1965), to which I refer with page numbers.

30 It is even more controversial whether Bayle was a religious believer. I assume nothing here about that debate.

31 We'll return to this view, which I'll call "Galilean humility", below (§8.1).

32 Thus the idea that "there are several worlds [that] may present different features and be differently governed" (p. 587). The concept of alternative worlds was to play a decisive role in the Enlightenment; cf. Fontanelle's *Conversations on the Plurality of Worlds* (1686). The appeal to different heavenly bodies in connection with cultural or political difference traces back at least as far as Lucian's *Veritae Historia*, which describes inhabitants of the Sun and the Moon in the same style that Herodotus and Pliny described inhabitants of foreign lands.

33 See, in connection with this, the Early Modern debate over "innate ideas". It seems to me that one of Descartes' innovations (cf. Chapter 4) was to get away from this issue, and in general away from the focus on disagreement (cf. Chapter 2), in his articulation of the skeptical argument.

34 In this connection, see also Hume's appeal to custom and habit (§3.1.2).

35 On the question of the compatibility of skepticism and fideism, see Popkin 1979, pp. xvii–xx, and Penelhum 1983.

36 A contested term; I understand "secularism" such that secularism implies that non-religious worldviews and ways of life are "live" options.

37 Annas and Barnes (1985, p. 8) say that Modern skeptics attacked knowledge and the Ancients attacked belief. But this can't be quite right. The "Cartesian skeptic" (§4.2.1) says that we have very little knowledge.

But the Ancient skeptic doesn't say that we have very little belief. Rather, she suspends judgments and gives up her beliefs. But the Modern skeptic doesn't "give up her knowledge", whatever that might mean. She gives up her *claims* to knowledge. But the Ancient skeptic did not merely give up her "claims to belief", whatever that might mean.

38 In a similar vein, Annas and Barnes (1985, p. 8) complain that Descartes' doubt is a "sham", because it has no influence on Descartes' actions; but if the apraxia objection (§1.4.2) can be overcome, this seems at least partially true of the Pyrrhonian's suspension of judgment.

39 This relates, of course, to questions of scope and target (§1.3.2).

40 "Galilean humility" described below (§8.1), is both non-rustic and non-urbane (§1.3.2): only the philosopher-scientist is in a position to acquire knowledge. This represents a remarkable reversal of the Pyrrhonian's stance.

Chapter 2

1 Cf. Gutting 1982, p. 83; Kelly 2005a, pp. 174–5; 2010, p. 112; Elga 2007, p. 488; Bergmann 2009, p. 336.

2 Cf. White 2005, p. 445; Feldman 2006, p. 231; 2007, p. 207; Christensen 2007, p. 192; cf. Elga 2007.

3 In connection with Chisholm's point, note that Barnes (1990) abandons the requirement, for legitimate employment of a standard C, that you are justified in believing that it is legitimate to employ C, in favor of the requirement that you not "return a negative or sceptical answer" to the question of whether it is legitimate to employ C (p. 35). Chisholm's point is that a negative answer might well undermine the legitimate employment of C, but that a skeptical answer (i.e. suspension of judgment) need not do so. For his part, Barnes disagrees (p. 143; cf. Hazlett 2012, pp. 212–15).

4 In addition to this, other important cases include cases of serial disagreement (Elga 2009, pp. 286–7) and cases of multi-peer disagreement (van Inwagen 2010, pp. 27–8).

5 Frances (2005) is aware of this objection, and thus (for example) formulates eliminativism as the view that "all occurrences of 'S believes P' are false" (p. 30; see also p. 36, pp. 69–70). But this is a semantic thesis, not a thesis in the philosophy of mind or psychology (which is what eliminativism purports to be). (Compare: what zoology tells us is that whales aren't fish, not that all occurrences of <x is both a whale and a fish> are false.) But isn't the relevant semantic thesis (and others like it) debated by experts? Perhaps, although to generate a skeptical conclusion (on Frances' view) it must be "obvious to most of us" that the contents of our beliefs are incompatible with the relevant semantic thesis (p. 32). Imagine that you're eating a cheeseburger. It's unclear whether this entails anything semantic, e.g. that the sentence "I'm eating a cheeseburger" would be true if you were to utter it.

Chapter 3

1   Hume's letters, and contemporary anecdotes, reveal that he was an atheist, and therefore that his expressions of fideism (e.g. *Enquiry concerning Human Understanding*, §XII.3, p. 163) were ironic.

2   Why do I proceed to examine Hume's *Enquiry* (1748) in advance of Descartes' *Meditations* (1641)? This historical reversal is due to the fact that the "Humean skeptical argument" (I shall argue) suffers from a serious flaw (§3.3) that does not affect the "Cartesian skeptical argument" (§4.2.1).

3   For citations from the *Enquiry* and the *Enquiry concerning the Principles of Morals*, I provide section and part, as well as page numbers in Hume 1975; for citations from the *Treatise* I provide book, part, and section, as well as page numbers in Hume 1978; for citations from the *Abstract* I provide page numbers in Hume 1978.

4   As Peter Millikan (2002, p. 109) argues, the argument of the *Enquiry* is both a better argument and more obviously a skeptical argument than the argument of the *Treatise*. For a much more thorough treatment of Hume's argument than the one I am about to give, see Millikan 2002, §§3–10.

5   Perhaps. For the Pyrrhonians, you don't choose to suspend judgment on the basis of the fact that you ought to suspend judgment, but rather are brought to suspension of judgment by the apparent equipollence of reasons. But this makes it obscure why it matters that appearances are "passive and unwilled", as it suggests that beliefs are "passive and unwilled" as well.

6   Perhaps. Although Hume distances himself from Pyrrhonism (*Enquiry*, §XII), it's unclear how different his philosophy is from theirs, for just as the Pyrrhonians were content to "go along" with their involuntary appearances, for practical purposes, Hume is content to "go along" with his involuntary beliefs, for practical purposes.

7   Compare the "argumentative constraint on knowledge", below (§3.2.2).

8   There seem to be other kinds of cases of knowledge without the ability to give a good argument. One kind of case: it seems like you can know something but be unable to articulate your reasons, as when you recognize someone but couldn't say what their distinguishing characteristics are (cf. §5.2.2). Another kind of case: non-human animals seem to know various things, but are completely unable to give arguments (cf. Hume, *Treatise*, I.iii.16, *Enquiry*, §IX).

Chapter 4

1   With the exception of "Galilean humility" (§8.1).

2   Although Augustine suggests that the Academics were actually secret Platonists (chapters 17–20); in this respect he resembles those contemporary secularists who are fond of thinking that historical Christians were secret atheists.

3 For English quotations from Descartes I am using John Cottingham's translation of the *Meditations* in Descartes 1984, Dugald Murdoch's translation of the *Rules for the Direction of the Mind* in Descartes 1985, Robert Stoothoff's translation of the *Discourse on the Method* in Descartes 1985, and Murdoch and Stoothoff's translation of the *Search for Truth by means of the Natural Light* in Descartes 1984. References are to page numbers in the Adam and Tannery edition of Descartes' works.

4 There is no direct evidence that Descartes was insincere in his religious assertions; contrast, in this connection, Hume (Chapter 3). It can be argued that Descartes engaged in dissimulation about religion in the *Meditations*, on the ground that some of his arguments are of such poor quality that they were not plausibly advanced in good faith (Curley 1986). If we take his arguments seriously, however, then there is no good reason to think that Descartes was insincere (cf. Popkin 1979, p. 172; Williams 1997, p. ix).

5 I follow the text of the *Meditations* here, but cf. the same line of reasoning laid out in the *Discourse on the Method*.

6 That said, the *Meditations* may be (as they say) "based on a true story": see *Discourse*, Part Two, 11. On the genre of the *Meditations*, see Rorty 1986; Williams 1997.

7 The worry is that "[m]y habitual opinions keep coming back", and thus the strategy of "pretending for a time that these former opinions are utterly false and imaginary" (22).

8 It is also worth noting that this is not really *Descartes'* insight; for a discussion of the argument in Plotinus, Augustine, and Avicenna, see Sorabji 2006, chapter 12.

9 Compare someone living before the invention of microscopes who advances a species of skepticism about microphysics, on which the microscopic nature of things is unknowable. Her argument would not generalize on the subject of knowledge, because of historical differences in access to microscopes and other such devices.

10 The necessity of mathematics is not the issue here; Descartes held mathematics to be contingent, and my argument here does not assume the contingency of mathematics.

11 Cf. the joke about the mathematician: she claims some lemma is obvious, is challenged by someone who wonders whether it is obvious, reflects on the lemma for an hour, and concludes, "Yes, it's obvious."

12 For an alternative argument for Cartesian skepticism that jettisons the first premise of the Cartesian skeptical argument, in favor of the underdetermination principle, see Brueckner 1994.

13 At least, not given how things stand right now. In some movies, characters are depicted as coming to know that they are "inside of" a computer simulation. It is unclear whether this is possible. Suppose you hear a voice: "Hello! It's me, the cunning demon of utmost power that's been deceiving you all this time." Why trust the testimony of this voice? Why think that what this voice is telling you is true?

14 I mean that one of these four must be the case. It is possible that more than one of these four is the case. In jargon: the possibilities are jointly exhaustive, but not mutually exclusive.

15 However, I shall argue that being a Cartesian skeptic has no ill effects (Chapter 9).

16 Some contemporary epistemologists appeal here to a "brain in a vat" scenario: you are nothing more than a brain, hooked up to a computer simulation. People sometimes suggest that *that* is somehow more "realistic" than the scenario Descartes describes. "Demons"? Ridiculous. But reality as computer simulation? Totally possible." If you take the "brain in a vat" possibility that seriously, the skeptic may have already won the argument. That said, many of Descartes' seventeenth-century readers would have found the demon scenario more "realistic" than do most contemporary readers (Popkin 1979, pp. 180–1).

17 I borrow the case from Elliot Sober, who uses it to make an entirely different point.

18 For citations from Berkeley's *Dialogues* I'll give page numbers from Berkeley 1979.

19 For another reason for suspicion about idealism as anti-skepticism, see Greco 2008, pp. 117–18.

20 It's beyond the scope of our study to consider Kant's "transcendental idealism" and its anti-skeptical credentials. On this topic, consult Stroud 1983; 2000a; Stern 2008; and cf. §4.5.6.

21 This is why Hilary Putnam (1981, Chapter 1) imagines that the computer and the vat were not intentionally created by anyone.

Chapter 5

1 For example, Scott Soames (2005) sympathetically describes the "ironic nature of Moore's presentation" (p. 23).

2 Many of Moore's essays were originally delivered as lectures, and they retain the style of addresses to an audience. See, in particular, "Hume's Theory Examined", "Proof of an External World", and "Four Forms of Scepticism".

3 This is why the bulk of Moore's paper "Proof of an External World" (1939) is orthogonal to the problem of Cartesian skepticism. The conclusion of Moore's argument in that paper is that external things exist; his target is idealism, and not skepticism. However, there is some important epistemological content in the last two paragraphs of the paper (pp. 148–50), to which we'll return (§5.2.2).

4 Compare the presuppositions of the other skeptical arguments that we've considered (§4.6).

5 There are other anti-skeptical strategies that reject the second premise. For example, you might argue that the second premise is false, because demon deception is unlikely (§4.5.4). For another, you might appeal to an "externalist" conception of evidence (cf. Williamson 2001, chapter 8). Finally, you might appeal to the idea that you are "entitled" to believe that you are not deceived by a demon, and argue that such "entitlement" amounts to knowledge (cf. §9.1.2).

6 For a quick survey leading up to the state of the art, see Sosa 1991; 2007; Goldman 1992; 2002; Greco 2010. Like all philosophical views, reliabilism is controversial. When evaluating anti-skeptical strategies, it is important not to get distracted by issues that may be orthogonal to the question of skepticism. For example, you might think that reliability comes in degrees, and conclude that the reliabilist owes us an account of *how* reliable a way of forming beliefs has to be, for true beliefs formed in that way to amount to knowledge. But it is obscure whether this bears on the status of reliabilism *as an answer to the problem of Cartesian skepticism*. The proposed problem for reliabilism may be a genuine problem for the view, but it does seem to bear on reliabilism's specifically *anti-skeptical* credentials. For criticisms of reliabilism that speak to said credentials, see Stroud 1994; Fumerton 1995, Chapter 6; Vogel 2000.

7 Note, in particular, that the proposed account faces the "Gettier problem", on which see Gettier 1963; Shope 1983.

8 Resistance to this idea dates back at least as far as Sextus Empiricus, who would compare the reliabilist to someone searching for gold in a dark room (*Against the Logicians*, 1.52) and to archers shooting at targets in the dark (2.325). In the dark one cannot tell whether one has grasped the gold or hit the target, and without knowledge that one's beliefs are reliably-formed, one cannot tell whether one's beliefs are true. If reliabilism is true, these comparisons are inapt: if someone *knows* that p, then she *knows,* or at least is in a position to know, that she has grasped or hit upon the truth.

9 I have avoided appealing to formalism and the apparatus of possible worlds in explaining the notion of safety. For those familiar with the jargon: S's belief (that p) is safe iff p $\Box \to$ S believes that p, i.e. iff in nearby worlds in which p, S believes that p.

10 For more on this point, see Hill 1996, pp. 579–80; Pryor 2004. Recall the neo-Moorean's rejection of the argumentative constraint on knowledge (§5.2.2).

11 For further discussion, see Sosa 1994; Stroud 1994; Vogel 2000; Van Cleve 2003. See also the "problem of easy knowledge" (Cohen 2002).

Chapter 6

1 On which see Hawthorne 2004, pp. 31–6.

2 It is easy to confuse the closure principle with a rule of inference called "*modus ponens*". *Modus ponens* says that you can infer the proposition that q from the propositions that p and that if p, then q. Closure says something different: it says that you can infer the proposition that S can know that q from the propositions that S knows that p and that the proposition that p entails the proposition that q.

3 One reason why this formulation isn't perfect: it seems to imply that you "can" recognize all entailments. But perhaps some entailments are beyond your ability to recognize. The same, *mutatis mutandis*, when it comes to your ability to perform deductions.

4 As with the notion of safety (§5.2.3), I've avoided appealing to formalism and the apparatus of possible worlds in explaining the notion of sensitivity. For those familiar with the jargon: S's belief (that p) is sensitive iff $\sim p \; \square \rightarrow \sim$(S believes that p), i.e. iff in nearby worlds in which $\sim p$, S doesn't believe that p.

5 See, for example, Nozick 1981, pp. 179–96; Sosa 1999; Williamson 2001, Chapter 7; Kripke 2011.

6 On which see Makinson 1965; Kyburg 1970; Hawthorne 2004, pp. 46–50.

7 See Vogel 1990b, pp. 13–15.

8 Compare John Hawthorne's (2004) appeal, in defense of closure, to a slogan used to advertise lottery tickets: "Hey, you never know" (p. 8).

9 Cf. Vogel 1990b, pp. 15–20.

Chapter 7

1 Perhaps not: the validity of *modus ponens* has been challenged, but for reasons that are orthogonal to the validity of the Cartesian skeptical argument.

2 For more on these issues, see Malcolm 1942; 1963; 1977. For a contemporary defense of Wittgenstein's approach to skepticism, see Wright 2004a.

3 See Cohen 1988; DeRose 1992; 1995; Lewis 1996. See also Schaffer 2004a; 2005a; 2007. Schaffer's "contrastivism" is importantly different from standard contextualism, but offers a similar approach to the problem of Cartesian skepticism.

4 These include Gricean approaches (Schaffer 2004b; Rysiew 2001; Hazlett 2009), sensitive invariantism (Stanley 2007; Hawthorne 2004; Fantl and McGrath 2009), and relativism about knowledge attributions (MacFarlane 2005).

5 Unless she rejects (1d) and defends nonclosure (Chapter 6).

Chapter 8

1 From William R. Shea and Mark Davie's translation in Galilei 2012, p. 119.

2 Consider, in particular, "quidditism" (Lewis 2009, pp. 209–12).

3 On that issue, see Molnar 2007; see also Langton 2001, p. 32.

4 On this issue, see Elgin 1996, pp. 122–9; Zagzebski 2001; Kvanvig 2003; Riggs 2003; Grimm 2006; 2010, forthcoming; Pritchard 2010.

5 On this point, see Grimm forthcoming.

6 See Zagzebski 2001; Riggs 2003; Grimm 2010, forthcoming.

7 On this issue see Elgin 1996, pp. 122–9; 2006; 2009; Zagzebski 2001; Kvanvig 2003; Riggs 2003; Grimm 2010; Pritchard 2010.

8 I've here adapted Stephen Grimm's (2010) case of the misunderstanding shaman.

Chapter 9

1 These issues are complicated by the fact that it is unclear that philosophers typically believe the positions that they defend. But there is meant to be some kind of difference between skepticism, which is not a "live" option, and, say, reliabilism, which is a "live" option.

2 For more on the consequences of anti-revisionism outside of epistemology, see Frances 2005, pp. 169–71. On the peculiar appeal of anti-revisionism in epistemology, see pp. 76–7.

3 As well, there is no threat to inquiry from Cartesian skepticism, given its modality (§4.2.3). Even if it is incoherent to seek what is impossible, it is not incoherent to seek what no one has.

4 Consider also the view that knowledge that p is necessary for proper assertion that p (Williamson 1996; 2001, chapter 11; DeRose 2002; Hawthorne 2004, pp. 21–4 and *passim*; Stanley 2005, p. 10 and *passim*; cf. Weiner 2005).

5 The authors cited here also defend the view that knowledge that p is sufficient for rationally treating the proposition that p as a reason for action.

6 Cf. the discussion of Jack Aubrey in Weiner 2005.

7 On the most natural way of imagining this case, you not only don't know that the French will attack at noon, but you also believe that you don't know that the French will attack at noon. So if what I've said about the case is right, then it is also a counterexample to the view that it is not rational to treat the proposition that p as a reason for action if you believe that you don't know that p.

8 On this kind of case, see Schiffer 2007; Hawthorne and Stanley 2008, pp. 581–6. See also Brown 2008a.

9 It is important here not to assume that someone who knows that p is necessarily more confident that p than someone who merely believes that p. A fool can be highly confident that p, but fail to know that p, while a sage might know that p, but without such a high degree of confidence. But even when someone is aware that her belief (that p) does not amount to knowledge, it seems that she still might be highly confident that p: think of

confidence that your team will win the championship game. The relationship
between knowledge, belief, and confidence is complex and deserves
further study.

10 For citations from Franklin I'll give page numbers from Franklin 2008.

Bibliography

Annas, J. and Barnes, J. (1985), *The Modes of Scepticism* (Cambridge: Cambridge University Press).

Aristotle (1984), *The Complete Works of Aristotle*, Vol. II (Princeton: Princeton University Press).

Austin, J. (1962), *Sense and Sensibilia* (Oxford: Oxford University Press).

Averill, E. (1985), "Color and the Anthropocentric Problem", *Journal of Philosophy* 82, pp. 281–303.

Averill, E. and Hazlett, A. (2012), "Color Objectivism and Color Projectivism", *Philosophical Psychology* 24(6), pp. 751–65.

Barnes, J. (1982), "The Beliefs of a Pyrrhonist", *Proceedings of the Cambridge Philological Society* 28, pp. 1–29; reprinted in M. Burnyeat and M. Frede (eds), *The Original Sceptics: A Controversy* (London: Hackett, 1997), pp. 58–91. (References above are to the 1997 text.)

—(1990), *The Toils of Scepticism* (Cambridge: Cambridge University Press).

Bayle, P. (1965), *Historical and Critical Dictionary: Selections*, trans. R. H. Popkin (Indianapolis, IN: The Bobbs-Merrill Company).

Bergmann, M. (2009), "Rational Disagreement After Full Disclosure", *Episteme* 6:3, pp. 336–53.

Berkeley, G. (1979), *Three Dialogues Between Hylas and Philonous* (London: Hackett).

Bermudez, J. L. (2008), "Cartesian Skepticism: Arguments and Antecedents", in J. Greco (ed.), *The Oxford Handbook of Skepticism* (Oxford: Oxford University Press), pp. 53–79.

Bett, R. (ed.) (2010), *The Cambridge Companion to Ancient Scepticism* (Cambridge: Cambridge University Press).

BonJour, L. (1978), "Can Empirical Knowledge Have a Foundation?", *American Philosophical Quarterly* 15(1), pp. 1–13.

Bouwsma, O. K. (1949), "Descartes' Evil Genius", *Philosophical Review* 58(2), pp. 141–51.

Brown. J. (2005), "Doubt, Circularity, and the Moorean Response to the Skeptic", *Philosophical Perspectives* 19, pp. 1–14.

—(2006), "Contextualism and Warranted Assertibility Manoeuvres", *Philosophical Studies* 130, pp. 407–35.

—(2008a), "Subject-Sensitive Invariantism and the Knowledge Norm for Practical Reasoning", *Noûs* 42(2), pp. 167–89.

—(2008b), "Knowledge and Practical Reason", *Philosophy Compass* 3(6), pp. 1135–52.

Brueckner, A. (1994), "The Structure of the Skeptical Argument", *Philosophy and Phenomenological Research* 54(4), pp. 827–35.

Burnyeat, M. (1980), "Can the Sceptic Live His Scepticism?", in M. Schofield,

M. Burnyeat and J. Barnes (eds), *Doubt and Dogmatism: Essays in Hellenistic Philosophy* (Oxford: Oxford University Press); reprinted in Burnyeat and Frede 1997, pp. 25–57. (References above are to the 1997 text.)

—(1982), "Idealism and Greek Philosophy: What Descartes Saw and Berkeley Missed", *Philosophical Review* 91(1), pp. 3–40.

Burnyeat, M. and Frede, M. (eds) (1997), *The Original Sceptics: A Controversy* (London: Hackett).

Byrne, A. and Hilbert, D. (2003), "Color Realism and Color Science", *Behavioral and Brain Sciences* 26, pp. 3–64.

Chalmers, D. (2005), "The Matrix as Metaphysics", in C. Grau (ed.), *Philosophers Explore* The Matrix (Oxford: Oxford University Press), pp. 132–76.

Chisholm, R. M. (1957), *Perceiving: A Philosophical Study* (New York: Cornell University Press).

—(1982), *The Foundations of Knowing* (Brighton: Harvester Press).

—(1989), *Theory of Knowledge*, 3rd edn (New York: Prentice-Hall).

Christensen, D. (2007), "Epistemology of Disagreement: The Good News", *Philosophical Review* 116, pp. 187–217.

—(2009), "Disagreement as Evidence: The Epistemology of Controversy", *Philosophy Compass* 4:5, pp. 756–67.

Cicero (2006), *On Academic Scepticism*, trans. C. Brittain (London: Hackett).

Cohen, J. (2004), "Color Properties and Color Ascriptions: A Relationalist Manifesto", *Philosophical Review* 113(4), pp. 451–506.

Cohen, S. (1988), "How to Be a Fallibilist", *Philosophical Perspectives* 2, pp. 91–123.

—(2002), "Basic Knowledge and the Problem of Easy Knowledge", *Philosophy and Phenomenological Research* 65(2), pp. 309–29.

Curley, E. M. (1978), *Descartes Against the Skeptics* (Cambridge, MA: Harvard University Press).

—(1986), "Is There Radical Dissimulation in Descartes' *Meditations*?", in A. O. Rorty (ed.), *Essays on Descartes'* Meditations (Berkeley: University of California Press), pp. 243–70.

Davidson, D. (2001), *Subjective, Objective, Intersubjective* (Oxford: Oxford University Press).

DeRose, K. (1992), "Contextualism and Knowledge Attributions", *Philosophy and Phenomenological Research* 52(4), pp. 913–29.

—(1995), "Solving the Skeptical Problem", *Philosophical Review* 104(1), pp. 1–52.

—(2009), *The Case for Contextualism: Knowledge, Skepticism, and Context*, Vol. 1 (Oxford: Oxford University Press).

Descartes, R. (1984), *The Philosophical Writings of Descartes*, Vol. II, trans. J. Cottingham, R. Stoothoff, and D. Murdoch (Cambridge: Cambridge University Press).

—(1985), *The Philosophical Writings of Descartes*, Vol. I, trans. J. Cottingham, R. Stoothoff, and D. Murdoch (Cambridge: Cambridge University Press).

—(1997), *Meditations on First Philosophy*, revised edition, trans. John Cottingham (Cambridge: Cambridge University Press).

—(1998), *Discourse on Method and Meditations on First Philosophy*, 4th edn, trans. D. A. Cress (London: Hackett).

Diogenes Laertius (1925), *Lives of Eminent Philosophers*, two volumes, trans. R. D. Hicks (Cambridge, MA: Loeb Classical Library, William Heinemann).

Dretske, F. (1970), "Epistemic Operators," *Journal of Philosophy* 67(24), pp. 1007–23.

Elga, A. (2007), "Reflection and Disagreement," *Noûs* 41(3), pp. 478–502.

Elgin, C. (1996), *Considered Judgement* (Princeton: Princeton University Press).

—(2006), "From Knowledge to Understanding," in S. Hetherington (ed.), *Epistemology Futures* (Oxford: Oxford University Press), pp. 199–215.

—(2009), "Is Understanding Factive?," in A. Haddock, A. Millar, and D. Pritchard (eds), *Epistemic Value* (Oxford: Oxford University Press), pp. 322–9.

Fantl, J. and McGrath, M. (2002), "Evidence, Pragmatics, and Justification," *Philosophical Review* 111(1), pp. 67–94.

—(2007), "On Pragmatic Encroachment in Epistemology," *Philosophy and Phenomenological Research* 75(3), pp. 558–89.

—(2009), *Knowledge in an Uncertain World* (Oxford: Oxford University Press).

Feldman, R. (1995), "In Defence of Closure," *Philosophical Quarterly* 45, pp. 487–94.

—(1999), "Contextualism and Skepticism," *Philosophical Perspectives* 13, pp. 91–114.

—(2006), "Epistemological Puzzles about Disagreement," in S. Hetherington (ed.), *Epistemology Futures* (Oxford: Oxford University Press), pp. 216–36.

—(2007), "Reasonable Religious Disagreements," in L. Antony (ed.), *Philosophers Without Gods* (Oxford: Oxford University Press), pp. 194–214.

Feldman, R. and Warfield, T. A. (eds) (2010), *Disagreement* (Oxford: Oxford University Press).

Frankfurt, H. (1970), *Demons, Dreamers, and Madmen: The Defense of Reason in Descartes'* Meditations (Indianapolis, IN: The Bobbs-Merrill Company).

Franklin, B. (2008), *Autobiography and Other Writings* (Oxford: Oxford University Press).

Frede, M. (1979), "The Sceptic's Beliefs." Originally published in *Neue Hefte für Philosophie* 15/16, pp. 102–29, and reprinted in Burnyeat and Frede 1997, pp. 1–24. (References above are to the 1997 text.)

—(1983), "Stoics and Skeptics on Clear and Distinct Impressions," in M. Burnyeat (ed.), *The Skeptical Tradition* (Berkeley: University of California Press), pp. 65–93.

Fogelin, R. (1985), *Hume's Skepticism in the Treatise of Human Nature* (London: Routledge & Kegan Paul).

—(1994), *Pyrrhonian Reflections on Knowledge and Justification* (Oxford: Oxford University Press).

—(2009), "Hume's Skepticism," in D. F. Norton and J. Taylor (eds), *The Cambridge Companion to Hume*, 2nd edn (Cambridge: Cambridge University Press), pp. 209–37.

Fumerton, R. (1995), *Metaepistemology and Skepticism* (Lanham, MA: Rowman & Littlefield).

—(2008), "The Problem of the Criterion," in J. Greco (ed.), *The Oxford Handbook of Skepticism* (Oxford: Oxford University Press), pp. 34–52.

Galilei, G. (2012), *Selected Writings*, trans. W. R. Shea and M. Davie (Oxford: Oxford University Press).

Garrett, D. (1997), *Cognition and Commitment in Hume's Philosophy* (Oxford: Oxford University Press).

Greco, J. (2003), "How to Reid Moore", *Philosophical Quarterly* 52(209), pp. 544–63.

—(2007), *Putting Skeptics in their Place: The Nature of Skeptical Arguments and their Role in Philosophical Inquiry* (Cambridge: Cambridge University Press).

—(2008), "Skepticism about the External World", in J. Greco (ed.), *Oxford Handbook of Skepticism* (Oxford: Oxford University Press), pp. 108–28.

—(2010), *Achieving Knowledge: A Virtue-Theoretical Account of Epistemic Normativity* (Oxford: Oxford University Press).

Grimm. S. (2006), "Is Understanding a Species of Knowledge?", *British Journal for the Philosophy of Science* 57, pp. 515–35.

—(2010), "Understanding", in S. Bernecker and D. Pritchard (eds), *The Routledge Companion to Epistemology* (Abingdon: Routledge), pp. 84–94.

—(forthcoming), "Understanding as Knowledge of Causes", *Synthese*.

Goldman, A. (1992), *Liaisons* (Cambridge, MA: MIT Press).

—(2002), *Pathways to Knowledge: Public and Private* (Oxford: Oxford University Press).

Gutting, G. (1982), *Religious Belief and Religious Skepticism* (South Bend: University of Notre Dame Press).

Hankinson, R. J. (1995), *The Sceptics* (Abingdon: Routledge).

Hawthorne, J. (2004), *Knowledge and Lotteries* (Oxford: Oxford University Press).

Hawthorne, J. and Stanley, J. (2008), "Knowledge and Action", *Journal of Philosophy* 105(10), pp. 571–90.

Hazlett, A. (2009), "Knowledge and Conversation", *Philosophy and Phenomenological Research* 78(3), pp. 591–620.

—(2012), "Higher-Order Epistemic Attitudes and Intellectual Humility", *Episteme* 9:3, pp. 205–23.

Hill, C. (1996), "Process Reliabilism and Cartesian Skepticism", *Philosophy and Phenomenological Research* 56(3), pp. 567–81.

Hume, D. (1975), *Enquiries concerning Human Understanding and concerning the Principles of Morals*, P. H. Nidditch (ed.), 3rd edn (Oxford: Oxford University Press).

—(1978), *A Treatise of Human Nature*, P. H. Nidditch (ed.), 2nd edn (Oxford: Oxford University Press).

van Inwagen, P. (2010), "We're Right. They're Wrong", in R. Feldman and T. Warfield (eds), *Disagreement* (Oxford: Oxford University Press) 2010, pp. 10–28.

Inwood, B. and Gerson, L. P. (trans) (1997), *Hellenistic Philosophy: Introductory Readings*, 2nd edn (London: Hackett).

Johnston, M. (1996), "Is the External World Invisible?", *Philosophical Issues* 7, pp. 185–98.

Kelly, T. (2005a), "The Epistemic Significance of Disagreement", *Oxford Studies in Epistemology* 1, pp. 167–96.

—(2005b), "Moorean Facts and Belief Revision, or Can the Skeptic Win?", *Philosophical Perspectives* 19, pp. 179–209.

—(2010), "Peer Disagreement and Higher-Order Evidence", in R. Feldman and T. Warfield (eds), *Disagreement* (Oxford: Oxford University Press), pp. 111–74.

Kim, J. (1982), "Psychophysical Supervenience", *Philosophical Studies* 41, pp. 51–70.

Klein, P. (1999), "Human Knowledge and the Infinite Regress of Reasons", *Philosophical Perspectives*, 13, pp. 297–325.

Kornblith, H. (2002), *Knowledge and Its Place in Nature* (Oxford: Oxford University Press).

Kvanvig, J. (2003), *The Value of Knowledge and the Pursuit of Understanding* (Cambridge: Cambridge University Press).

Kyburg, H. E. (1970), *Probability and Inductive Logic* (New York: Macmillan).

Langton, R. (2001), *Kantian Humility: Our Ignorance of Things in Themselves* (Oxford: Oxford University Press).

—(2004), "Elusive Knowledge of Things in Themselves", *Australasian Journal of Philosophy* 82(1), pp. 129–36.

Langton, R. and Lewis, D. (1998), "Defining 'Intrinsic'", *Philosophy and Phenomenological Research* 58, pp. 333–45.

Lewis, D. (1983), "Extrinsic Properties", *Philosophical Studies* 44, pp. 197–200.

—(1984), "Putnam's Paradox", *Australasian Journal of Philosophy* 62(3), pp. 221–36.

—(1996), "Elusive Knowledge", *Australasian Journal of Philosophy* 74(4), pp. 549–67.

—(2009), "Ramseyan Humility", in D. Braddon-Mitchell and R. Nola (eds), *Conceptual Analysis and Philosophical Naturalism* (Cambridge, MA: MIT Press), pp. 203–22.

Long, A. A. and Seddy, D. N. (1987), *The Hellenistic Philosophers, Volume 1: Translations of the Principal Sources with Philosophical Commentary* (Cambridge: Cambridge University Press).

MacFarlane, J. (2005), "The Assessment Sensitivity of Knowledge Attributions", *Oxford Studies in Epistemology* 1, pp. 197–233.

McDowell, J. (1994), *Mind and World* (Cambridge, MS: Harvard University Press).

Makinson, D. C. (1965), "The Paradox of the Preface," *Analysis* 25(6), pp. 205–7.

Malcolm, N. (1949), "Defending Common Sense", *Philosophical Review* 58(3), pp. 201–20.

—(1942), "Moore and Ordinary Language", in P. A. Schilpp (ed.), *The Philosophy of G.E. Moore* (Chicago, IL: Open Court), pp. 345–68.

—(1963), "George Edward Moore", in N. Malcolm, *Knowledge and Certainty: Essays and Lectures* (New York: Prentice-Hall), pp. 163–83.

—(1977), "Moore and Wittgenstein on the Sense of 'I know'", in N. Malcolm, *Thought and Knowledge* (New York: Cornell University Press), pp. 170–98.

Millikan, P. (2002), "Hume's Sceptical Doubts concerning Induction", in P. Millikan (ed.), *Reading Hume on Human Understanding* (Oxford: Oxford University Press), pp. 107–73.

Molnar, G. (2007), *Powers: A Study in Metaphysics* (Oxford: Oxford University Press).

Montaigne, M. (2003), *The Complete Essays*, trans. M. A. Screech (London: Penguin Classics).

Moore, G. E. (1925), "A Defence of Common Sense", in J. H. Muirhead (ed.), *Contemporary British Philosophy*, second series (London: Allen & Unwin, 1925), pp. 193–223; reprinted in G. E. Moore, *Philosophical Papers* (London: Allen & Unwin, 1959), pp. 32–59. (References above are to the 1959 text.)

—(1939), "Proof of an External World", *Proceedings of the British Academy* 25, pp. 273–300; reprinted in G. E. Moore, *Selected Writings* (London: Routledge, 1993), pp. 147–70.

—(1953), "Hume's Theory Examined", in G. E. Moore, *Some Main Problems of Philosophy* (London: Allen & Unwin), pp. 108–26; reprinted in G. E. Moore, *Selected Writings* (London: Routledge, 1993), pp. 59–78. (References above are to the 1993 text.)

—(1959), "Four Forms of Scepticism", in G. E. Moore, *Philosophical Papers* (London: Allen & Unwin), pp. 196–226.

—(1993), "Letter to Malcolm" (28 June 1949), in G. E. Moore, *Selected Writings* (London: Routledge, 1993), pp. 213–16.

Nagel, T. (1999), "Davidson's New *Cogito*", in L. E. Hahn (ed.), *The Philosophy of Donald Davidson* (Chicago, IL: Open Court), pp. 195–206.

Norton, D. F. (2002), "Of the Academical or Sceptical Philosophy", in P. Millikan (ed.), *Reading Hume on Human Understanding* (Oxford: Oxford University Press), pp. 371–92.

Nozick, R. (1981), *Philosophical Explanations* (Harvard University Press).

Pappas, G. (2008), "Berkeley's Treatment of Skepticism", in J. Greco (ed.), *The Oxford Handbook of Skepticism* (Oxford: Oxford University Press), pp. 249–64.

Penelhum, T. (1983), "Skepticism and Fideism", in M. Burnyeat (ed.), *The Skeptical Tradition* (Berkeley: University of California Press), pp. 287–318.

Perin, C. (2010), "Scepticism and Belief", in R. Bett (ed.), *The Cambridge Companion to Ancient Scepticism* (Cambridge: Cambridge University Press), pp. 145–64.

Popkin, R. (2003), *The History of Scepticism from Erasmus to Spinoza* (Berkeley: University of California Press).

Popper, K. (1963), *Conjectures and Refutations: The Growth of Scientific Knowledge* (London: Routledge & Kegan Paul).

Pritchard, D. (2010), "Knowledge and Understanding", in D. Pritchard, A. Millar, and A. Haddock, *The Nature and Value of Knowledge: Three Investigations* (Oxford: Oxford University Press), pp. 3–87.

Pryor, J. (2000), "The Skeptic and the Dogmatist", *Noûs* 34(4), pp. 517–49.

—(2004), "What's Wrong With Moore's Argument?", *Philosophical Issues* 14, pp. 349–78.

Putnam, H. (1981), *Reason, Truth, and History* (Cambridge: Cambridge University Press).

Quine, W. V. O. (1969), "Epistemology Naturalized", in W. V. O. Quine, *Ontological Relativity and other Essays* (New York: Columbia University Press), pp. 69–90.

Reed, B. (2008), "Certainty", *Stanford Encyclopedia of Philosophy* (Palo Alto, CA: University of Stanford Press).

Reid, T. (1983), *Inquiry and Essays* (London: Hackett).

Rorty, A. O. (1986), "The Structure of Descartes' *Meditations*", in A. O. Rorty (ed.), *Essays on Descartes'* Meditations (Berkeley: University of California Press), pp. 1–20.

Rorty, R. (1979), *Philosophy and the Mirror of Nature* (Princeton: Princeton University Press).

Russell, B. (1954), *The Analysis of Matter* (Mineola, NY: Dover Publications).

—(1959), *The Problems of Philosophy* (Oxford: Oxford University Press).

Rysiew, P. (2001), "The Context-Sensitivity of Knowledge Attributions", *Noûs* 35(4), pp. 477–514.

Schaffer, J. (2004a), "From Contextualism to Contrastivism", *Philosophical Studies* 119, pp. 73–103.

—(2004b), "Skepticism, Contextualism, and Discrimination", *Philosophy and Phenomenological Research* 69(1), pp. 138–55.

—(2005a), "Contrastive Knowledge", *Oxford Studies in Epistemology* 1, pp. 235–71.

—(2005b), "Quiddistic Knowledge", *Philosophical Studies* 123(1–2) (2005), pp. 1–32.

—(2007), "Knowing the Answer", *Philosophy and Phenomenological Research* 75(2), pp. 383–403.

Schmitt, C. B. (1983), "The Rediscovery of Ancient Skepticism in Modern Times", in M. Burnyeat (ed.), *The Skeptical Tradition* (Berkeley: University of California Press), pp. 225–51.

Sellars, W. (1956), "Empiricism and the Philosophy of Mind", *Minnesota Studies in the Philosophy of Science* 1, pp. 253–329.

Sextus Empiricus (2000), *Outlines of Scepticism,* trans. J. Annas and J. Barnes (Cambridge: Cambridge University Press).

—(2005), *Against the Logicians*, trans. R. Bett (Cambridge: Cambridge University Press).

Smith, N. (1905a), "The Naturalism of Hume (I)", *Mind* 14(54), pp. 149–73.

—(1905b), "The Naturalism of Hume (II)", *Mind* 14(55), pp. 335–47.

Soames, S. (2005), *Philosophical Analysis in the Twentieth Century, Volume I: The Dawn of Analysis* (Princeton, NJ: Princeton University Press).

Sorabji, R. (2006), *Self: Ancient and Modern Insights about Individuality, Life, and Death* (Chicago: University of Chicago Press).

Sosa, E. (1991), *Knowledge in Perspective: Selected Essays in Epistemology* (Cambridge: Cambridge University Press).

—(1994), "Philosophical Scepticism and Epistemic Circularity", *Proceedings of the Aristotelian Society Supplement* 68, pp. 263–90.

—(1997), "How to Resolve the Pyrrhonian Problematic: A Lesson from Descartes", *Philosophical Studies* 85:2/3, pp. 229–49.

—(1999), "How to Defeat Opposition to Moore", *Philosophical Perspectives* 13, pp. 141–53.

—(2000), "Skepticism and Contextualism", *Philosophical Issues* 10, pp. 1–18.

—(2007), *A Virtue Epistemology: Apt Belief and Reflective Knowledge, Volume 1* (Oxford: Oxford University Press).

Stanley, J. (2004), "On the Linguistic Basis for Contextualism", *Philosophical Studies* 119 (1–2), pp. 119–46.

—(2007), *Knowledge and Practical Interests* (Oxford: Oxford University Press).

Stern, R. (2008), "Kant's Response to Skepticism", in J. Greco (ed.), *The Oxford Handbook of Skepticism* (Oxford: Oxford University Press), pp. 265–85.

Striker, G. (1996), *Essays in Hellenistic Epistemology and Ethics* (Cambridge: Cambridge University Press).

—(2010), "Academics versus Pyrrhonists, reconsidered", in Bett 2010, pp. 195–207.

Stroud, B. (1977), *Hume* (London: Routledge & Kegan Paul).

—(1983), "Kant and Skepticism", in M. Burnyeat (ed.), *The Skeptical Tradition* (Berkeley: University of California Press), pp. 413–34.

—(1984), *The Significance of Philosophical Scepticism* (Oxford: Oxford University Press).

—(1994), "Scepticism, 'Externalism', and the Goal of Epistemology", *Proceedings of the Aristotelian Society Supplement* 68, pp. 291–307.

—(2000a), *Understanding Human Knowledge: Philosophical Essays* (Oxford: Oxford University Press).

—(2000b), *The Quest for Reality: Subjectivism and the Metaphysics of Colour* (Oxford: Oxford University Press).

Unger, P. (1975), *Ignorance: A Case for Scepticism* (Oxford: Oxford University Press).

Van Cleve, J. (1984), "Reliability, Justification, and the Problem of Induction", *Midwest Studies in Philosophy* 9(1), pp. 555–67.

—(2003), "Is Knowledge Easy—or Impossible? Externalism as the Only Alternative to Skepticism", in S. Luper (ed.), *The Skeptics: Contemporary Essays* (Farnham: Ashgate), pp. 45–59.

Vogel, J. (1990a), "Cartesian Skepticism and Inference to the Best Explanation", *Journal of Philosophy* 87(11), pp. 658–66.

—(1990b), "Are There Counterexamples to the Closure Principle?", in M. D. Roth and M. Ross (eds), *Doubting: Contemporary Perspectives on Skepticism* (Dordrecht: Kluwer Academic Publishers), pp. 13–27.

—(1993), "Dismissing Skeptical Possibilities", *Philosophical Studies* 70(3), pp. 235–50.

—(2000), "Reliabilism Leveled", *Journal of Philosophy* 97(11), pp. 602–23.

—(2004), "Skeptical Arguments", *Philosophical Issues* 14, pp. 426–55.

Vogt, K. (2010a), "Ancient Skepticism", *Stanford Encyclopedia of Philosophy* (Palo Alto, CA: University of Stanford Press).

—(2010b), "Scepticism and Action", in R. Bett (ed.), *The Cambridge Companion to Ancient Scepticism* (Cambridge: Cambridge University Press), pp. 165–80.

Weatherson, B. and Marshall, D. (2012), "Intrinsic vs. Extrinsic Properties", *Stanford Encyclopedia of Philosophy* (Palo Alto, CA: University of Stanford Press).

White, R. (2005), "Epistemic Permissiveness", *Philosophical Perspectives* 19, pp. 445–59.

Williams, B. (1978), *Descartes: The Project of Pure Inquiry* (London: Routledge).

—(1983), "Descartes' Use of Skepticism", in M. Burnyeat (ed.), *The Skeptical Tradition* (Berkeley: University of California Press), pp. 337–52.

Williams, M. (1995), *Unnatural Doubts: Epistemological Realism and the Basis of Scepticism* (Princeton: Princeton University Press).

—(2008), "Hume's Skepticism", in J. Greco (ed.), *The Oxford Handbook of Skepticism* (Oxford: Oxford University Press), pp. 80–107.

—(2010), "Descartes' Transformation of the Sceptical Tradition", in R. Bett (ed.), *The Cambridge Companion to Ancient Scepticism* (Cambridge: Cambridge University Press), pp. 288–313.

Williamson, T. (2000), *Knowledge and Its Limits* (Oxford: Oxford University Press).

Wittgenstein, L. (1969), *On Certainty* (London: Harper & Row).

Woodruff, P. (2010), "The Pyrrhonian Modes", in R. Bett (ed.), *The Cambridge Companion to Ancient Scepticism* (Cambridge: Cambridge University Press), pp. 208–32.

Wright, C. (2000), "Cogency and Question-Begging: Some Reflections on McKinsey's Paradox and Putnam's Proof", *Philosophical Issues* 10, pp. 140–63.

—(2002), "(Anti-)Sceptics Simple and Subtle: G.E. Moore and John McDowell", *Philosophy and Phenomenological Research* 65(2), pp. 330–48.

—(2004a), "Wittgensteinian Certainties", in D. McManus (ed.), *Wittgenstein and Scepticism* (London: Routledge), pp. 22–55.

—(2004b), "Warrant for Nothing (and Foundations for Free)?", *Proceedings of the Aristotelian Society Supplement* 78, pp. 176–212.

Zagzebski, L. (2001), "Recovering Understanding", in M. Steup (ed.), *Knowledge, Truth, and Duty: Essays on Epistemic Justification, Responsibility, and Virtue* (Oxford: Oxford University Press), pp. 237–51.

Index

Page references in **bold** denote locations of important definitions

Aenesidemus 5, 7, 16
Agrippa 10
Agrippa's trilemma 10–12, 40, 68,
    102 *see also* five modes, the;
    Humean skeptical argument
Annas, J. 16, 32, 33, 187, 188, 189
a priori vs. a posteriori **64**
apraxia objection, the 23–7, 177–9, 190
Aquinas, T. 55
Arcesilaus 5, 16, 17, 188, 189
Aristotle 24, 25, 28, 37, 188
Armstrong, D. 110
Arnauld, A. 75, 95
Augustine of Hippo 29, 72, 191, 192
Averill, E. 161, 164
Avicenna 192

Barnes, J. 5, 16, 17, 20, 21, 22, 23, 25,
    26, 32, 33, 38–42, 187, 188, 189,
    190
Bayle, P. 17, 23, 30, 31, 55, 161, 189
Beattie, J. 33, 179
Beauchamp, T. L. 64
"begging the question" *see* circularity
Bergmann, M. 190
Berkeley, G. 55, 97–8, 193
Bermudez, J. L. 9, 28, 72
Bett, R. 187
Bouwsma, O. K. 99
Brittain, C. 188
Brown, J. 178, 196
Brueckner, A. 87, 192
Burnyeat, M. 9, 21, 22, 25, 27, 28, 188
Byrne, A. 162

Calvin, J. 29
Carneades 5, 33, 188, 189
Cartesian dualism 98–9

Cartesian skeptical argument 9–10,
    80–9, 91, 92, 93–101, 102,
    107, 109–10, 112, 117, 124, 127,
    129, 133, 134, 139–40, 141–2,
    163, 169, 173, 174–5, 191 *see
    also* Descartes, R.; problem
    of Cartesian skepticism;
    skepticism, Cartesian
Castellio, S. 29, 31
Chalmers, D. 100
Chisholm, R. 13, 47–8, 112–13, 190
Christensen, D. 50, 190
Christianity 6, 29, 32, 71
Cicero 16–7, 22, 23, 28, 188
circularity 95–6, 120–23
closure principle 102, 127–38, **128**,
    194
    closed under entailment 131
    multi-premise 135
Cohen, J. 162
Cohen, S. 148–9, 153–5, 194, 195
conservativsm 26, 31, 177 *see also*
    revisionism
contextualism **144**, 144–55 *see also*
    knowledge
Copernicus, N. 71
Cottingham, J. 192
Curley, E. 93, 96

Davie, M. 195
Davidson, D. 99–100
Democritus 4
DeRose, K. 147, 148–9, 151, 153–5,
    195, 196
Descartes, R. viii, ix, 13, 30, 32, 33,
    55, 71–80, 82, 85, 87, 89–91, 94,
    95–6, 102, 138, 161, 163, 189,
    192 *see also* Cartesian skeptical

argument; problem of Cartesian skepticism; skepticism, Cartesian
Diogenes of Appolonia 4
Diogenes Laertius 4, 6, 16, 17, 21, 24, 187
disagreement 9, 75, 189
    Peer 42–50
    Expert 50–3
    see also mode from dispute, the
doxastic involuntarism **62**
Dretske, F. 129, 130–2, 134

Elga, A. 190
Elgin, C. 196
entitlement 175, 194
Epicurus 4
epistemic peerhood **43**, 48–9
epistemic superiority **51**
externalism *see* internalism

fallacy of equivocation 142, 151–3
Fantl, J. 177, 195
Feldman, R. 43–5, 135, 151, 155, 190
fideism 29–30, 189
five modes, the 10–13, 84 *see also* Agrippa's trilemma; mode from dispute, the
Fogelin, R. 63
Fontanelle, B. 189
Frances, B. viii, 51–2, 90, 190, 196
Frankfurt, H. 82, 96
Franklin, B. 183–4, 196
Frede, M. 14, 22, 25, 32, 187
Frege, G. 107
Fumerton, R. 194

Galilean humility 160–4, **162**, 165, 166, 167, 189, 190, 191 *see also* Galileo, G.
Galileo, G. 71, 161, 170, 195 *see also* Galilean humility
Garrett, D. 63
Gassendi, P. 29, 73, 75, 85
Gettier, E. 194
Gettier problem 194
Goldman, A. 194
Greco, J. 74, 86, 90, 98, 193, 194
Grimm, S. 196

Grube, G. M. A. 187
Gutting, G. 190

Hankinson, R. J. 15, 188
Hawthorne, J. 151, 178, 194, 195, 196
Hazlett, A. 48, 164, 190, 195
Heraclitus 4
Hicks, R. D. 187
Hilbert, D. 162
Hill, C. 194
Hobbes, T. 75
Hume, D. ix, 13, 30, 31, 32, 33, 34, 38, 55–64, 101, 108, 179, 181–3, 188, 189, 191, 192 *see also* Humean skeptical argument
Humean skeptical argument 64–9, 93, 102, 191 *see also* Agrippa's trilemma; Hume, D.
humility, intellectual 47–8

idealism 97–8
indirect realism 98–9
inductive knowledge 64–7, **65**
infallibilism 30, 33, **89**, 89–91, 174 *see also* knowledge
inference to the best explanation 96–7, 175, 194
internalism 40–2, **41**, 47, 90 *see also* knowledge
intrinsic property **164**, 164–7
Inwagen, van 190

Jefferson, T. 31
Johnston, M. 163

Kant, I. 164, 166, 193 *see also* Kantian humility
Kantian humility **164**, 164–7 *see also* Kant, I.
Kelly, T. 46, 190
knowledge
    acquaintance knowledge **159**, 160–4, 165–6
    argumentative conception of 115
    argumentative constraint on **67**, 67–9, 90, 191, 194
    non-argumentative conception of 114–15
    practical **159**

propositional **159**, 165–6
safety theory of 118
see also contexutalism; infallibilism;
    internalism; reliabilism;
    understanding
knowledge-belief principle **17**
knowledge requirement view **178**,
    177–9
Kornblith, H. 101
Kripke, S. 195
Kvanvig, J. 196
Kyburg, H. E. 195

Langton, R. 164, 165, 166, 196
Lewis, D. K. 100, 111, 164, 165, 166,
    167, 195
Locke, J. 31, 161
Lucian 189
Luther, M. 29

MacFarlane, J. 195
Makinson, D. C. 195
Malcolm, N. 142–4, 195
Mappes, T. A. 64
Marshall, D. 164
McGrath, M. 177, 195
medical empiricism 4
Mersenne, M. 29, 73, 75, 83, 85, 95
methodism **113**
Millikan, P. 64, 191
mode from dispute, the 13, 37–42,
    75 *see also* disagreement; five
    modes, the; problem of the
    criterion
Molnar, G. 196
Montaigne, Michel de 29–32, 34, 55,
    187, 189
Moore, G. E. 67, 107–13, 120, 121,
    142–4, 193
    Moore's proof **122**, 123
    see also Moorean facts;
        neo-Mooreanism
Moorean facts **110**, 110–11 *see also*
    Moore, G.E.
Murdoch, D. 192

Nagel, T. 99
neo-Mooreanism 113–20, **114**, 171,
    194

neo-Moorean argument **113–14**,
    121–2, 124, 139–40
    see also Moore, G. E.
Neruda, P. 187
Newton, I. 60–1
Norton, D. F. 63
Nozick, R. 86, 87, 123, 129, 132–4, 195
    Nozick's argument **134**, 139–40

Pappas, G. 97
paradox of inquiry 12
particularism **113**
Paul the Apostle 32
Penelhum, T. 189
Perin, C. 21, 25
Philo of Larissa 33
Plato 4, 5, 12, 187
Plotinus 192
Popkin, R. 28, 31, 33, 38, 72, 83, 85,
    90, 189, 192, 193
Popper, K. 39, 90
Pritchard, D. 196
problem of Cartesian skepticism 91–2,
    92, 94–5, 97–8, 99, 101, 107,
    141–2, 150, 151–5, 159 *see also*
    Cartesian skeptical argument;
    Descartes, R.; skepticism,
    Cartesian
problem of the criterion 12, 39–42,
    102 *see also* mode from
    dispute, the
Protagoras 4
Pryor, J. 119, 194
Putnam, H. 100, 193
Pyrrho of Elis 5, 6, 24, 26
Pythagoras 4

Quine, W. V. O. 101

Rawls, J. 45
Reed, B. 89
Reid, T. 42–3, 49, 94, 101, 122
reliabilism **115**, 115–18, 194 *see also*
    knowledge
revisionism 176, 178 *see also*
    conservativism
Riggs, W. 196
Rorty, A. O. 192
Rorty, R. 98

Ross, W. D. 188
Russell, B. 96, 107–8, 161, 162, 164, 165
Rysiew, P. 195

safety **118**, 194 *see also* knowledge,
    safety theory of
Sanchez, F. 29
Schaffer, J. 195
Schiffer, S. 196
Schmitt, C. B. 189
Screech, M. A. 189
secularism 32, 189
self-refutation objection, the 19–23,
    93, 177
self-undermining objection, the 23,
    93, 177
sensitivity **132**, 195
    sensitivity principle **132**
Sextus Empiricus 4, 6, 8, 9, 11, 12, 13,
    17, 18, 20, 21, 25, 26, 28, 37, 62,
    177, 179, 187, 194
Shea, W. R. 195
Shope, R. 194
skepticism
    Academic vs. Pyrrhonian 5–6, **18**,
        16–9, 19–20, 23, 24, 27, 29, 63,
        94, 177
    Ancient 3–13, 32–4, 160
    Cartesian 33, **82**, 84–5, 93, 94, 176
    in the Early Modern period 9, 23,
        28–34, 38, 179
    mitigated vs. unmitigated **17**, 22,
        24, 29, 33, 85, 87, 93, 173–6
    modality of **19**, 84, 196
    order of **14**, 13–5, 189
    as a paradox viii
    "radical" 84–5
    rustic vs. non-rustic **15**, 19, 22, 25,
        26, 27–8, 30, 74, 160
    scope of **15**, 15–6, 82–4, 100, 190
    urbane **15**, 160
    see also Descartes, R.; Cartesian
        skeptical argument; problem of
        Cartesian skepticism
Smith, N. 63

Soames, S. 193
Sober, E. 193
Socrates 4–5, 23, 177
Sorabji, R. 192
Sosa, E. 68, 96, 118, 150–1, 155, 194,
    195
soundness **82**
Stanley, J. 178, 195, 196
Stern, R. 193
Stoicism 3, 4, 5, 6, 24, 25
Stoothoff, R. 192
Striker, G. 17, 27–8, 188
Stroud, B. 34, 63, 86, 127–8, 176, 193,
    194
suspension of judgment **5**, 6, 14, 19,
    24, 25, 73–4, 94, 187, 188

ten modes, the 7–10
Thales 4

underdetermination principle 87, 192
understanding 160, 167–71
    explanatory **167**
    see also knowledge
Unger, P. 90, 91
uniqueness principle **44**

validity **82**, 141–2, 151–3
Van Cleve, J. 67, 194
virtue argument 179–81
Vogel, J. 87, 96, 194, 195
Vogt, K. 25, 32, 188

Weatherson, B. 164
Weiner, M. 196
White, R. 190
Williams, B. 9, 74, 85, 89, 90, 94, 96,
    188, 192
Williams, M. 175
Williamson, T. 137, 194, 195, 196
Wittgenstein, L. 49, 101, 142–4
Wright, C. 175, 195

Zagzebski, L. 171, 196

CPSIA information can be obtained
at www.ICGtesting.com
Printed in the USA
LVOW01s1748100117
520460LV00008B/55/P